A COMPREHENSIVE GUIDE TO
Wheelock's Latin

UPDATED TO WHEELOCK'S 6TH EDITION (REVISED)

DALE A. GROTE

D0711907

Bolchazy-Carducci Publishers, Inc.
Wauconda, Illinois USA

Editor
Laurie Haight Keenan

Contributing Editor
Georgia Irby-Massie

Cover Design
Cameron A. Marshall

Page Design & Typography
Adam Phillip Velez

Cover Graphic
"Roman study with scrolls or volumina,
tablets for writing, chair, table, lamp, etc."
Plate 276 from Thomas Hope, *Costumes of the Greeks and Romans*
(New York: Dover Publications, 1962)

Bolchazy-Carducci Publishers, Inc.
1000 Brown Street, Unit 101
Wauconda, Illinois 60084 USA
www.bolchazy.com

Printed in the United States of America
2006
by United Graphics

ISBN-13: 978-0-86516-486-4
ISBN-10: 0-86516-486-X

Library of Congress Cataloging-in-Publication Data

Grote, Dale A.
    A comprehensive guide to Wheelock's Latin: newly revised for Wheelock's 6th edition
/Dale A. Grote
        p. cm.
    Rev. ed. of: Comprehensive study guide for Wheelock's Latin. c1995.
    ISBN 0-86516-486-X (pbk.: alk. paper)
    1. Wheelock, Frederic M. Wheelock's Latin grammar. 2. Latin
language—Grammar—Problems, exercises, etc. 3. Rome—Civilizations—Problems,
excerises, etc. I.Grote, Dale A. Comprehensive study guide for Wheelock's Latin. II.
Title.

PA2087.5 .G76
478.2'421—dc21

00-050805

FOR MY FATHER,
WHO ENJOYS EXPLAINING THINGS

MEO MAGISTRO
PRIMO ATQVE
OPTIMO

CONTENTS

KEY **291**

Answers to Selected Exercises

FOREWORD

Many American classicists of my generation first learned Latin from Wheelock, and I suppose that most of them had an experience not dissimilar from mine. I had spent the better part of my sophomore year beginning ancient Greek and, realizing that I'd come to the Classics late in my college career, determined that the only thing to do was to teach myself Latin over the course of the summer. It seemed a reasonable enough prospect: I knew I could harass my Greek professors if I needed help (why else, after all, does one go to a small college?); I figured myself to be a real crackerjack at languages (a notion of which I was soon disabused); and there wasn't much else to do in a small college town in Minnesota during the summer doldrums. At least, not unless one owned a flashy jacked-up pickup truck in which to drive around, which I didn't. So I started in on my self-tutoring. I was working the graveyard shift at a local greasy-spoon that served an odd assortment of burgers, subs, fries, and Greek food. I would arrive at work around midnight, fry through the wee hours, clean the place around three, serve eggs and pancakes to the railroad workers at five, become tired and irascible at seven, and stumble home to a small, hot apartment at eight. I'd go to sleep, but inevitably wake too early, usually in mid-afternoon. Somehow, between shifts I did a chapter of Wheelock every weekday till I was done. It was a strange summer.

The fact that even I made it through Wheelock's 40 chapters in just a few months, however, are a testament to the book's strong points. Wheelock has long been admired for its direct presentation of grammar, its reliance on real Latin texts, its concise organization, and its clear paradigms. It was an ideal book for me, and it makes admirable sense that Harper Collins chose to include it in their new series of college outlines, books designed for students who might be autodidacts. The same qualities, naturally, have made it a favorite of college professors and their students for several decades.

When I began my teaching career at Oberlin College, therefore, I turned almost instinctively to Wheelock for my beginning Latin text. It would be, I thought, like rediscovering an old friend. I wasn't wrong, but it turns out that the chum I spent my (relatively) alert hours with that summer had picked up a few quirks along the way. Some were merely charming. (I recommend that every teacher of Wheelock begin her class by pointing the students to footnote 2 in the preface, in which Wheelock explains that "Caesar's works were studiously avoided because there is a growing opinion that Caesar's military tyranny over the first two years is infelicitous, intolerable, and deleterious to the cause ... ") Others were more troubling.

I found that my students, a bright lot, did not have the active knowledge of English grammar necessary to fully comprehend Wheelock's brief and direct explanations. What had been crystalline for me was cryptic to them, and I found myself spending an inordinate amount of time explaining, e.g., what an agent is rather than showing how it is used in Latin. The Latin Teachers' Nightmare began: we were falling behind.

Miraculously, a mild-mannered hero appeared on the scene through the magic of Internet. Dale Grote, hailing from the far reaches of North Carolina, announced on the wires that, having experienced the same problems that were plaguing me, he had written a workbook to accompany Wheelock. It contained fuller explanations of the grammar, useful exercises, additional etymological information, and best of all, it was available on-line. Dale suggested that we inhabitants of this brave new world download his stuff, and pass it on to our students as an optional supplement to Wheelock. Crossing my fingers, I did just that.

The results were tremendous. Not every student requested, or needed, Grote's Wheelock. But those students who did need extra help and who did Grote's exercises with dedicated regularity immediately improved. I found that my class time was being used more efficiently, and that I was able to relax and open things up more. We got back on schedule, and my nervous tics slowly subsided to their normal level. Discussions began to center on grammatical niceties and even points of literary and cultural interest. Most important, my students liked this Grote fellow, with his careful explanations, sympathetic outlook, and wry sense of humor. He allowed them to experience Wheelock, perhaps not in the idyllic grease-and-burger fogged way that I had, but in a way that was, after all, pleasant and instructive. Coincidentally, it was spring.

In closing, allow me to quote a favorite passage from Sterne's *Tristram Shandy*:

I am convinced, Yorick, continued my father, half reading and half discoursing, that there is a North-west passage to the intellectual world; and that the soul of man has shorter ways of going to work, in furnishing itself with knowledge and instruction, than we generally take with it. —But alack! all fields have not a river or a spring running besides them; —every child, Yorick! has not a parent to point it out. —The whole entirely depends, added my father, upon the auxiliary verbs, Mr. Yorick. Had Yorick trod upon Virgil's snake, he could not have looked more surprised.

I do not know if the auxiliary verbs really are a shortcut to the intellectual world. I suspect not. Alas, I do know that there is no Northwest passage to the learning of Latin. That continental crossing is achieved only by much difficult, and sometimes stultifying work. But Wheelock remains among the best available maps; and while not every student will need the supplementary notes provided in this book, those that do will find that Grote creates a well-marked path over the unfamiliar territory of Latin Grammar. This book has been much-needed over the past five or ten years, and I am extremely pleased to see it available. With Grote's help, I hope, Wheelock will continue to be the standard text for another generation of sleep-deprived, energetic students.

Kirk Ormand

PREFACE

This is a *help-when-you-need-it* book. There are several implications of such a description. One: it won't be for everyone. It will be of no use whatsoever to geniuses or the teachers of geniuses. Two: it won't be for anyone all of the time. No one is confused all the time, but most are confused some of the time (except for geniuses; *vide* point one above). Three: it probably won't please some teachers of Latin because of its repetitiveness and casual diction. It wasn't written for the successful, but for the struggling and frightened; its style is meant to calm and reassure. Four: it is not meant to encroach upon class time. The book is best mentioned only once in the term, preferably on the first day as an optional aid for the bewildered or the about-to-be bewildered. Five: it will not in all likelihood be read in its entirety but in fragments. Confusion descends on different students at different times for different reasons. Accordingly, nearly all the chapters include some review of earlier material that is pertinent (hence the charge of repetitiveness). Six: it has no other purpose than to be a faithful companion to the venerable Wheelock. It doesn't raise new issues or make things worse by flirting with novel explanations. There will be no talk of kernels or lexical fields.

These notes are a condensation of twenty years experience helping baffled students through Wheelock's magisterial forty chapters. They are also expressive of my twin personal convictions that nearly all college students are capable of learning Latin well enough to benefit from its study, and that, after almost fifty years, Wheelock is still the best text around to do it with.

Finally, typos are like ants at a picnic: no matter how many you squash, there are always more. This text has benefitted greatly in this regard by several Argus-eyed readers over the years. Chief among them are Laurie Haight Keenan, editor and classicist at Bolchazy-Carducci, Dr. R. Scott Smith at the University of New Hampshire, my former student Daniel Wahl, the autodidacts Joe Riegsecker and Tom McCurdy, the whole list of Internet users of my book and online materials, and particularly to Karen Mahmoud, who stamped out the last remaining ant colonies.

Dale Grote, UNC Charlotte

1

Getting Started: Verbs

VERBS: THE BASICS

What is a verb? (This isn't a trick question). Think back to your 9th grade grammar class. You might remember this lapidary sentence from your childhood: *A verb is an action word.* Despite its simplicity, this definition of a verb isn't a bad place to start. A verb is a kind of a word, and it very often indicates an action. We need add only one refinement to have a good working definition of a verb that'll get you on your way to learning Latin. In addition to indicating an action, a verb can also indicate just a state of being where there isn't much (or any) action going on.

In this sentence, *the horse ate his oats*, the verb is *ate* and clearly this is an action. Now look at another sentence: *George was six feet tall*, the verb is *was* and nothing is really going on. The verb in this sentence is telling you that George is six feet tall. George isn't doing anything. So, for now, our definition of a verb is a word that indicates an action or state of being.

Fine. Now let's take a step into a little more complexity. Sometimes you'll see English indicating the action or state of being with a cluster of words instead of just one word. Consider the ideas of action or state of being that are indicated in these sentences: *This **would have been** helpful, I **was looking** at my horse, You **have seen** this before.* So where are the verbs? Let's consider. In each of these examples, you can see that there's really only one action or state of being that's indicated in these sentences. In the first, the basic verbal idea is that of existence. In the second, the verbal idea is that of looking. And in the third, the verbal idea is that of seeing.

But the sentences depict the verbal ideas in ways that are more complicated than can be expressed with just one word. The basic verbal idea needs to be qualified, or helped out, with additional words. These extra words are called *helping* or *auxiliary* verbs. (I'll call them auxiliary verbs, from the Latin word *auxilium* which means *help*.) In the second sentence, *I **was looking** at my horse*, the core of the verbal idea is *look*, but in this sentence the speaker wants it to be in the past, so he/she puts the auxiliary verb *was* in front of *look* and then even adds the ending *-ing* to the form *look*. In the third sentence, *you **have seen** this before*, the basic verb is *see*. The speaker adds the auxiliary verb *have* to put it into the past, and uses a slightly different form of the verb *see*, *seen*, because that's what the grammar of English calls for in that position.

Is this clear? A basic verbal idea is modified to fit into the sentence, and English modifies its verb according to its own rules, according to its own grammar: *I see, I do see, I am seeing, I will see, I was seeing, I saw, I have seen, I have been seen, I would have seen*, and so on. This modification of a verb to show different aspects or conditions of the action is called *conjugation* (*kahn juh GAY chion*); and a verb is said to *conjugate* (*KAHN juh gate*) when it's modified to exhibit these different conditions.

Collect your thoughts for a moment. Do you understand that verbs are words that indicate an action or state of being? Do you understand that verbs conjugate to express the different ways the action or state of being is to be understood in a sentence? Good. Now you're ready to think about Latin verbs.

LATIN VERBS: THE BASICS

For the most part, almost exclusively, Latin verbs conjugate by attaching things to the end. This is different from English, right, where conjugation is mainly achieved by putting words in front of the verb. Look at the Latin translation for the English verb *to see* in some of its forms:

	Singular		**Plural**	
1st	videô	*I see*	vidêmus	*we see*
2nd	vidês	*you see*	vidêtis	*you see*
3rd	videt	*he/she/it sees*	vident	*they see*

A quick note about pronouncing Latin may be in order at this point. We know two things about the way ancient Latin would have sounded: (1) we don't know exactly what it sounded like, and (2) if it sounded like modern Italian or church Latin, the Roman grammarians who first wrote Latin down were out of their minds. Just listen to your teacher and imitate what you hear. If you're working independently, you can go to the book's Web site, www.languages.uncc.edu/classics /Wheelock, and listen to RealAudio sound files for some extra work.

So what's changing and what's staying the same in the Latin verb? You should be able to see that there's a part of the Latin verb that's staying the same, which has variable endings added to it. You should also be able to deduce what these endings are signifying. But what does all this mean? What's meant by the *1st, 2nd,* and *3rd* off to the left?

Let's look at the numbers to the left first. Any time language takes place, there are two necessary participants. There is the one who is speaking, and there's the one to whom the speech is directed. There's a performer, and there's an audience. In the technical vocabulary of grammar, we call these *person.* The word *person* was a good choice. It means literally *through-sound* (*per-sona*), from the Latin word *persôna*, which means, among other things, a character in a play. So if you imagine that language is a kind of performance, you can see how the people involved in it could be the actors. The one who is the primary orientation around which the speech takes place is called the 1st person. The speaker refers to himself as *I* in English. If the speaker is identifying himself with a group, then that's considered to be a 1st person plural. English uses the word *we* for this.

The perceived audience, the one to whom the speech is directed, is called the 2nd person, and in English it's represented with the word *you*. When the 2nd person is plural, standard English again uses the word *you*. That is, English makes no *formal* distinction between the singular and the plural. (The American southern *y'all*, as useful as it could be, is not yet considered to be standard.)

It is also possible that these two participants, the1st and 2nd person, are talking about something or someone who's not there or who's not seen as one of the two necessary actors in speaking: the speaker and the audience. That's called the *third* person, and English uses the words *he, she, it,* or *they*, if it's plural.

I could go on and on about this concept of person. It's actually quite interesting, but let's keep it simple for now. Here's what you should know about person to get through the first chapter: Latin puts something at the end of the verb to change the person of the verb. We call these endings, surprisingly enough, *personal endings*. Here they are:

	Singular		Plural	
1st	**-ô**	*I*	**-mus**	*we*
2nd	**-s**	*you*	**-tis**	*you*
3rd	**-t**	*he/she/it*	**-nt**	*they*

Now try your hand at changing the person and number of a few other Latin verbs. The verb meaning *warn, advise* in Latin has the stem **monê-**, and the verb meaning *owe, ought* in Latin has the stem **dêbê-**. So have a look at these forms and translate them into English.

Latin	English	Latin	English
dêbêmus		monet[1]	
dêbêtis		monês	
dêbent		moneô	

CONJUGATIONS OF LATIN VERBS

You now know the single most important characteristic of Latin verbs: they conjugate by adding suffixes to a stem. You also now know the most common kind of suffix of verbs: the personal ending. Next you need to know something more about the stems.

The Latin equivalent for the English *see* has the stem **vidê-**, to which you add the personal endings. Notice that the last letter of the stem is a vowel; it's **-ê-**. This

---

[1]You may be wondering why the **-ê-** is short before the personal ending. It just happens that Latin didn't like to have long vowels before a final **-t, -nt,** or **-ô**.

is called its stem vowel, or its thematic vowel. It's the vowel which shows up before the personal endings. Not all Latin verbs have the -ê- as its thematic or stem vowel. There are four groups of Latin verbs, called *conjugations*, determined by the vowel that appears at the end of the stem. The verbs you've been working with have stems that end in -ê. Verbs whose stems end in -ê are called *second conjugation* verbs. If the stem of the verb ends in -â, then it's called a *first conjugation* verb. Verbs whose stems end in short -e are called *third conjugation*, and verbs whose stems end in -î are called *fourth conjugation*. Look at the following examples:

Conjugation:	**1st**	**2nd**	**3rd**	**4th**
Stem:	laudâ-	valê-	agĕ-	venî-

You have worked already with second conjugation verbs. Now let's have a look at an example of a first conjugation verb. The stem of the Latin verb that means *love* is **amâ-**. To conjugate it, we add the personal endings, following the same rules that apply to second conjugation verbs. Fill in the stem and personal endings in the blanks on the following chart but hold off filling in the conjugated forms for now.

	Stem	Personal Ending	Conjugated Form
Singular			
1st			
2nd			
3rd			
Plural			
1st			
2nd			
3rd			

If you follow the rules of conjugation that apply for second conjugation verbs, you should write the form **amaô** for the first person singular. But listen to how easily the two vowels **â** and **ô** can be simplified into a single **ô** sound. Say **âô** several times quickly and you'll see how similar these two sounds are. Over time, Latin simplified the sound **âô** to just **ô**. The final written form therefore is **amô**, not **amâô**. That might appear to be an exception to the rule which says you should add the personal ending to the stem. But if you remember how similar the two sounds are, you'll see that it's still trying to follow the rule. So write **amô** for *I love*. Aside from this small irregularity, however, the personal endings are attached directly to the stem without any alteration or loss of the stem vowel. Complete the table above and compare it to the one that appears in Wheelock, Chapter 1. (See note 1 above for the rules about the long marks.)

THE ENGLISH PRESENT TENSES

The conjugated forms of the Latin verbs you're working with are in the present tense, which should be simple enough. But there is a small difficulty translating the Latin present tense into English that always drives beginning students nuts. Look at the following conjugated forms of the English verb *see*: *I see, I am seeing, I do see.*

Each of these forms refers to present time and is, therefore, a present tense, but each is different. We're so accustomed to these different present tenses in English that we can hardly explain what the different meanings are, even though we're instantly aware that there is a distinction being made. *I see* is called the *simple present* tense; *I am seeing* is called the *present progressive*; and *I do see* is called the *present emphatic*. And just how do we use these different forms?

One way we use the emphatic and progressive present tenses is to ask questions. Here's a present tense statement: *George sees Betty* Now put that into a question. What did you say? You said **Does** *George see Betty?* Do you see what you did? You recast the original simple present tense into the present emphatic, and then put the auxiliary verb in front of George. That's one way English asks simple questions. It uses one of the compound present tenses. Another way we use the emphatic tense is in negatives. Like so: *I see Betty* becomes *I **do** not **see** Betty.* Finally, we can use the emphatic to be, well, emphatic: *I do like green eggs and ham, I do, I do.*

The progressive tense can be used to indicate an aspect of continuity of an action. For example, you can say *I run* meaning that you run for exercise. But if you say *I am running* it means you're running right now.

The point of this is that Latin has only one present tense, but it can be translated into any of the three English present tenses—simple, emphatic, progressive—depending on what sounds right to your native ears. So, when we see **laudâs**, for example, it can be translated into English as *you praise, you do praise*, or *you are praising*. We have to let our native sense of the simple present, the present progressive, and the present emphatic tell us which to use.

THE IMPERATIVE

Another conjugated form of Latin verbs is the *imperative*. Its name is its definition. <u>Look</u> here, <u>Watch</u> out, <u>Stop</u> that, etc. A problem with the English imperative is that it's not clear whether the command is being given to one person or to more than one. Of course, context helps us out, but there is no way to indicate in the verbal form itself whether the command is directed to one person or to a hundred. Latin, however, does have separate forms for a singular imperative and for a plural imperative, just as it has a singular and plural form for the second person which English lacks. To form the imperative of any Latin verb, follow these rules:

Singular	Plural
stem	stem + **te**

THE INFINITIVE

Finally, the last conjugated form of the verbs you get in this chapter is the *infinitive (in FIN in tiv)*. Infinitive forms are those which do not specify a person. You can't say of an infinitive first, second or third person. There are many verb forms that are *infinite*, as you'll see, and which, therefore, could be called *infinitive*. But in common usage, the word *infinitive* is generally limited to forms which are translated into English as *to x* (where *x* is the meaning of the verb). To form the infinitive of Latin verbs, an **-re** suffix is added to the stem. Try a few:

Stem	Infinitive Ending	Infinitive Form	Translation
laudâ-			
monê-			
amâ-			
vidê-			

DICTIONARY CONVENTIONS FOR VERBS

As you can see, each verb has at least ten different forms (there are many, many more which you'll learn later). For obvious reasons, it would be impossible for a dictionary to list all the different forms a verb could have. That is, you can't look up **laudant** just as it is any more than you could look up a conjugated English verb, such as *they are prevaricating*, under *they* in an English dictionary. The dictionary has to simplify the way it lists the information you're going to need to make it manageable.

At some point, either by instruction or experience, you learned the conventions of an English dictionary. You know that *they are prevaricating* is a conjugated form of the basic verb *prevaricate*, and you know that this is so even if you have no idea what the verb *prevaricate* means. In just this way, you have to be trained in the conventions of a Latin dictionary, so that you won't spend fruitless hours digging around in the dictionary looking in vain for the information you need.

What are the conventions for a Latin dictionary? If you see a form like **laudant** in a text you're reading and want to look it up, how do you do it? What is its *dictionary* form? What is the form under which this form will be listed?

You might suppose that the dictionary form for a Latin verb would be the stem. For the form **laudant**, you'd think the dictionary entry would be **laudâ-**. If you thought that, you were almost right. The first entry in a dictionary for a verb is *not* the stem. It's the first person singular. Surprised? There is a reason for it, and I'll explain it to you later. But for now, if you want to look up **laudant**, you first have to picture what it'll look like in the first person singular. You'll have to undo the form **laudant** by taking off the third person plural ending **-nt** and then by adding the first person singular ending **-ô** to get the form **laudô**.

A consequence of this is that when we talk about Latin verbs, we refer to them in their first person singular. So in class you'll hear *The Latin verb for the English verb to see is* **videô.** Or if you're asked a question like *What is* **laudant** *from*? You'll be expected to answer **laudô.**

Do you understand this? I know I'm repeating myself, but many of my students never seem to appreciate the need for a little thinking *before* they rip open the dictionary. The result is that they stagger around for a while in the dictionary, and then either come up with nothing, or they latch onto anything that looks like the word they wanted to find. You must learn to ask your sources of information meaningful questions. And that means asking questions they are equipped to answer and being able to understand the information they return to you. A dictionary cannot answer the question *What is* **laudant**? But it can answer the question, *Is* **laudô** a verb, and if it is, what does it mean?

Let's go through this slowly. Let's look up a verb that first appears to you in a conjugated form: **salvête.**

(1) You have to recognize that **salvête** is a conjugated form, and that the separable suffix is **-te.**

(2) You remember that verbs conjugate by adding endings to the stem, so **salvê-** is the stem. But you can't look it up under the stem alone, because a dictionary lists verbs under the first person singular. You must reconstruct the first person singular to look up this verb.

(3) Next ask yourself what the conjugation of a verb like **salvê-** is going to be, first or second conjugation? Since the final vowel of the stem is **-ê-,** the verb you're looking at is a second conjugation verb. And what does the first person singular of a second conjugation verb look like? It's **salvê + ô salveô.**

(4) Now you've simplified the verb to something you can look it up under: **salveô.** So you look it up.

(5) The second entry for a verb in the Latin dictionary is its infinitive form. After **salveô,** therefore, you see **salvêre.** Since you know that an infinitive is the stem plus the ending **-re,** you can easily see the true stem of the verb simply by dropping off the final **-re** infinitive ending. This confirms the fact that the verb you're looking up is a second conjugation verb.[2]

(6) The translation given for **salveô** is *to be well; to be in good health.* Now translate **salvête.** With the personal ending brought back in the translation, it is *be well* or, more idiomatically, *hello.*

I know this may seem tedious at first, but concentrate on internalizing each one of these steps. You'll benefit immensely when the grammar becomes more complicated. The moral of all this is that you should never go browsing around in the dictionary hoping to find something that might match the word you're looking up. You must think carefully about what you're looking for *before* you turn the first page of the dictionary. This may seem obvious, but the source for a number of common errors beginning students make in their translations stems directly from an indiscriminate, thoughtless use of the dictionary.

---

[2]This may seem like an unnecessary step and that the second entry is entirely superfluous. As you'll see later, however, having the infinitive form given to you is critical to determining the conjugation of the verb. For now, simply get accustomed to looking at both entries when you look up a verb.

VOCABULARY PUZZLES

níhil You might have noticed by now that words of more than one syllable have a little accent mark over one of them. This is not a feature of the Latin language and doesn't change the meaning of the word. They're just stress marks that tell you where to put the stress accent. I'll never use them in my notes, and you'll never see them in written Latin.

amô, amâre, amâvî, amâtum Take a look at the first verb in this chapter's vocabulary list. You'll notice that it has four, not two, entries. It is possible for a verb to have four different entries. I told you about the first two in my notes here because those are the only ones that need concern you for the first several chapters. The last two are used in the formation of tenses you're not going to learn for quite a while. If I were you, I'd pay no attention to the last two entries for now. I won't be talking about them until we get to the tenses that use them.

dêbeô, dêbêre [dêbuî, dêbitum] This verb has an apparently odd combination of meanings, *to owe; should, must, ought,* until we remember that our English verb *ought* is really an archaic past tense of the verb *to owe.* As with the English verb *ought,* the Latin verb **dêbeô** is often followed by an infinitive to complete its meaning: *I ought to see* = **Dêbeô vidêre.** An infinitive which completes the meaning of another verb is called a *complementary infinitive.*

servô, servâre Despite its appearance, this verb doesn't mean *to serve.* It means *to save.* If you think of its English derivatives, you can keep it straight. *Conservation, preservation* and so on all have the basic idea of *save* in them, not *serve.*

ONE LAST THING

Now I'm going to do something I'll never do again in the rest of the book. I'm going to help you with a sentence in Wheelock's *Sententiae* ("thoughts" or "sentences") for this chapter. After fifteen years of having almost all my students mess up the very first sentence of the semester, I can't stand it any longer. And the truth be told, it's not really the fault of the student. Wheelock hits you with a sentence right off that you're not prepared for. Here it is:

Labor mê vocat.

What's so hard about this? Well, you recognize all the words in the sentence, and recognize that the verb is **vocat**, which is in the third person singular. Remembering what you've learned, you want to translate the verb as **vocâ**—*call*—**t** he/she/it or *he/she/it calls.* Right? So what then becomes of the **labor**? The most common mistranslation is *he/she calls me to labor,* because you want to translate **vocat** as *he/she calls,* and then you have to find a way to fit **labor** in. What you don't know is that you're supposed to plug *he/she/it* into the sentence if and only if you *don't already have* a word in the sentence that's performing the action. In this sentence, we do. It's **labor**. So the sentence is *labor calls me* and you don't repeat the *it* that's at the end of the verb in the personal ending **-t**. Now take a quick look at sentence number 8: **Rûmor volat**, and number 10: **Apollô mê servat**. Same thing, right? You don't translate the meaning of the **-t** personal ending. You already have something that's performing the action.

2

What's a Case?

WHAT'S A NOUN? WHAT'S A PRONOUN?

In Chapter 1, you learned the most important lesson in all of Latin: *Things happen at the end of words that you have to pay attention to.* Then you studied personal and other endings that are attached to the stem of verbs. In this chapter, you're going to see that things happen at the end of nouns and adjectives that you have to pay attention to.

First, what's a noun? I remember being taught that a noun is the name for a person, place or thing. That's just fine. A noun is a kind of word which we use to name things. You know, like *tree, horse, house, girl, boy, truth* and so on. Naturally, the complete picture is a heck of a lot more complicated than this, and as you progress we'll have to refine and qualify what you have here, but this will do for now. A noun is word that names a person, place, thing, or idea.

Next, closely related to nouns are words which we call *pronouns*. What are they? You might recognize the *pro-* part of the word from our word *pro,* as in our expression *pro or con.* It means *for* or *on behalf of* or *in place of.* So when we say *pronoun,* we're talking about a word that is, literally, " *pro* a noun", taking the place of a noun. So what are they good for?

Imagine hearing someone talking like this: *Unicorns are mythical beasts. Unicorns don't exist. No one has ever seen a unicorn . . .* This is terribly cluttered. We don't talk like this. Instead, once you understand what's being talked about, we don't have to repeat the noun *unicorn* again and again. We can refer to it with a kind of shorthand, with a *pronoun.* We'd say: *Unicorns are mythical beasts.* **They** *don't exist. No one has ever seen* **one**.

The words *they* and *one* are standing in for the noun *unicorn(s),* and so they're called *pronouns:* pronouns! Let's set this knowledge aside for a while. We'll return to it soon. Next point . . .

INFLECTION IN ENGLISH

Consider the following sentence: *The girl saw the boy.* How can you tell that this sentence does not mean that the boy is seeing the girl? The answer is obvious to an English speaker. *Girl* comes before the verb, and *boy* comes after it. This arrangement tells us that the *girl* is performing the action of the verb, and the *boy* is receiving the action. We say that the one who is performing the action of the verb is the *subject* of the verb. We call the thing that's receiving the action of a verb the *object* of the verb.

This isn't too hard, is it? In English, we generally show these functions (subject and object) by position relative to the verb. The subject of the verb tends to come before the verb, and the object tends to come after it. Turn the original sentence around. Suppose you want the girl to be the object of the verb and you want the boy to be its subject. You'd say *the boy* saw *the girl,* and that would be that.

Now rewrite these sentences replacing the nouns *girl* and *boy* with the appropriate pronouns.

Original	With Pronouns
The girl saw the _boy_.	_____ saw _____.
The boy saw *the girl*.	_____ saw _____.

Did you have any problem with this? Probably not. You probably wrote *She saw him,* and *He saw her* almost without thinking about it. That's because you're a native English speaker, and you just have a feel for English grammar. But let's have a closer look at what you've done.

In the first sentence, you replaced *the girl* with *she,* but in second you replaced *the girl* with *her.* Why? Why are you using different forms of the pronoun? I mean, both pronouns *she* and *her* are referring you to the same thing, namely, the girl. So both pronouns are standing in for the same noun. Why the different pronouns?

And how about *the boy.* In the first sentence, you used *him,* but in the second you used *he.* Why the difference? I know what you're thinking; you're thinking that it sounds right that way. But that's not good enough. You have to *understand* what the difference is. Think about it.

In the first sentence, *the girl* was the subject of the verb, so you used *she* to replace it. That means that the English pronoun *she* is used if the noun it's replacing was the subject of the verb. In the second sentence, *the girl* was the *object* of the verb, and so you used *her* to replace it. That means that the English pronoun *her* is used to replace a noun that would have been the object of the verb. Similarly, we use *he* to replace a subject of a verb, but *him* to replace the object of a verb.

This is very interesting, isn't it? There is something about the *forms* of the words *she* and *he* that makes them sound like subjects to our ears. We can say _she is running down the road_ but we can't say *I saw _she_.* And we'd never say *him likes bananas,* unless we're trying to be amusing. There's something about the *forms* of the words *him/her* that makes them sound like the objects of verbs, not the subject. What's going on here?

Up above I said that English uses position to show what grammatical role a word is playing in its sentence. For the most part, that's how we do it. But sometimes the words themselves will change to show a different grammatical role. *He* has a form that tells you it's going to be the subject of a verb. *Him* shows you that it's being used as the object.

You need some technical terms to describe what's happening. Here goes. When a word changes its form to show you how it's being used in a sentence, we say that the word is *inflecting* (*in FLEK ting*), and we call this whole phenomenon *inflection* (*in FLEK shion*).[3] So we'd say *"her"* is an <u>inflected</u> form of the pronoun *"she."* Or we could say *the pronoun "he"* <u>inflects</u> *to "him."*

This inflection in the pronouns (change of form to show grammatical function) is very useful for helping us understand each other. In English, inflection is almost exclusively limited to the pronouns. The rest of the time we mostly rely on position to tell us what the words in the sentence are doing to each other. But nouns inflect too. For example:

Grammar	Noun's Form	Grammar	Noun's Form
Subject	apple	*Subject*	apples
Possessor	apple's	*Possessor*	apples'
Object	apple	*Object*	apples

Let's pull all this together so that we can get on with Latin. Languages that rely primarily on inflection to show grammatical relationship are called *inflected* languages. That makes sense! English, though it has some inflection, is not an inflected language because it mainly shows grammatical role by position. Latin, however, *is* an inflected language because it relies almost entirely on changes in the words themselves to indicate their grammatical function in a sentence. And since Latin is what we're studying, let's turn to it now.

INFLECTION IN LATIN

Fortunately, the inflection of Latin nouns is a pretty simple affair. The words don't change completely when they inflect, the way that *we*, for example, in English becomes *our* or *us*. Instead, Latin nouns inflect by adding different endings, so you can still see most of the word.

A Latin noun has two parts. It's going have the part that contains the meaning of the noun (the thing it's pointing to) and then attached to the end of it there's going to be the part that tells you what the word is doing in the sentence. An attentive Roman would have heard two things in his nouns: the meaning of the word *and* what it's doing in the sentence. In other words, if English worked the way Latin did, you'd have this in an English sentence:

The girl (subject) sees the horse (object).

Do you see? Attached to the noun is a little marker that tells you how the noun is being used in the sentence. So instead of having just the word for *girl*, you'd also get with it a sound at the end that indicates its particular use in a sentence. That's what you have to train yourself to hear (or to see) in Latin nouns. You have to get used to paying attention both to the beginning of the word, which tells you what the noun means, and then to the end of the word, which tells you what the noun is doing in its sentence.

---

[3] Don't confuse this with verbs. We say that verbs *conjugate* when they change their forms, but we say that nouns *inflect* (*in FLEKT*).

This is going to take some adjustment, and, to be honest with you, a fair number of students of Latin never really catch on to this. What happens is they'll read just enough of the letters of the word to get the definition, and they'll stop and forget to look at the ending, which is where they'd find out what the word is doing. Then they try to find a way to force the noun into a meaningful English translations. In the first several chapters you can get by with this because the sentences are short and the words are practically like English. You can translate them by just getting the vocabulary and then shuffling the words around until you can get some sense out of them. But if you acquire this bad habit, when the sentences start getting more peculiar and more complicated, you'll have to go back and retrain yourself. Better to do it right when you start. Don't stop reading a word until you get to the end and note its ending. Okay, enough exhortation. Back to work.

WHAT IS A CASE?

As native English speakers, you probably instinctively recognize three different grammatical roles a word can play in a sentence. You recognize that a word can be doing something (the subject), it can be owning something (possessive), or having something done to it (object). Don't think too hard about this, because if you do, you'll get confused. Just follow along for a while, okay? There are three different grammatical roles that English sort of accepts and recognizes.

Think about the pronoun *they, their, them*. There are different forms of the third person plural pronoun because the pronoun is recognizing three different grammatical roles it can be playing in the sentence.

The different grammatical functions a word can have in a sentence are called *cases*. We say, therefore, that *they* is in the *subjective case*, because in this form, the word is going to play the grammatical role of being the *subject* of the verb. Further, the form *their* is said to be in the *possessive case*, and *them* is in the *objective case*.

Why are these roles called *cases*? The word *case* is actually a kind of interesting one to use. It comes from the Latin word **cadô** which means *to fall*. There's a Platonic explanation for this. Originally, the Platonically trained grammarians conceived of a word as a representation on earth of something that existed in the mind (or in the world of Forms and Ideas). That is, *dog*, in the sense of *dogness*, is an idea that exists in a perfect world of forms and ideas. But when you use the word *dog* in a sentence, the idea of *dogness* has fallen away a little bit from its perfect idea, because now it's down here with us, being mixed with other things in a sentence. So a *case*—grammatical role—can be thought of as a falling away, a falling down of the idea of the word into the imperfect world of coming to be and passing away. Interesting, isn't it?

To return to our work, in English there are four recognizable cases, that is grammatical functions, a word can have: the subjective, the possessive, the objective, and indirect object.[4] So we say there are four cases in English. In Latin there are six

---

[4] The indirect object case in English is indicated entirely by position and not by a distinct form. In the sentence, *I gave him a dollar*, the word *him* is in the indirect object case which is indicated by its location before the direct object *dollar*. But the word *him* can also be used as a direct object. *I see him.* Similarly, *she showed us some courage.*

different cases. That is, Latin recognizes six different roles a word can play in a sentence, and therefore each word will have six different possible endings to indicate which of the six possible cases the word is in.

I know this sounds terrifying, but try to stay calm. These cases have easily understood English translations, and the different endings follow a pattern that you'll grow accustomed to. We'll start very, very slowly.

Before I show you the endings, let's first discuss what these cases are and what grammatical role they define. Here are the Latin cases. (Don't try to memorize them all at once here. Just read through the list; there will be plenty of time to firm up your familiarity of them.)

Latin	Approximate English Equivalent
Nominative (*NAH mi nuh tiv*)	Subjective Case
Genitive (*JEH ni tiv*)	Possessive Case
Dative (*DAY tiv*)	Object of words like *to* or *for* or Indirect Object
Accusative (*ah KWU zah tive*)	Objective Case
Ablative (*A blah tiv*)	Adverbial Usages: *by, with*
Vocative (*VAH kuh tiv*)	Direct Address

You may be wondering why there are different names in English and in Latin for cases that are nearly identical. Why does Latin grammar say *nominative* when English grammar says *subjective*. You may well wonder, but I have absolutely no idea. Here's a more detailed discussion of the cases.

Nominative

Nominative comes from the Latin word which means *name*. We can see this root in lots of English words, like *nominate, denomination, nomenclature*. The *nominative* case in Latin is considered, in the Platonic sense, to be the least fallen of the cases. So when you refer to a word in Latin, you'll use the word in its nominative case; that is, its *name* case. So to answer the question *what's the Latin word for horse?* you'd say *the Latin word for horse is **equus*** (and *equus* is in the nominative case).

Genitive

The word *genitive,* as in *genitive* case, is related to the word that means generation or source. You know that in Latin the genitive case shows possession, but how does the idea of possession tie into the idea of *source?* You need to think of the object that belongs to someone as coming from him. Think of the expression *John's newspaper.* There's John, and then his possession is the newspaper. So if you want the newspaper, you first have to consider John. The newspaper comes from John. And so John is the source or origin of the newspaper in this narrow sense. I know, I know, this is a bit of a stretch. But as you'll see later, the Latin genitive case really does have uses that are properly described as source or origin. You're just trying to get started in Latin. If I hit you with all the variations and possibilities right away, you'd give up.

Dative

What's next? The *dative* case. What is the etymology of the word *dative*? It comes from the Latin verb that means *to give*. It's lurking under our word *donation*. (Yes, we *do* get our word *date* from it, but explaining how a word meaning *to give* can produce a word that means a point on a calendar is pretty complicated and not worth the effort here.) So you can think of the *dative* case as the *giving* case in the sense that the word in the dative case is having something *given* to it.

Accusative

Tracking down a meaningful etymology of the word *accusative* is really horrid. If I were you, I'd skip over this paragraph. Just note that a word in the accusative case is going to be the direct recipient of the action in a verb or it's going to be the object of a preposition. If you're ambitious enough to follow along, here we go. The word *accusative* has the word for *cause* or *reason* in it. So in what sense can the object of a verb be said to *cause* the action of the verb? Think of it this way. Suppose I kicked a ball. *Ball* is in the accusative case, right, because it's the object of the verb *kick*. So far so good. But how can you say that the ball caused anything? Well, what happened in the sentence? *I kicked*; that's what happened. But what was the reason, the cause of the act of kicking? No one can answer the question completely, but it had at least something to do with the ball, since it was the ball that received the action. In this sense, I acted, that is *kicked*, because of something I wanted to do to the ball. So the ball attracted or evoked an action from me—it was the *cause* of the action. We chaff at this because we're inclined to think of the *reason* for something as the *purpose* for something. Calling the *ball* the purpose for the action makes no sense to us. Presumably, we kicked the ball not because it was there, but because we wanted it to go somewhere. But if you realize that the ball is what allowed the action to happen, then you can get a glimmer of how it could be called the *cause*, the *ac+cause*, the *accusative*. I told you you should have skipped this paragraph.

Ablative

Etymology is no use at all for understanding the meaning of the *ablative* case. Let's just forget it. When you see a word in the ablative case, and if it's not the object of a preposition (a word like **in** or **dê**), use our prepositions *by* or *with* and then translate the word.

Vocative

Finally, the word *vocative* comes from the Latin verb **vôcô**, which you got in the first chapter. So the *vocative* case is the case a noun is in if you're *calling* to it. The vocative is the *calling* case. I sometimes call it the *hey* case: *Hey George* in Latin would be expressed in Latin simply by putting the word *George* in the vocative case.

CASE ENDINGS OF THE FIRST DECLENSION

To review, a Latin noun will have a stem that tells you what the word means, and an ending that tells you what role it's playing in the sentence. So to be able to work with a noun, you're going to have to recognize both its first part, and what kind of ending can be attached to it. Let's look now at how a Latin noun inflects to show all these different cases.

A noun will be able to be in one of six cases, singular or plural. Does that mean that potentially every noun will have as many as twelve different case endings that can be added to its stem? That's about the size of it. That's the bad news. There is some good news. The good news is that nouns will share these case endings. That is, nouns will not have their own exclusive set of case endings that mean something for that noun only. If that were true, you'd have to know the case endings which would be different for each and every noun in the language, and if that were true, the Romans themselves could never have learned their language. No. Instead, there are 5 patterns of cases in Latin, that we call *declensions (deh KLEN shion)*. So the noun for *girl,* for example, will get its case endings from the declension it belongs to, and will never get endings from any of the other four. All nouns belong to one, and only one declension. What this means for you is that eventually you'll have to memorize the pattern of case endings for all five declensions, and then learn how to tell what declension a noun belongs to. Once you've done that, you'll be able to put the right endings on that noun. Let's look at how the word for *girl* (**puella**) inflects through its different cases:

	Singular		**Plural**	
Nom.	puell**a**	*girl*	puell**ae**	*girls*
Gen.	puell**ae**	*of the girl*	puell**ârum**	*of the girls*
Dat.	puell**ae**	*to/for the girl*	puell**îs**	*to/for the girls*
Acc.	puell**am**	*girl*	puell**âs**	*girls*
Abl.	puell**â**	*by/with the girl*	puell**îs**	*by/with the girls*
Voc.	puell**a**	*girl*	puell**ae**	*girls*

The stem of the Latin word is clearly visible. It's **puell-** to which different endings are being attached. The endings are:

	Singular	Plural
Nom.	-a	-ae
Gen.	-ae	-ârum
Dat.	-ae	-îs[5]
Acc.	-am	-âs
Abl.	-â`	-îs
Voc.	-a[6]	-ae

This pattern of endings is called the *first declension*. Hence, we can say that **puella** is a *first declension* noun. Not surprisingly, the other declensions are called the second, third, fourth, and fifth declensions. They are distinguished from one another in part by the thematic, or characteristic, vowel that appears in their endings. In the first declension, the thematic vowel is clearly **-â-**, since it's visible in almost all the case endings. (Don't panic if sometimes the vowel is short. There are some positions in Latin in which a vowel cannot be long, even if it wants to be. In the first declension, the **-a-** *wants* to be long, but is sometimes prevented from being so because of the rules of Latin pronunciation.)

Now try your hand *declining* another first declension noun, **pecûni-**, *money*. Don't forget, all you're doing is adding the additional case endings to the stem.

	Stem	+	Case Ending	→	Inflected Form
N/V.	pecûni-	+		→	
Gen.		+		→	
Dat.		+		→	
Acc.		+		→	
Abl.		+		→	
Plural					
N/V.		+		→	
Gen.		+		→	
Dat.		+		→	[7]
Acc.		+		→	
Abl.		+		→	

---

[5]Originally the dative and ablative plural endings were **-aîs**, but over time this was simplified to **-îs**.

[6]The nominative and vocative endings are so often identical that declensions list them together under *N/V*.

[7]Don't let your English sense of sound mislead you. The form is in fact **pecûniîs** with a doubled **i**. It would have been pronounced something like this: *peh KOO neh ees*.

GENDER

All Latin nouns possess what is called *gender*. That is, a noun will be masculine, feminine, or neuter. I really wish that grammarians had chosen a different word for this feature of Latin nouns. They could have called it *up, down,* and *sideways* or *plus, minus,* or *zero.* They could have called it anything, but they chose the word *gender* which has created all kinds of useless speculation. Students wonder why the word for *virtue* is feminine when it means *manly* virtue in Latin. It's a complete waste of time. Grammatical gender of nouns is not biological gender. Never was. It's just that Latin nouns have an extra property which grammarians decided long ago to call *gender.* So don't ask.

Unlike case, a noun's gender is something it cannot change any more than it can change its meaning. A noun may change its case or number; but it will never change its gender. This is a fixed feature. And just like its meaning, you must be told what gender a noun is when you look it up in the dictionary. You can't guess what the gender of a noun will be with any certainty. This is important to remember, because although the vast majority of *first* declensions nouns just happen to be feminine, not all of them are. You must *memorize* the gender of each noun just as you have to learn and memorize its meaning.

DICTIONARY CONVENTIONS FOR NOUNS

This leads us to another matter. To learn a Latin noun thoroughly, you must know several things. You must know (1) its meaning, (2) its gender, (3) its stem, and (4) its declension. So how are Latin dictionaries laid out to tell you all these things and where do you look to find them? Latin dictionaries use the following conventions for listing nouns:

(1) The first entry in the dictionary is the noun in the nominative, singular case.

(2) The second entry is the genitive singular ending.

(3) The last entry is the gender of the noun.

Are you wondering about (2)? Are you wondering why the dictionary gives you the genitive singular of the noun after it's just given you the nominative singular? I mean, is there any doubt as to which declension the noun **pecûnia** belongs? It ends in an -**a**- so it's a first declension because that's the nominative singular ending of the first declension. Right? Well, that kind of thinking will be good for this chapter, but there's more coming and you'll soon see why it's essential that you be given the genitive case for the noun. If you're really curious about it, read the next paragraph. If you're not, or if you can wait, skip it.

There are two reasons you must be given the genitive of the noun. The first is that some declensions have a nominative case ending that is the same as the nominative case ending of another declension. For example, many nouns in the second declension end in **-us** in the nominative, but so do many nouns that belong to the third declension, and nearly all nouns in the fourth declension do. So if you look up a word in the dictionary and the nominative entry ends in **-us**, you still don't know what declension it belongs to. With a nominative ending like that, it could be either second, third, or fourth, and you need to know what declension it is in order to be able to understand what the case ending is telling you. And how does the genitive case help you out on this? Unlike the nominative case endings, the genitive cases endings are distinctive for each declension. The genitive singular ending of the first declension is **-ae**, that of the second declension is **-î**, that of the third is **-is**, that of the fourth is **-ûs**, and that of the fifth is **-eî**. If you know the genitive singular of a noun, you know what declension the noun belongs to and how the endings are attached to it.

Let's gather up what we've learned about dictionary entries for nouns. The first entry is the nominative singular, the second is the genitive case ending—which tells you the declension to which the noun belongs, and the third is the gender:

Nominative	Genitive	Gender	→	Actual Entry
patria	-ae	*f.*	→	patria, -ae *f.*
pecûnia	-ae	*f.*	→	pecûnia, -ae *f.*
poêta	-ae	*m.*	→	poêta, -ae *m.*

AGREEMENT OF ADJECTIVES AND NOUNS

Moving along, we have one other thing to clear up in this chapter. You might remember from high school grammar that an adjective is a word that modifies or qualifies a noun. In the expression *red leaf*, *leaf* is the noun and *red* is telling you something more about it. That's pretty simple. Here are some more: *a tall building, a difficult sentence, the rocky coast*, and so forth.

Now consider this sentence: *A red leaf with a brown stem fell off the tall tree onto the flat ground.* There is no question about which adjectives are modifying which nouns. That's because in English we tend to put the adjectives right next to the noun they're modifying. No one would think the author is trying to say that the ground is red or that the stem is flat. Position makes this clear. In Latin, however, where position is used differently, adjectives have to be matched up with their nouns in a different way. Instead of using position, Latin adjectives take on some of the characteristics of the nouns they're modifying; i.e., they undergo changes to match the noun they're modifying. We call this *agreement*.

So what properties do nouns have in a Latin sentence? Well, they have case, and they have number (singular or plural) and they have gender (masculine, feminine, or neuter). So each noun has number, gender, and case. That means that an adjective has to be able to acquire the number, gender, and case of the noun it's modifying.

So how does it do that? It does it by declining. And in this respect it resembles a noun. Nouns decline to get different numbers and cases; so do adjectives. But there is an important difference. Latin nouns are either masculine, feminine, or neuter by nature, and they can never change their gender. The noun **porta, -ae**, *f.*, is forever feminine. The noun **poêta, -ae**, *m.*, is forever masculine, etc. But for adjectives to be useful, they have to be able to become any one of the three genders; i.e., adjectives have to be able to be masculine, feminine, or neuter to match the gender of the noun they're modifying. And how do they do that? They accomplish this by using endings from different declensions (and you'll learn these other declensions in the next couple of chapters). So here are two critical differences between adjectives and nouns:

(1) each adjective can have any of the three genders, but each noun can have only one gender;

(2) each noun will belong only to one declension, but adjectives can span declensions.

You'll see much more of this later; but for now you need to know that adjectives use endings of the first declension to become feminine, and, therefore, to modify nouns which are feminine in gender. So try this. Decline the expression *big rose*:

	Singular		Plural	
	magna	**rosa**	**magna**	**rosa**
N/V.	magna	rosa	magnae	rosae
Gen.	magnae	rosae	magnārum	rosārum
Dat.	magnae	rosae	magnīs	rosīs
Acc.	magnam	rosam	magnās	rosās
Abl.	magnā	rosā	magnīs	rosīs

Look at these endings for the adjective and the noun. They look alike, don't they? But this is dangerously deceptive. Get this in your head: *agreement means same number, gender, and case, not look-alike endings*, even though in this limited example and in all the examples in this chapter they do look alike.

VOCABULARY PUZZLES

tua, mea The words **tua**, *your,* and **mea**, *my,* are the first and second person singular possessive *adjectives,* and they consequently must *agree* in number, gender, and case with whatever is being possessed. **Tu-** and **me-** are the stems of the word, and the **-a** is the adjectival suffix. What causes students concern is that they can't quite bring themselves to make the adjectival suffix of the singular possessive adjectives plural. For example, they balk at **meae rosae**, *my roses),* because they assume somehow that the entire word **me-** must become plural. This isn't necessary. Think of it this way: the **tu-** or **me-** part of these words refers to the person doing the possessing, the adjectival suffix refers to whatever is being possessed.

fâma, ae f. Look at this word. Does it look totally unfamiliar, or can you see a little something in there that you've seen before? Certainly there is. There's the English word *fame* there staring back at you. The Latin definition for the word is *rumor, report; fame, reputation.* Is this going to be hard for you to remember? It shouldn't be; it's practically English. Look at some of the other vocabulary items. Can you see English there too? All of these words are such clear English derivatives that they should be a snap to recognize.

What's my point? There's an old story about an American in China who spoke Chinese fluently. He went up to two old Chinese men and asked them in perfect Chinese for directions to the train station. The old men just shrugged their shoulders indicating they didn't understand him. As the American was walking away, he overhead one of the old men saying to the other, "That's funny, but I could have sworn he was asking for directions to the train station." What's the moral? The old Chinese men were so convinced that no American could speak Chinese that they doubted the evidence of their senses.

In Latin, too, many beginning students get themselves into a foreign state of mind, and simply fail to recognize the English that's plainly in front of them. Instead, they rip into the dictionary to look up words like **poêta** or **philosophia**, when it should be obvious what they mean.

True, some Latin words with English derivatives take a little thought and require you to expand your English vocabulary somewhat. The English word *impecunious* (from **pecûnia**) isn't one that comes up every day, so you have to stretch a little. But you should be dictionary-lazy. You should hate to turn to the dictionary to find the definition of a word. You should dig into a Latin word in a sentence and try to see whatever English there is in it. It won't work all the time, but it will work 90% of the time in these early lessons, and about 60% of the time after that. Be lazy! Think!

3

Second Declension Nouns; What's an Adjective?

THE SECOND DECLENSION

You'll have no trouble understanding the concepts in this chapter, *if* you've been paying attention to the specialized vocabulary of grammar. Can you tell me what a *declension* is? And don't say "A declension is, like, endings, like, -**a**, and -**ae**, and, like, **puella**, and, like ... cases?" Learning the meaning of the technical vocabulary of any discipline is the key to everything *in* the discipline. If you can't define the word *declension* you don't *understand* what a declension is, and you're not taking the first few steps in Latin the way you should. This faulty learning will get you into deep trouble very soon, when the syntax of the sentences you're reading will demand a complete mastery of the grammatical concepts underlying them. (Face it, any nitwit can read the five-word sentences you've been getting so far.) Have I terrified you? Good. So what's a declension? Can you come up with a crisp, meaningful definition? Try this: *A declension is a pattern of case endings.* Hold on to this. Remember it.

Latin has five declensions; that is, five different patterns of case endings. And each noun will belong to only one declension. **Puella -ae**, *f.*, for example, is a first declension noun. It will always be a first declension noun. It will never get endings from the second, the third, the fourth, or the fifth declensions. Membership in a declension is simply one of the unalterable features of a noun that you must learn (or recognize) when you study and memorize a noun.

Let's look again at a paradigm for the first declension endings and compare them to endings of the second declension. Decline the noun **puella, -ae**, *f.* and compare its case endings to those of the second declension noun **amîcus**, which I'll decline for you. (You can find the first declension endings in Wheelock, pp.11-2.)

	Singular		**Plural**	
Nom.	puella	amîc**us**	puellae	amîc**î**
Gen.	puellae	amîc**î**	puellārum	amîc**ôrum**
Dat.	puellae	amîc**ô**	puellīs	amîc**îs**
Acc.	puellam	amîc**um**	puellās	amîc**ôs**
Abl.	puellā	amîc**ô**	puellīs	amîc**îs**
Voc.	puella	amîc**e**	puellae	amîc**î**

As you can plainly see, **-a-** is the dominant, also called the *thematic*, vowel of the first declension. With the exception of the dative and ablative plural, all the case endings have an **-a-** plainly visible in them. Now let's compare the first declension with the second. Although it's a little more difficult to see in places, the dominant vowel of the second declension is **-ô-**.[8] Once you see this difference between the first and second declension, you can detect some of the similarities:

(1) The accusative singular of both declensions adds **-m** to the thematic vowel: **-am** and **-um** (originally **-ôm**).

(2) The ablative singular is just the long thematic vowel **-â-** and **-ô-**.

(3) The genitive plural is the ending **-rum** added to the thematic vowel: **-ârum** and **-ôrum**.

(4) The dative and ablative plural are formed alike: First Declension **âîs** → **îs**; Second Declension: **ôîs** → **îs**

(5) The accusative plural in both declensions is the thematic vowel + **-s**: **-âs** and **-ôs**.

SECOND DECLENSION NOUNS IN -ER AND -IR; STEM CHANGES

As I said, this is the *basic* pattern of endings for nouns of the second declension, and all second declension nouns will *basically* use these endings. There are second declension nouns, however, that do not follow this pattern precisely, but which use slight variations of it. Not all second declension nouns end in **-us** in the nominative singular. Some end in **-er** and one common noun ends in **-ir**.

So if the nominative case can look different (**-us, -er, -ir**), then how can you tell that a noun belongs to the second declension when you look it up in the dictionary? Ahhh ... good question! Remember in Chapter 2 when I told you that the dictionary *must* give you the genitive case so that you can be certain you know what declension it belongs to? At the time, you didn't believe me and just pretended you did. *Now* you know why.

Let's say you find a word in the dictionary whose first entry ends in **-er**. What declension is it? It doesn't have the **-us** ending that looks so familiar as a second declension ending. What do you do? What's the next entry for a noun going to be? It's the genitive, or some short-hand way of telling what the genitive singular case ending will look like. And, as you also remember, the genitive singular ending is always discrete—it's always different for each declension. **-ae** is the genitive singular ending of the first declension. What's the genitive singular ending of the second declension? Look back a page or so, if you've forgotten. I'll wait.

---

[8]The **-u-** of the nominative singular **-us** and the accusative singular **-um** was originally an **-ô**. The original dative and ablative plurals of the second declension were **-ôîs**, which was simplified to **-îs**, just as the original **-âîs** of the first declension was simplified to **-îs**.

The genitive singular ending of the second declension is **-î**. So . . . if a noun belongs to the second declension, there will be a **-î** indicated in the second entry in the dictionary. Let's look at the dictionary entries for a couple of second declension nouns:

Nominative	Genitive	Gender	→	Actual Entry
amîcus	-î	*m.*	→	amîcus, -î *m.*
puer	-î	*m.*	→	puer, -î *m.*

Try your hand at declining both these nouns, and then say them aloud in all their cases. Try **amîcus, -î** *m.* first:

	Singular		Plural
Nom.	amīcus	*Nom.*	amīcī
Gen.	amīcī	*Gen.*	amīcōrum
Dat.	amīcō	*Dat.*	amīcīs
Acc.	amīcum	*Acc.*	amīcōs
Abl.	amīcō	*Abl.*	amīcīs
Voc.	amīce	*Voc.*	amīcī

Now decline the noun **puer, -î**, *m.*

	Singular		Plural
Nom.	puer	*Nom.*	puerī
Gen.	puerī	*Gen.*	puerōrum
Dat.	puerō	*Dat.*	puerīs
Acc.	puerum	*Acc.*	puerōs
Abl.	puerō	*Abl.*	puerīs
Voc.	puer	*Voc.*	puerī

Let's try another second declension noun that ends in **-er** in the nominative singular: **ager, agrî**, *m., field*. The nominative is the **-er** type you saw in **puer**, but look at the genitive singular. Instead of just giving you an abbreviation for the genitive singular ending, **-î**, the dictionary is telling you something more. Here you have a full form, **agrî**, for the genitive entry of the noun. The case ending obviously is **-î**, so the noun belongs to the second declension. If you take off the genitive singular ending **-î** you're left with **agr-**, and what's that?

We need to pause here and refine what we mean by a *stem* of a noun. As you probably recall, the stem of a noun is the basic form of the noun to which you add the case endings. But despite the attractive notion that the *stem* of a noun is the nominative singular minus the case ending, the stem of a noun is really the form which is the root of all cases *except* the nominative singular. What's that? The nominative case is something of an exception. Remember the word *nominative* has the word *name* buried in it. The *nominative* case, therefore, is the *name* case of the word. It's almost as if the nominative case is what the word is *before* it starts to decline. In fact, there's a technical term for all the cases except the nominative (singular). We can call all the cases excluding the nominative the *oblique* cases. Why use the word *oblique*? The etymology of the word will tell you: it means something like *leaning away*. So the *oblique* cases are the ones that are *falling* or *leaning* away from the nominative, which, presumably, is standing up straight.

Back to work. We were talking about the stem of nouns. Can you understand this sentence: *it is possible that the stem used in the oblique cases may not be identical to the one in the nominative singular.* Sure, that makes sense. It means that the stem that you can see in the nominative singular of the noun might have to be changed (slightly) when you start declining it. We call such a noun—when the stem changes from the nominative to the oblique cases—a *stem-changing* noun.

So what's the true stem of the noun **ager**? The stem, the true stem, of the word is found not by looking at the nominative entry, but by dropping the genitive singular ending from **agrî**, leaving **agr-**. So the true stem of this word is **agr-**, not **ager-**. Hence, we say that **ager** is a stem-changing noun because the stem is not apparent in the nominative entry. The moral is, therefore, you need to memorize the stem of the noun from the dictionary entry if you want to know the noun completely.

There is another way to see the true stem of a noun that works sometimes. English derivatives typically come from the stem of a noun, not the nominative. So if English derivatives don't have the -e in them, then the Latin noun was probably a stem-changing noun. So how about some English derivatives from **ager**: *agriculture, agronomy, agribusiness.* There you have it. Decline **ager, agrî**, *m*. (Wheelock, p. 18)

	Singular		Plural
Nom.	ager	Nom.	agrī
Gen.	agrī	Gen.	agrōrum
Dat.	agrō	Dat.	agrīs
Acc.	agrum	Acc.	agrōs
Abl.	agrō	Abl.	agrīs
Voc.	ager	Voc.	agrī

If a noun is *not* a stem-changing noun, then the dictionary will simply put the genitive ending in the second entry. But if it *is* a stem-changing noun, the dictionary must indicate that. Examine the following nouns and see how the dictionary conveys the necessary information:

Entry	Stem	Meaning
gener, -î, *m.*	gener-	*son-in-law*
magister, -trî, *m.*	magistr-	*teacher*
socer, -î, *m.*	socer-	*father-in-law*
liber, -brî, *m.*	libr-	*book*
vesper, -î, *m.*	vesper-	*evening*
signifer, -î, *m.*	signifer-	*standard bearer*

The noun **vir, -î,** *m.*, represents another class of second declension nominative singular endings. Is there a stem change indicated in the genitive singular? No, there isn't. So it behaves just like **puer.** Decline it.

	Singular		Plural
Nom.	vir	*Nom.*	virī
Gen.	virī	*Gen.*	virōrum
Dat.	virō	*Dat.*	virīs
Acc.	virum	*Acc.*	virōs
Abl.	virō	*Abl.*	virīs
Voc.	vir	*Voc.*	virī

SECOND DECLENSION NOUNS ENDING IN -IUS

Nouns whose stem ends in an **-i-** need a closer look. What can you tell me about the noun **filius, -iî,** *m*? You should be able to see that it's a second declension noun and that the stem is **fili-** (**filius** minus the **-î** of the genitive singular). But the second entry ends in two **-i**'s. What's that all about? Don't be disturbed. Often when a stem ends in an **-i-** the dictionary likes to reassure you that despite its odd appearance, the genitive singular form really ends with two **i**'s: **filiî.** Similarly, the dative and ablative plurals: **filiîs.** It may look odd, but there was a noticeable difference in the way the two **i**'s would have been pronounced. The first is short, the second is long, so **filiî** would have been pronounced *FEE leh ee.* But, in fact, even the Romans weren't very comfortable with this arrangement; and often the **i**'s were simplified to one long **-î-**: to **filî** or **filîs.** To be consistent, Wheelock always uses the double **i.**

In the vocative singular, however, the **-i-** at the end of the stem does cause a change. **Filius** is an **-us** ending second declension noun, so the vocative singular should be **filie.** But short **i** and short **e** are so similar in sound that some simplification was inevitable. The final form is not **filie** but **filî.** So also in the name **Virgilius**: not **Virgilie,** but **Virgilî.** Decline **filius, -iî,** *m.*

	Singular		Plural
Nom.	fīlius	Nom.	fīliī
Gen.	fīliī	Gen.	fīliōrum
Dat.	fīliō	Dat.	fīliīs
Acc.	fīlium	Acc.	fīliōs
Abl.	fīliō	Abl.	fīliīs
Voc.	fīlī	Voc.	fīliī

ADJECTIVES

Let's review for a moment.

(1) You remember that adjectives are words that qualify nouns, and that an adjective will *agree* with the noun it modifies.

(2) By *agreeing* we mean that it will have the same number, gender, and case as the noun it's modifying.

(3) You also know that an adjective must be able to modify nouns of all three genders, and that to modify a feminine noun an adjective uses the case endings from the first declension.

Now translate and decline *great wisdom. Wisdom* in Latin is **sapientia, -ae**, *f.*, a feminine noun of the first declension, as you can tell from the entry. *Great* is the adjective modifying *wisdom* so it must agree in number, gender, and case with **sapientia**.

The stem of the adjective is **magn-**, and the case endings you must use are those of the first declension, since **sapientia** is feminine.

	Singular		Plural	
	magn-	**sapienti-**	**magn-**	**sapienti-**
N/V.	magna	sapientia	magnae	sapientiae
Gen.	magnae	sapientiae	magnārum	sapientārum
Dat.	magnae	sapientiae	magnīs	sapientiīs
Acc.	magnam	sapientiam	magnās	sapientiās
Abl.	magnā	sapientiā	magnīs	sapientiīs

So you can see what happens to the adjective when it needs to be feminine, and it needs to be feminine when it's modifying a feminine noun. The adjective picks up first declension endings.[9] And what happens when an adjective needs to

[9]Notice! an adjective is different from a noun because a noun *can't* get endings from different declensions, but an adjective can. We don't say that such and such an adjective *belongs* to the first or second declensions. These adjectives are free agents; they have dual citizenship; they belong to the first *and* to the second declensions.

modify a masculine noun? To modify a masculine noun an adjective uses the case endings from the second declension. So if **magn-** is modifying a noun that's masculine, you can expect to see the case endings **-î, -ô, -um, -ô** and so on attached to its stem. We'll do some drills on this in a moment.

That's fine and good, but we have a problem. Which of the three singular nominative forms of the second declension do they use: **-us, -er,** or **-ir**? The answer is that some adjectives will use **-us** and some will use **-er.** (None uses **-ir**.) All the adjectives we'll be looking at for the next two chapters use the **-us** ending and decline after that pattern. In Chapter 5 you'll get the **-er** type; so I'll postpone discussion of that kind until then (although there's nothing really very complicated about it).

To return. Let's suppose you want to modify the noun **poêta, -ae,** m., with the adjective for *great.* Look up *great* in the dictionary and write down what you see.

great _____

What kind of an entry is this? The convention for listing an adjective is different from that for a noun. The first entry tells you how an adjective modifies a masculine noun, the second tells you how it modifies a feminine noun, and the third how it modifies a neuter noun (and we'll learn about that in the next chapter).

Let's look at the first entry. **Magnus** tells you that the adjective uses the **-us** type endings from the second declension to modify a masculine noun; the **-a,** which stands for the nominative singular of the first declension, tells you that it uses first declension endings to modify feminine nouns; the **-um** tells you which endings to use for neuter nouns.[10] Now, how did you find the stem of **-us** type nouns of the second declension? Do you remember? You can cheat a little and simply drop off the **-us** ending of the nominative, and that's the stem. What's the stem of the adjective **magnus, -a, -um**? I hope you guessed **magn-**. So an entry like this is a shorthand way of saying this:

	Singular			Plural		
	Masculine	**Feminine**	**Neuter**	**Masculine**	**Feminine**	**Neuter**
Nom.	magnus	magna	[magnum]	magnî	magnae	[magna]
Gen.	magnî	magnae		magnôrum	magnârum	
Dat.	magnô	magnae		magnîs	magnîs	
Acc.	magnum	magnam		magnôs	magnâs	
Abl.	magnô	magnâ		magnîs	magnîs	
Voc.	magne	magna		magnî	magnae	

[10]We'll fill out the neuter endings in the next chapter.

So decline *great poet*. (**WARNING**: Remember that agreement means same number, gender, and case; not forms which look alike!)

	Singular		Plural	
	great	**poet**	**great**	**poet**
N/V.	magnus	poēta	magnī	poētae
Gen.	magnī	poētae	magnōrum	poētārum
Dat.	magnō	poētae	magnīs	poētīs
Acc.	magnum	poētam	magnōs	poētās
Abl.	magnō	poētā	magnīs	poētīs

Does anyone's chart start out **magna poêta**? That's wrong, wrong, wrong. Why? Consider. When an adjective has to modify a noun that's feminine, what endings does it use? Answer: first declension. What gender is **poêta**? Answer: masculine. So first declension endings on the adjective **magn-** are wrong, because (1) that makes the adjective feminine, and (2) the noun it's modifying is masculine. Okay, so what declension endings are you going to put on the adjective to make it agree with **poêta**, which is masculine? Answer: second.

One last detail. Now that you know that the adjective will use second declension endings of the **-us** type, consider the vocative singular *oh great poet*. Well, the vocative singular of **poêta** is the same as the nominative: **poêta**. And indeed, as I told you a little earlier, most of the time the vocative of nouns will be the same as their nominatives. But the **-us** type second declension is the one exception to this rule. The vocative of nouns, and adjectives, using this declension is not the same as the nominative; it's not **-us** added to the stem. It's **-e** added to the stem. So think about how you have to write *oh great poet* again. You have to write **magne poêta**. Got it?

APPOSITION

Consider this English sentence: *Daniel, my brother . . .* You can easily see that *brother* is giving you more information about *Daniel;* that is, *brother* is modifying or qualifying *Daniel*. In this sense, at least, *brother* is acting like an adjective because it's giving you more information about another word. But since *brother* is a noun, not an adjective, it cannot qualify another noun in quite the same way an adjective does. We call this modifying relationship between nouns *apposition (A poh ZI chion)*. We would say *brother* is in *apposition* to *Daniel*.

In Latin also, nouns can be set in apposition to each other for modification. One noun is modifying another noun—something like an adjective modifying a noun. But a noun cannot agree with the noun it's modifying the same way an adjective does. And why not? Think. An adjective agrees with the noun it's modifying, and agreement means they have the same number, gender, and case. And in order for an adjective to modify nouns of different genders, it has to be able to change its own gender. But nouns all have gender inherent in them, so one noun that's in apposition to another can't be made to agree with the noun it's modifying.

Look. Suppose you want to say "my daughter, the poet" in Latin. You'd write **mea puella poêta**. The word **puella** is feminine, but the word in apposition to it, **poêta**, is masculine. It did not, nor could it, change its gender.

But it *can* acquire the case of the noun it's modifying, and that's what it does in Latin. A noun apposite, or in apposition to, another noun, will have the same case as the noun it's modifying, but it will not change its number or gender to suit that of the noun it's modifying.

In Latin, when a noun is in apposition to another noun, the noun doing the modifying will agree with the modified noun in case. **Gaium, meum fîlium, in agrîs videô,** *I see Gaius, my son, in the fields*. **Gaium** is accusative because it's the direct object of the verb **videô**. Therefore the word for *son* must also be in the accusative case, since it's telling us more about Gaius, and Gaius, as the object of the verb *to see*, is in the accusative case.

READING A LATIN SENTENCE (AKA WORD ORDER)

Many of my students have a very difficult time understanding a very simple concept about Latin. To wit: it's a foreign language. Another way of saying this is: it's not English. Of course, everyone has an intuitive sense that this is so. If Latin were English, it wouldn't be taught in departments of foreign languages by people with years of specialized training. But really understanding what this means, really being able to grasp the full range of its implications, has often proven impossibly elusive to many otherwise very bright young minds.

Latin's system of case inflections has one important implication for word order. It won't be necessary to show grammatical function by position. Accordingly, Latin word order won't be the same as English's, and, more disturbingly, word order in Latin will exhibit considerable flexibility. This is not to say, I should point out, that word order means nothing in Latin. It's just that it means something different. Take this sentence, for example: **videô in agrîs amîcôs meôs**, *I see my friends in the fields*. Grammatically, it is equivalent to this one: **in agrîs meôs amîcôs videô**. The difference is one of rhetorical emphasis, even though the word for word English translation is the same.

Some students never quite recover from this. They want their Latin to follow precise rules at all times, and the shock that it's not always so can be nearly fatal. Sometimes adjectives follow their nouns, sometimes they precede their nouns, and sometimes they're several words away. Sometimes the object precedes a verb, sometimes it comes after. Sometimes the finite verb is at the beginning of a sentence, sometimes at the end, and sometimes in the middle. Your only salvation is going to be to have the case endings and verb forms memorized so thoroughly that it doesn't matter where they come in the sentence. You'll always know what grammatical function each of them has.

VOCABULARY PUZZLES

dê + abl.; **in** + abl. Like English, prepositions in Latin will take the noun they're governing in a case other than the nominative. We wouldn't say in English *with I* or *to she*; we say *with me* and *to her*. But, in Latin, some prepositions will have to be followed by the accusative case; others by the ablative case. (And some can be followed by both, though the meanings change slightly.) Therefore, whenever you learn a preposition, you must also memorize the case it takes.

paucî, -ae This is an adjective, but unlike other adjectives, the word for *few* has no singular forms. (That's logical. How could a word that means *few* be singular?) The dictionary starts its listing in the nominative plural. As you can see, the **-î** and the **-ae** endings are the second and first declension nominative plural endings, respectively. So this adjective declines like **magnus, -a, -um** with the exception that it has no singular forms.

meus, -a, [-um] The adjective means *my*, and it agrees with whatever is being owned. The stem is **me-**. It has an irregular vocative singular ending. Instead of **mee**, you have **mî**. So it's **mî amîce** for *hey, my friend*.

Rômânus, -a, [-um] This is an adjective, but it can be used as a noun, like our word *American*. It's an adjective—like *American pie* or *we're an American band*—but it can also be used for a person: *she's an American* or *the Americans are coming*. Hence, **Rômânî** can mean *the Romans*, and **Rômâna** can mean a *Roman woman*. On the other hand, we can also say **Rômâna patria**, *the Roman fatherland*; or **Rômânî librî**, *Roman books*.

4

More about the Second Declension; Sum; What's a Predicate?

NEUTERS OF THE SECOND DECLENSION

Let's recall some basic facts of the second declension. The second declension is the pattern of case endings which has an **-ô-** for its thematic vowel. The nominative singular has three possible forms—**-us**, **-er**, and **-ir**. Sometimes nouns which end in **-er** in the nominative undergo a stem change from the nominative to the genitive singular. To find the real stem of the noun, you simply drop off the genitive ending **-î** from the second entry in the dictionary. Finally, you may remember that the vast majority of nouns ending in **-us**, **-er**, and **-ir** in the nominative singular are masculine.

What you learned in the last chapter was not the whole story on the second declension. The second declension is divided into two parts: the part you know, and a set of endings that you're going to learn now. This second part contains only neuter nouns. The endings of this pattern are nearly identical to those of the second declension you already know. That's why despite the differences, these endings are best thought of coming from the second declension. The differences are

(1) the nominative singular ending is always **-um**;

(2) the stem is found by dropping off the nominative **-um** ending, and there is never a stem change;

(3) the neuter nominative and accusative plural endings are **-a**.

You don't have to worry about the vocative singular; it's the same as the nominative singular. Remember, the only place in Latin where the vocative differs from the nominative is in the singular of **-us** ending second declension nouns and adjectives. So, a dictionary entry for a noun of this type will look like this: **xum, -î**, *n*. (where **x** is the stem). Here are some examples for you to decline and a second declension noun of the **-us** type for comparison (Wheelock 24-5).[11]

---

[11]Remember that when the stem ends in a **-i-** (**cônsil*i*um**) the dictionary will often repeat the final **-i-** along with the genitive singular, just to reassure you that the noun has forms where the **-i-** is doubled: **cônsiliî, cônsiliîs**.

	numerus, -î, *m.*	**perîculum, -î,** *n.*	**cônsilium, -iî,** *n.*
Nom.	numerus	perîculum	cônsilium
Gen.	numerî	perîculî	cônsiliî
Dat.	numerō	perîculō	cônsiliō
Acc.	numerum	perîculum	cônsilium
Abl.	numerō	perîculō	cônsiliō
Voc.	numere	*same as nom.*	*same as nom.*
Plural			
N/V.	numerî	perîcula	cônsilia
Gen.	numerōrum	perîculōrum	cônsiliōrum
Dat.	numerîs	perîculîs	cônsiliîs
Acc.	numerōs	perîcula	cônsilia
Abl.	numerîs	perîculîs	cônsiliîs

ADJECTIVES

You recall that adjectives are words which modify nouns, and that in Latin an adjective must agree with the noun it's modifying. By *agreeing*, we mean it must have the same number, gender, and case. This means that an adjective must be able not only to change its case and number, but also change its gender, right? That's because nouns come in all three genders. An adjective wouldn't be very handy if it could modify only, say, feminine nouns. To be truly useful, an adjective has to be able to attribute its quality to nouns of all three genders. Now, to acquire number and case, an adjective declines through a declension—just like nouns—but how does an adjective change gender? An adjective changes gender by using different declensional patterns. Like this: if an adjective needs to modify a feminine noun, it uses endings from the first declension; if it has to modify a masculine noun, it uses the second declension endings which are used by **-us** and **-er** ending nouns. You have some experience with this already. You've put first and second declension endings on adjectival stems before. But how do you imagine an adjective will modify a neuter noun? Let's look at a dictionary entry for a typical adjective: **magnus, -a, -um.**

The first entry, as you recall, tells you which declension the adjective uses to modify a masculine noun. It tells you this by giving you the nominative singular ending of the declension it uses. The second entry is the nominative singular ending of the declension the adjective uses to modify a feminine noun. The third entry is the nominative singular ending of the declension the adjective uses to modify a neuter noun.

So there you have it. How does the adjective **magnus, -a, -um** modify a neuter noun? It uses the **-um** neuter endings of the second declension; so **magnus**, when it's modifying a neuter noun, will follow the same pattern as a noun like **perîculum, -î,** *n.* Write out all the possible forms of the adjective *great* (Wheelock 25-6).

	Masculine	Feminine	Neuter
Nom.	magnus	magna	magnum
Gen.	magnī	magnae	magnī
Dat.	magnō	magnae	magnō
Acc.	magnum	magnam	magnum
Abl.	magnō	magnā	magnō
Voc.	magne	magna	magnum
Plural			
N/V.	magnī	magnae	magna
Gen.	magnōrum	magnārum	magnōrum
Dat.	magnīs	magnīs	magnīs
Acc.	magnōs	magnās	magna
Abl.	magnīs	magnīs	magnīs

THE VERB SUM

The verb *to be* is irregular in Latin; i.e., it doesn't follow the normal pattern of conjugations of other verbs. Wheelock says it's best just to memorize the forms by sheer effort and rote. That's a perfectly acceptable suggestion. But the verb is actually much more regular than it may first appear. If you wish, you may try to follow my discussion about the verb to get a glimpse behind its seemingly bizarre appearance. If not, just memorize the forms outright and skip over the paragraphs in between the lines of asterisks.

****

For those of you going on with me, let's recall a couple of things. A verb conjugates by adding personal endings to the stem of the verb. You find the stem of the verb by dropping the **-re** ending of the infinitive, and what you're left with is the stem. The final vowel of the stem tells you the conjugation of the verb: **-â-** for a first conjugation; **-ê-** for the second conjugation, etc. Let's have a look at the infinitive of the verb *to be* to find its stem. The infinitive is **esse.** What kind of an infinitive is this?

We need to back up a little. Although you were told otherwise, the real infinitive ending of a Latin verb is not **-re** at all, but **-se.** Why does the **-se** become **-re**? Like this. It's an invariable rule of Latin pronunciation that an **-s-** which is caught between two vowels—we call it *intervocalic* (*in ter voh KAH lik*)—turns into a **-r-.** So the *real* infinitive of the verb *to praise* is **laudâ + se laudâse.** But because the **-s-** of the true infinitive ending is in between the **-â-** and the **-e-,** it changes to an **-r-.** The final form, therefore, is what you recognize: **laudâre.** Okay, so let's return to **esse.**

If we drop off the infinitive ending, the real infinitive ending, **-se**, we're left with the stem **es-** for the verb. But the stem has no final vowel like other verbs. For this reason we call **esse** an *athematic verb*, because its stem ends in a consonant, not a vowel. To conjugate the verb, we should therefore add the personal endings directly to the final **-s** of the stem. This is what the formula should be (don't fill in the conjugated form yet).

	Stem	+	Personal Ending	→	Conjugated Form
1st	es	+	m[12]	→	sum
2nd	es	+	s	→	es
3rd	es	+	t	→	est
Plural					
1st	es	+	mus	→	sumus
2nd	es	+	tis	→	estis
3rd	es	+	nt	→	sunt

Try to pronounce the final form for the first person singular: **esm**. Do you hear how you're automatically inserting a **u** sound to make the word pronounceable? It sounds like **esum**. Now try to pronounce the first person plural: **esmus**. The same thing happens between the **s** and the **m**, doesn't it. You almost *have* to insert a **u** sound. Now pronounce **esnt**. Same thing, right? You almost *have* to put in a **u** sound before all the personal endings that start with an **-m-** or an **-n-**, and that will be the first person singular and plural, and the third person plural. There's something else. Wherever the form is lengthened by this additional **u** sound, the first **-e** of the verb stem **es-** is dropped off. So it becomes just **s-**. Okay, you're ready to write out the conjugated forms. Now look at the remaining forms, the second person singular and plural, and the third person singular. Is there any trouble adding an **s** or a **t** to the final **s-** of the stem? No. In fact, in the second person singular, the **s** of the personal ending just gets swallowed up by the **s** of the stem: **es + s es**. Fill out the conjugated forms and check your work (Wheelock 26).

****

As with other Latin verbs, the basic form of *to be* is considered to be the first person singular, and that's how the verb will be listed in the dictionary, followed by the infinitive. The entry will be: **sum, esse**. So when I want to refer to the Latin verb *to be*, I'll say: the verb **sum**. You can also see why it's going to be important to memorize all these forms well. You can't look up **estis** or **es**. You must reduce these conjugated forms to a form that will appear in the dictionary: you must know that these forms are from **sum**.

---

[12]Don't be alarmed by this ending; it's a perfectly normal alternative form for **-ô**. You'll see it a lot.

SUBJECTS AND PREDICATES

We divide sentences into two parts: the subject, which is what's being talked about, and the predicate (*PREH dee kit*), what's being said about the subject. Basically, the subject is the subject of the verb, and the predicate is the verb and everything after it. For example, in the sentence *Latin drives me crazy because it has so many forms*, **Latin** is the subject, and everything else is the predicate. Of course, the full story of subject and predicate is more involved than this, but this will get us by for now.

TRANSITIVE AND INTRANSITIVE VERBS: PREDICATE NOMINATIVES

In Latin, the subject of a verb is in the nominative case. You know that. So it may seem to follow that whenever a noun is in the nominative case, it will be the subject of a verb, and, hence will always be in the subject of the sentence. But while it's true that all subjects of verbs with person will be in the nominative case, it does not follow that all nouns in the nominative will be subjects. We do find nouns in the nominative case in the predicate. When we do, we call them, logically enough, *predicate nominatives*. But how does it happen that a nominative case shows up in the predicate? Here's the answer.

We divide verbs into two broad classes: verbs that transfer action and energy from the subject to something else (the object), and verbs in which there is no movement of energy from one place to another. Consider this sentence: *George kicked the ball*. Here George expended energy—he kicked—and this energy was immediately applied to an object—the ball—which was changed as a result of what George did to it. We call a verb like this a *transitive* verb because there is a *transition* of energy. Now look at this sentence: *The river is wide*. Is the river doing anything in this sentence to anything else? Does the verb *is* imply that the subject is acting on something else? No. There is no movement of activity from the subject to something else. Verbs like this are called **in**transitive because there is no transition of energy. Consequently, they don't take direct objects because there's nothing being acted upon. Some more examples of intransitive verbs:

*The dog **was running** away.*

*We'll all **laugh**.*

*Krusty the Klown **didn't seem** very happy.*

Sometimes it's hard to tell whether a verb in English is transitive or intransitive. The problem comes about because English can use the same verb transitively or intransitively. Like this. You can say *George is singing*. That's a perfectly good sentence, and it's clear that George isn't affecting anything else by singing. He's just participating in the action. So since there's no movement of energy from George to something else, we'd have to say that the verb *singing* is not transitive. But we could also say *George is singing a song*. Now this is different. Here George is singing, but his action is directed toward something, namely, the song. So in this instance, the song is the direct object of the verb, and so we'd have to say that the verb of this sentence is being used *transitively.* Maddening, isn't it. A rule of thumb is this: Ask yourself, *Can I 'x' something?* (where *x* is the verb you're investigating). If that sounds right, then the answer is *yes,* the verb is transitive; if *no,* then it's intransitive. *Can I see something?* Yes; therefore the verb *to see* is being used transitively. *Can I fall something?* No; therefore, *to fall* is not being used transitively.

SUM AS A COPULATIVE VERB

The verb *to be* is obviously an intransitive verb—there is no movement of energy from the subject to an object—but it has an interesting additional property. What are we actually doing when we use the verb *to be?* We are in effect modifying the subject with something in the predicate. In the sentence *The river is wide, river* is the subject and *wide* is an adjective in the predicate that is modifying *river.* Even though it's on the other side of the verb and in the predicate, it's directly tied to the subject. In Latin, therefore, what case would *wide* be in? Think of it this way. *Wide* is an adjective, and it's modifying the *river,* even though it's in the predicate. Adjectives in Latin must agree in number, gender, and case with the nouns they modify, so *wide* has to be in the nominative case. It's modifying *river,* right? What the verb *to be* does is to tie or link the subject directly to something in the predicate, and for that reason we call the verb *to be* a *linking* or *copulative* (*CAH pew lah tiv*) verb. This principle has a special application in Latin, which has a full case system. When the verb **sum** links the subject with an adjective in the predicate, the adjective agrees with the subject:

Dônum	est	magnum.		Dôna	sunt	magna.
nominative	=	nominative		nominative	=	nominative
neuter	=	neuter		neuter	=	neuter
singular	=	singular		plural	=	plural

When **sum** links the subject with a *noun* in the predicate, however, we have a bit of a problem. You know, like *this child is a monster.* Nouns have fixed gender, so the noun in the predicate can't agree with the subject noun in quite the same way an adjective can. A noun in the predicate has its own gender which it cannot change. But a noun in the predicate that is tied to the subject by **sum** will agree with the subject in *case.* Think of the verb **sum** as an equal sign, with the same case on both sides:

<u>My life is war.</u>

Mea vîta	est	bellum (*war*).
nominative		nominative
feminine		neuter
singular		singular

ADJECTIVES AS NOUNS

Think about the underlined words in these English sentences:

(1) The <u>poor</u> will always be with you.

(2) Only the <u>good</u> die young.

(3) He expects only the <u>best</u>.

These sentences make perfectly good English, but there is something interesting going on. What kind of words are *poor, good,* and *best*? What part of speech are they? They're adjectives, of course, as you can easily tell by putting them into different expressions: *you're driving me to the <u>poor</u> house,* where *poor* is modifying *house; he's one <u>good</u> apple,* where *good* is modifying *apple; we had the <u>best</u> time in Miami!* where *best* is modifying *time.* Remember, adjectives modify nouns, and you can see how they're doing that in these three sentences. Now go back to the original three. What are these adjectives agreeing with, or modifying? What does *poor* tell you more about? What noun does *good* modify? What does *best* go with? Obviously, they're modifying nothing. How can that be?

Let's look at it another way. What is the subject of the first sentence? Or, to put it a different way, what is the subject of the verb *will be*? The answer is, *the poor.* What about the second sentence? What is the grammar of the word *good*? That is, what grammatical role is the word playing? Once again, it's the subject of the verb of the sentence: *die.* Finally, what's the grammar of *best* in the third sentence? That's easy enough; it's the direct object of the verb *expect.* But these are roles that nouns usually play. How can we account for the fact that these adjectives are used like nouns?

You've perhaps already drawn the correct conclusion. It's possible for adjectives to be used in place of nouns, or without nouns, provided that there's a pretty clear reference for them. The adjectives are still agreeing with a noun, but the noun just isn't explicitly stated. In the first sentence, what do you suppose *poor* is most likely agreeing with? Probably *people,* right? So the full sentence would be *the poor <u>people</u> will always be with you.* You can similarly expand the second sentence to *only the good <u>people</u> die young.* What about the third? Here the omitted word is a little more difficult to identify exactly. This could mean *the best <u>thing</u>* or *the best <u>outcome</u>* or *the best <u>pie</u>* or something else that the context would supply. In any case, the adjective is implying some noun that must be understood with the adjective.

When adjectives appear in a sentence without a noun, we say that the adjective is being used as a *substantive* or that the adjective is being used *substantively* (sub stan TIVE uh lee). *Substantive* is just another word for a noun. So what is really meant is the adjective is being used as a noun.

There are a couple more features that you have to keep in mind when you're dealing with an adjective being used as a substantive in Latin. That's because Latin can be much more specific in terms of the number and gender of nouns and adjectives than English can be. Consider how we'd translate this English sentence into Latin: *the greedy are bad.* The verb is *are,* so it will come from the Latin verb *sum.* It'll be third person plural. The subject is *greedy* so it'll come form the Latin adjective *avârus, -a, -um* and we'll put it into the nominative plural. But what gender should we choose? Well, what noun do you think the adjective is implying? Probably *people*, so we'll make the adjective masculine (masculine is the default gender for referring to a group of people which probably has both genders in it). Then the adjective *bad*, since it agrees with *greedy*, will be nominative, plural, and masculine. So here's the Latin sentence: **Avârî sunt malî.** That wasn't so hard.

But now look at this sentence: **Avârae sunt malae.** Now what do you have? Now the gender of the adjectives is feminine, so clearly the speaker is referring you to feminine nouns that have been left out. How do you translate it? It has to be something like *greedy women are bad.* Do you see? Because Latin is an inflected language, it can be more precise referring to things that have been left out. Study these examples, and see whether you're catching on.

Magister vêra docet, *the master teaches true [things] or the truth.*

Bonî vêra amant, *the good love true [things] or the truth.*

Iuvat parvam, *he is helping the small one [woman].*

Nôn stultôs iuvâmus, *we don't help the stupid [people].*

Nôn stultâs iuvâmus, *we don't help the stupid [women].*

Stultî multa timent, *the stupid [people] fear many [things].*

Bellam amâtis, *you love the beautiful [female].*

Bellôs amâtis, *you love the handsome [males].*

Oculî meî multa stulta vident, *my eyes see many stupid [things].*

Oculî meî multôs stultôs vident, *my eyes see many stupid [people].*

VOCABULARY PUZZLES

Look at these two dictionary listings: **bellum, -î,** *n., war;* **bellus, -a, -um,** *beautiful.* The first is an entry for a noun, the second an entry for an adjective. What are the differences? An entry for a noun starts with the nominative singular form, then it gives you the genitive singular. It actually starts to decline the noun for you so that you can tell the noun's declension and whether the noun has any stem changes you should be aware of. The final entry is the gender, since nouns have fixed gender which you must be given. For a noun, therefore, you must be given (1) the nominative form, (2) the stem, (3) the declension, and (4) the gender.

An entry for an adjective, by contrast, has different information to convey. For an adjective, you must know which declension it'll use to modify nouns of different gender, and that's what the **-us, -a, -um** is telling you. But there is an important omission from the adjective listing. There is no gender specified; and why should that be? It's because adjectives can *change* their gender. As you'll see later, this is the one sure sign that a word you're looking at in a dictionary is an adjective: it has declension endings listed but no gender.

You may also be concerned that, given the similar appearance of these two words, you may mix them up in your sentences. Certainly there will be some overlap of the two forms. For example, **bella** is a possible form of both the noun **bellum** and the adjective **bellus, -a, -um**. But there are also many forms that **bellus, -a, -um** can have that **bellum, -î**, *n.*, can never have. For example, **bellârum** can't possibly come from a second declension neuter noun. Neither can **bellae, bellâs, bellôs, bellâ**, and some others. If you see **bell-** something in your text, first ask yourself whether the case ending is a possible form from the neuter noun for war. If not, then it's from the adjective for *pretty*. In the instances where the forms do overlap, you'll have to let context and your good judgment tell you which it is. Let's try one.

Bella pecûniam multam habet.

This one's a little tricky. First off, the form **bella** could be from the neuter noun that means *war*. If it is, then **bella** is either nominative or accusative plural. Let's try nominative plural first. If it's nominative, then it's likely to be the subject of the verb. And if it's the subject of the verb, then the verb must be plural. Are you with me? If **bella** is nominative plural, then it's the subject of the verb and the verb must be plural. So you can expect an **-nt** ending on the verb of the sentence. But the verb of this sentence is singular. Therefore, you can conclude that **bella** isn't nominative. That leaves you with accusative plural if it's from **bellum, -î**, *n.* In that case, it would be object of the verb **habet**. So let's see about that. The verb is singular, and there is no nominative case, right? We ruled out **bella** as nominative because it would be plural and the verb is singular. And **pecûniam multam** is certainly not nominative with the **-am** ending. So we have to plug in a pronoun to hold the place of the subject of **habet**. Let's use *he*. At this point then we have *he has much money wars*. Does that make sense? No, it doesn't. Back to the drawing board.

What progress have we made? Remember, if **bella** is from **bellum, -î**, *n*, then it has to be either nominative or accusative plural. But we've just ruled out both possibilities. Therefore, what can we conclude? We can conclude that **bella** is not from **bellum, -î**, *n.*, and so it must be from **bellus, -a, -um**.

Now, if it's from **bellus, -a, -um**, what number, gender, and case could it be? If you can't come up with the answers fairly quickly, then you need to go back and review your case endings. The adjective **bella** could be (1) nominative singular feminine, (2) nominative plural neuter, or (3) accusative plural neuter. But we've already ruled out the possibility that it can be nominative plural or accusative. Do you remember that? We're left with (1) nominative singular feminine. Let's try it: *the beautiful [female] has much money*. Does that make sense? Of course it does.

I know this is tedious. Sometimes Latin will flow easily, but at other times you have to zero in on difficult little problems. Most importantly, you have to be thinking constantly about what you're doing, especially at the beginning when your problems are few.

5

The Future and Imperfect Tenses

FUTURE TENSE OF FIRST AND SECOND CONJUGATION VERBS

You weren't told this before, but there is a place between the stem of a verb and the personal endings where there is meaning. This is where Latin can put tense markers. In this chapter, you'll learn the tense markers for the future and imperfect tenses of verbs of the first and second conjugations.

When you want to put an English verb into the future tense, you use the stem of the verb and put *will* in front of it: *I see* becomes *I **will** see*; *they have* becomes *they **will** have*; etc. We call the additional word *will* a *helping verb*, or, more learnedly, an *auxiliary verb*. No matter what you call it, the *will* is changing the way the listener will understand the action of the verb *to see* and *to have*.

In Latin, the future tense is formed differently. The formula for forming the future tense of first and second conjugation verbs in Latin is this:[13]

stem + **be** + personal endings.

If you've studied a little Latin before, you're probably gasping for breath right now. Stay with me. It's all going to make sense.

The stem of the verb, you remember, is what's left over after you've dropped off the **-re** of the infinitive (the stem includes the stem vowel). The **-be-** is the sign of the future and is attached directly to the stem. Then you add the normal personal endings you used in the present tense directly to the tense sign **be**. So let's start to conjugate the future tense of a first and a second conjugation verb. Here are the tables. (Don't fill in the conjugated forms just yet.)

Future of the first conjugation: laudô, laudâre

	Stem	**Tense Sign**	**Personal Ending**	**Conjugated Form**
1st	laudā	be	ō	laudābō
2nd	laudā	be	s	laudābis
3rd	laudā	be	t	laudābit
Plural				
1st	laudā	be	mus	laudābimus
2nd	laudā	be	tis	laudābitis
3rd	laudā	be	nt	laudābunt

[13]This rule applies *only* to the first and second conjugation verbs; the third and fourth conjugation verbs form the future tense in another way.

Future of the second conjugation: moneô, monêre

	Stem	Tense Sign	Personal Ending	Conjugated Form
1st	monē	be	ō	monēbō
2nd	monē	be	s	monēbis
3rd	monē	be	t	monēbit
Plural				
1st	monē	be	mus	monēbimus
2nd	monē	be	tis	monēbitis
3rd	monē	be	nt	monēbunt

All this seems quite logical and straightforward. But there is one glitch: the short **-e-** of the tense sign **-be-** undergoes some radical changes when you start attaching the personal endings. Here's what happens.

(1) Before the **-ô** of the first person singular, the short **-e-** disappears completely, leaving **-bô**.

(2) Before the **-nt** of the third person plural, it becomes a **-u-**, leaving the form **-bunt**.

(3) And before all the other endings, it becomes an **-i-**, for **-bis, -bit, -bimus**, and **-bitis**.

As you can see, the short **-e-** in fact never stays what it truly is in any of these forms. And you may very well be wondering to yourself why I'm showing you all this. Why can't you simply memorize the future endings as **-bô, -bis, -bit, -bimus, -bitis**, and **-bunt**, without having to look any deeper into its history? The answer is you can certainly remember just the final forms if you wish, but this problem of the short **-e-** changing to other vowels occurs repeatedly in Latin; and instead of memorizing by rote each time you come across it, it just seems easier to learn the rule governing the changes, rather than encountering the changes each time as unique phenomena. It's hard to believe now, but knowing the deeper rules will make your life simpler in the future. Now that you know the rules, go back and fill in the conjugated forms of the future tense (Wheelock 31-2).

THE FORM OF THE IMPERFECT TENSE

The imperfect tense is formed precisely according to this same formula: stem + tense sign + personal endings. So to form the imperfect tense all you need to know is its tense sign and the personal endings it uses. The tense sign for the imperfect tense is **-bâ-**,[14] Finally, the imperfect tense uses the alternative ending **-m** in place

---

[14]You can remember the tense sign like this: *After four years of college, you'll get a B.A., but you'll still be* **imperfect**. My students hate that one. Here's another one: the **-â-** of **-bâ-** stands for *already happened*, or *been already*, as distinct from the **-i-** of the future, which stands for *in the future*.

of **-ô** for the first person singular ending. This makes some sense. Suppose the imperfect were to use **-ô** for the first person singular. What would happen? Well, think back. What happens in the first person singular of first conjugation verbs, whose stem vowel is long **-â-**? The **-â-** elides with the **-ô-** and is lost: **laudâ + ô → laudô.** Now if the imperfect were to use **-ô** instead of **-m**, the same thing would happen and the ending of the verb would be **-bô**, which is the same as the future. So, perhaps to avoid confusion, the imperfect tense uses the **-m**. But maybe not. Anyway, here is the formula for forming the imperfect tense:

stem + **bâ** + personal endings.

And here are a couple of things to remember:

(1) The stem vowel of the verb lengthens.

(2) The stem vowel for third i-stem and fourth conjugation verbs is **-iê-**.

(3) The first person singular ending is **-m**.

Now conjugate the imperfect tense for the first two conjugations (Wheelock 452).

Imperfect of the first conjugation: laudô, laudâre

	Stem	Tense Sign	Personal Ending	Conjugated Form
1st	laudā	bā	m	laudābam
2nd	laudā	bā	s	laudābās
3rd	laudā	bā	t	laudābat
Plural				
1st	laudā	bā	mus	laudābāmus
2nd	laudā	bā	tis	laudābātis
3rd	laudā	bā	nt	laudābant

Imperfect of the second conjugation: moneô, monêre

	Stem	Tense Sign	Personal Ending	Conjugated Form
1st	monē	bā	m	monēbam
2nd	monē	bā	s	monēbās
3rd	monē	bā	t	monēbat
Plural				
1st	monē	bā	mus	monēbāmus
2nd	monē	bā	tis	monēbātis
3rd	monē	bā	nt	monēbant

THE MEANING OF THE IMPERFECT TENSE

Forming the imperfect tense is just about the easiest thing in the world. What drives students and their teachers crazy is translating it. The imperfect tense refers to a past action which, presumably, has already been completed by the time the speaker is talking about it. However, the imperfect tense also indicates an action that was *going on* in the past over a period of time or that occurred again and again in the past, and hence is not viewed by the speaker as ever having reached a definite point of completion. Let's look at some examples of the English imperfect tense. You'll have an instinctive sense for the imperfective idea in the verbs, but try to develop some consciousness about it.

Even though the game **was** *still* **going on**, *I left the stadium.*

David always **used to like** *to go to the zoo.*

She **would** *always* **come** *on Tuesdays.*

In the first example, contrast the imperfect tense *was going on*, with the preterit, or simple past *left*. The fact that *I left* is viewed by the speaker as an action that had a definite end; it's something he did in a finite amount of time and something he completed. The fact that the game was still going on, however, is viewed as the general context in which he performed the action of leaving. The game was going on before he left; and, presumably, it continued to go on after he left. The game is viewed as an action with no explicitly conceived beginning and no definite ending. Now, of course, the game did start at some definite time in the past, and it's probably over by now, but the way the speaker chose to represent it for his own needs was as an action that extended over an indefinite period of time. In another context he might say, *The game* **started** *at 3:30 and* **ended** *at 7:00.* The point is, there's nothing *inherently* imperfective about the game. The speaker's portrayal of it will make it either perfect or imperfect.

In the second and third examples, we have something slightly different. Here, English expressions *used to like* and *would come* are indicating things that occurred repeatedly in the past. The Latin imperfect has this sense as well. Because a repeated or habitual action also has the sense of incompleteness—he or she never stopped doing whatever he or she used to do—the imperfect tense is also used to express this meaning: repeated or habitual action. When you're translating an imperfect tense into English, try out these different approaches—*used to* **x**, *was* **x**-*ing*, or *would* **x** (where *x* is the meaning of the verb) and see which one feels the best.

FIRST AND SECOND DECLENSION ADJECTIVES IN -ER

Look at this adjective: **stultus, -a, -um**. Do you remember what this entry is telling you? An adjective spans the first and second declensions to get the endings it needs to modify nouns of different genders. This entry is telling you that the adjective for *stupid* (stem: **stult-**) uses second declension **-us** type endings when it modifies masculine nouns, first declension endings when it modifies feminine nouns, and the **-um** category of neuter endings of the second declension to modify neuter nouns.

Now let's look a little more closely at the second declension. It has two parts, you may remember: the section reserved entirely for neuter nouns—those ending in **-um** in the nominative singular—and the section used by masculine and feminine nouns (the vast majority are masculine). There is a variety of nominative singular endings in this second group: **-us**, **-er**, and **-ir**. The nouns that followed the **-us** type second declension presented no problems. To find the stem, you simply dropped off the **-us** ending of the nominative case. But for the second declension nouns which end in **-er** in the nominative singular, you had to be more careful. For some of them, the stem was the form of the nominative singular, but for others the **-e-** of the **-er** dropped out from the stem. Then you used the reduced form for all the other cases. The dictionary has to tell you which **-er** ending nouns have stem changes; and it does so in the second entry for the noun: **puer, -î,** *m.;* **liber, -brî,** *m.;* **ager, agrî,** *m.* The stem of **puer** is **puer-**, the stem of **liber** is **libr-**, the stem of **ager** is **agr-**. Okay, so much by way of review.

Now look at this word as it appears in the dictionary: **lîber, -a, -um**. What is this? Is it a noun or an adjective? You can tell it's an adjective because there is no gender listed for it. Remember, an adjective has to be able to change its gender, so it has no fixed gender, as a noun does. An entry for an adjective has to tell you how it will acquire different genders—which declensional patterns it will use to become masculine, feminine, and neuter—and, you may recall, the first entry shows you the masculine nominative, the second the feminine nominative, and the third the neuter nominative.

So have a look again at this adjective. The second entry looks familiar—it's the nominative singular ending of the first declension. This tells you that the adjective **lîber** becomes feminine by using first declension endings. The **-um** should look familiar, too. That's its neuter ending, telling you it uses the **-um** endings of the second declension to modify neuter nouns. But what's the first entry? You know that this is telling you how the adjective becomes masculine, but what about the **-er**?

You've probably already figured out by now that the adjective is going to use the second declension endings to modify masculine nouns, and that it's going to use the **-er** ending in the nominative singular. So for *free soul,* you would write **lîber animus**. But what is the true stem of the adjective? Remember that **-er** ending nouns of the second declension often change their stems when they move out of the nominative singular. The dictionary tells you about that in the second entry for the noun in the genitive singular. That is, the dictionary actually starts declining it for you. But how will it tell you whether an adjective in **-er** has a stem change?

The rule is this: an adjective in **-er** that changes its stem (i.e., drops the **-e**) will use the changed stem in all genders and numbers and cases *except* for the nominative and vocative masculine singular. So all you need to see to know whether the adjective is going to change its stem is the next entry—the feminine nominative singular. Look at this entry: **pulcher, -chra, -chrum**. There, do you see it? The second entry shows you not only how the adjective becomes feminine, but also that the stem for all other cases except the masculine nominative singular is **pulchr-**. Look at this adjective: **noster, nostra, nostrum**. Stem change, right? Now look at this again: **lîber, -a, -um**. There is no stem change since it is not indicated in the second entry. The stem is **lîber-** throughout its inflection.

DRILL

Translate and decline the expression *our free fatherland*: **noster, -tra, -trum,** **līber, -a, -um, patria, -ae,** *f.*

	our	free	fatherland
Nom.	nostra	lībera	patria
Gen.	nostrae	līberae	patriae
Dat.	nostrae	līberae	patriae
Acc.	nostram	līberam	patriam
Abl.	nostrā	līberā	patriā
Plural			
Nom.	nostrae	līberae	patriae
Gen.	nostrārum	līberārum	patriārum
Dat.	nostrīs	līberīs	patriīs
Acc.	nostrās	līberās	patriās
Abl.	nostrīs	līberīs	patriīs

VOCABULARY PUZZLES

animus, -ī, *m.* In the singular the word means *soul, spirit,* the vapory seat of self-awareness. But in the plural it often takes on another meaning. It may mean *courage,* like our expression *high spirits, spirited,* as in *the losing team put up a spirited struggle.* It happens often in Latin that a word will acquire new meanings in the plural. Cf., the meaning of the English word *manner* in the singular with its meaning in the plural: *manners.*

noster, -tra, -trum This is an adjective which means *our.* That is, the adjective agrees with the thing that belongs to us. Therefore, it has a plural form only if the noun it's agreeing with is plural. Students are often lured into thinking that **noster** will have only plural case endings because *our* is first person plural. Remember, **noster** will have plural cases endings only if it's agreeing with a plural noun: **noster filius,** *our son,* or **nostrī filiī,** *our sons.*

igitur Wheelock tells you it's postpositive. That means it never is the first word in a Latin sentence (and it's usually the second word.) Despite our tendency to put the English *therefore* at the beginning of the sentence, **igitur** is never first. Remember.

-ne We form questions in English by juggling word order around, and by using auxiliary verbs. But Latin doesn't have that option since word order doesn't work in the same way. To ask a question in Latin, put **-ne** at the end of the first word of the sentence. The word to which it is attached becomes the point of inquiry of the question: **Amâsne mê?** *Do you love me?,* **Mêne amâs?** *Is it **me** you love (and not someone else)?*

propter + acc. As you know, prepositions in Latin take certain cases. **Propter** takes the accusative case—always—and we translate it, *because of.* Don't be thrown off by our English translation. **Propter** does not take the genitive case in Latin. It takes the accusative.

satis When we say *I have enough money,* we use *enough* as an adjective modifying *money.* In Latin the word for *enough* is a noun, not an adjective. Latin follows **satis** with the genitive case, and says in effect *I have enough **of** money,* **Habeô satis pecûniae.** You'll be pleased to know that **satis** does not decline—it is always **satis** no matter how it's being used in the sentence.

6

More about Sum

SUM, ESSE: FUTURE TENSE

You're going to get a fuller look at the irregular verb **sum** and its companion verb **possum.** You have already learned the present tense of the irregular verb **sum**. And those of you who followed my expanded notes on these forms know the whole truth about it. I recommend that those of you who skipped them go back and read them now (38-9). They will help you with this discussion.

Do you remember how you formed the future tense of the first and second conjugation verbs? It was something like this: stem + tense sign + personal endings → conjugated forms. The verb **sum** follows this formula exactly, but it has a tense sign for the future you haven't seen before. Let's start at the beginning:

(1) The stem of the verb *to be* is **es-**.

(2) The tense sign for the future is short **-e-**. (For the first and second conjugations, the tense sign of the future was **be-**, and the short **-e-** of the tense sign underwent changes when the personal endings were added to it. Do you remember what they were (page 46)? The short **-e-** future tense sign will undergo the same changes.)

(3) The personal endings are the same ones you've been using all along.

Let's set up a construction table for the future of **sum**. For now, fill in all the information except the conjugated form.

	Stem	Tense Sign	Personal Ending	Conjugated Form
1st	es	e	ō	erō
2nd	es	e	s	eris
3rd	es	e	t	erit
Plural				
1st	es	e	mus	erimus
2nd	es	e	tis	eritis
3rd	es	e	nt	erunt

Now, it is a rule of Latin pronunciation that whenever an **-s-** is between two vowels (when it's *intervocalic*, as the professionals say), it changes from **-s-** to **-r-**. Now look at the stem of **sum**: Es- plus the tense sign **-e-** will put the **-s-** between two vowels, so the **-s-** of the stem will become an **-r-**: **ese- ere-**. That, then, will be the base to which you add the personal endings. Now fill out the conjugated forms—and remember the changes the short -e- is going to go through. Compare your work to Wheelock 37-8. How did you do?

SUM, ESSE: IMPERFECT TENSE

The imperfect tense is formed along the same lines as the future tense: stem + tense sign + personal endings conjugated forms. Obviously, since this is a different tense, the tense sign is not going to be the same as the future tense sign. The tense sign of the imperfect is **-â-**. One other slight difference is that the imperfect tense uses the alternate first person singular ending: **-m** instead of the expected **-ô**. And don't forget the rule of **-s-**: when it's intervocalic, it changes to **-r-**. Fill out the following table and check your forms against Wheelock's on pages 37-8.

	Stem	Tense Sign	Personal Ending	Conjugated Form
1st	es	ā	m	eram
2nd	es	ā	s	erās
3rd	es	ā	t	erat
Plural				
1st	es	ā	mus	erāmus
2nd	es	ā	tis	erātis
3rd	es	ā	nt	erant

POSSUM: PRESENT, FUTURE, IMPERFECT TENSES

In Latin, the verb *to be able* is a combination of the adjective base **pot-**, *able*, plus the forms of the verb **sum**. To say *I am able*, Latin took the adjective **pot-** and combined it with the present tense of **sum**. To say *I will be able*, Latin used **pot-** plus the future of **sum**. To say *I was able*, Latin used **pot-** plus the imperfect of **sum**. For the verb **possum**, then, it is the verb **sum** that provides the person, number, and the tense.

In the present tense, there is one catch: wherever the verb **sum** starts with an s-, the -t- of **pot-** becomes an -s- also. So you see **possum** instead of **potsum** (from pot + sum), and so on. (When a consonant turns into the consonant which it is next to, we call this *assimilation*. So we would say *t* assimilates to *s*.)

The one real oddity of the verb is its infinitive. We might expect **potesse** (**pot + esse**) according to the rules, but the form **posse** is just one of those unexpected moments in life when things get out of control. You might want to remember it this way: the English word *posse* is a group of citizens who have been granted power to make arrests; that is, they have *ableness*. Fill out the following charts for the verb **possum, posse** (Wheelock 38).

	Present Tense	Future	Imperfect
1st	possum	poterō	poteram
2nd	potes	poteris	poterās
3rd	potest	poterit	poterat
Plural			
1st	possumus	poterimus	poterāmus
2nd	potestis	poteritis	poterātis
3rd	possunt	poterunt	poterant

The only real difficulty with **possum** is the English translations for it. If you stick with *to be able, will be able,* and *was/were able,* you'll get through just fine. You can also translate **possum** with the English verb *can*. But *can,* although it's popular in English, is loaded with oddities. For one, it has no future tense—*I will can??*—and, secondly, the imperfect tense is *could,* which is also a conditional of some kind or another in English: *I **could** see your house from there.* Try to stay with *to be able* for now, but be aware of the possibilities of *can*.

THE COMPLEMENTARY INFINITIVE

If you were to walk up to a stranger and, out of the blue, say *I am able,* you'd be answered with a pause and a blank stare of anticipation. The stranger would be expecting you to complete your thought: *Yes, you're able **to do** what?* That's because *to be able* requires another verb to complete its sense, and the form the completing verb will have is the infinitive. It needs a completing infinitive (or *complementary infinitive*). This is true in Latin as well. **Possum** in all its forms will be followed by another verb in the infinitive form: **Poterunt *vidêre* nostrôs fîliôs,** *they will be able **to see** our sons.* This isn't new. Do you remember the verb **dêbeô**? When it means *ought* it takes a complementary infinitive to complete its sense. **Rômânî amîcôs adiuvâre dêbent,** *the Romans ought to help their friends.* You'll see many more verbs and other words that require a complementary infinitive.

VOCABULARY PUZZLES

liber, -brî, *m.* How are you going to keep the noun for *book* distinct in your mind from the adjective for *free,* **lîber, -a, -um**. For one, the **-i-** in **liber, -brî ,** *m.,* is short, but it's long in **lîber, -a, -um**. Next, there is a stem change in **liber, -brî,** *m.,* but not in **lîber, -a, -um**. So if you see an inflected form **libr-** *something,* then you know the word means *book(s).* Remember this by recalling their English derivatives: li**br**ary is from the stem-changing **liber, -brî**, *m.,* and *liberty* is from **lîber,** in which there is no stem change.

vitium, -iî, *n.* Please don't confuse this with the word for *life,* **vîta, -ae**, *f.* Keep them straight this way: *vicious,* as in *Sid Vicious,* which comes from **vit*i*um**, has an *-i-*

after the *-t*, but *vital*, which comes from **vîta**, does not. **Vitia** means *vices* or *crimes*; **vîta** means *life*.

Graecus, -a, -um Like **Rômânus, -a, -um**, this adjective can be used as a noun: **Graecus** can be translated as *a Greek man*, and **Graeca** as *a Greek woman*, or as an adjective: **Graecus liber**, *a Greek book*.

-que As Wheelock tells you, this word (called an *enclitic* because it *leans on* another word) is attached to the end of the second word of two that are to be linked. Think of it this way: **x yque → x et y**.

ubi If **ubi** comes first in a sentence which is a question, always translate it as *where*. **Ubi es?** (Where are you?) But when it is in the middle of a sentence, it can be translated as either *where* or *when*, and does not (necessarily) mean that a question is being asked. You must try them both out to see which of the two possibilities makes the most sense.

însidiae, -ârum, *f.* We translate this word, although it is always plural in Latin, as the singular *plot*, or *treachery*. It's going to happen often that ideas which are conceived of as plural in Latin are thought of as singular in English. So the sentence *the plot is evil* would be **insidiae <u>sunt</u> malae** in Latin.

7

The Third Declension

CASE ENDINGS OF THE THIRD DECLENSION

The third declension is generally considered to be a **pôns asinôrum** (literally *bridge of asses*, which means a severe test of ability and resolve). I disagree. The third declension, aside from presenting you a new list of case endings to memorize, really involves no grammatical principles you haven't already been working with. I'll take you through it slowly, but most of this chapter is actually going to be review.

The third declension has nouns of all three genders in it, and they're fairly well distributed. Unlike the first and second declensions, where the majority of nouns are either feminine or masculine, the genders of the third declension are equally divided. So you really must pay attention to the gender markings in the dictionary entries for third declension nouns. A contributing complication is that the case endings for masculine and feminine nouns are identical. The case endings for neuter nouns are also of the same type as the feminine and masculine nouns, except for where neuter nouns follow their peculiar rules:

(1) The nominative and the accusative forms are always the same;

(2) The nominative and accusative plural case endings are short **-a-**.

You may remember that the second declension neuter nouns have forms that are almost the same as the masculine nouns—except for these two rules. In other words, there is really only one pattern of endings for third declension nouns, whether the nouns are masculine, feminine, or neuter. It's just that neuter nouns have a peculiarity about them. Find the third declension case endings on pages 43–4 in Wheelock (the last two columns) and write them down here. I know, I know, what's the point? Trust me, writing these forms out on your own as you're studying them will help with your memorization.

	Singular		Plural	
	Masc./Fem.	**Neuter**	**Masc./Fem.**	**Neuter**
N/V.	—	—	-ēs	-a
Gen.	-is	-is	-um	-um
Dat.	-ī	-ī	-ibus	-ibus
Acc.	-em	—	-ēs	-a
Abl.	-e	-e	-ibus	-ibus

Now let's go over some of the hot spots on this list. The nominative singular of all three genders is left blank because there are so many different possible nominative forms for third declension nouns that it would take half a page to list them all.[15] You needn't fret over this though, because the dictionary's first entry for a noun is the nominative singular. You'll have to do a little more memorization with third declension nouns because you simply can't assume that it'll have a certain form in the nominative just because it's third declension—as you could with first declension nouns, where they all end in -a in the nominative.

You'll also notice that there's a blank left in the accusative singular of neuter nouns. Can you guess why that should be? Remember, the accusative form of neuter nouns will be exactly the form of the nominative. So there's a blank in the accusative slot for neuter nouns. It'll be whatever the nominative is.

STEMS OF THIRD DECLENSION NOUNS

One very distinctive characteristic of nouns of the third declension is that nearly all of them are stem-changing nouns. The concept of stem-changing nouns is not new for you. You've already worked with it in the second declension with nouns ending in **-er** in the nominative.

Look at this entry for a second declension noun: **ager, agrî**, *m.*. The first entry for a noun is the nominative singular, the second is the genitive where you learn two things: (1) the declension of the noun (by looking at the genitive ending) and (2) whether there is a stem change from the nominative to the other cases. In this instance, we learn that **ager** is a second declension noun—because the genitive ending is **-î**—and that there is a stem change. The stem of the noun is **agr-**, to which you add the case endings. Now look at an example entry for a third declension noun: **rêx, rêgis**, *m.* Use your experience with second declension **-er** type masculine nouns to draw out all the important information you need about this noun. What's its stem? Now close the Wheelock book and decline it (Wheelock 43-4).

	Singular	Plural
N/V.	rēx	rēgēs
Gen.	rēgis	rēgum
Dat.	rēgī	rēgibus
Acc.	rēgem	rēgēs
Abl.	rēge	rēgibus

---

[15]In older editions of Wheelock (4th edition or less), you'll see an **-s** next to the stem **rêg-**. You may be tempted to think that **-s** is the case ending of the third declension. Let me explain. It is true that many masculine and feminine nouns add an **-s** to the stem to form the nominative singular. For example, the stem of the word for king is **rêg-** in Latin. If you add an **-s** to the stem you get **rêgs** and the combination of consonants comes out as an **-x-**. Try pronouncing it yourself. So the nominative form is **rêx**. So also **pâx** which comes from **pâc + s**. But I recommend that you forget the **-s** thing for now. If you go on in Latin and study its morphology some day, then you can worry about it.

How did you do? The nominative form is just what's listed in the dictionary—there is no ending in the nominative singular to add. Next, the stem of **rêx** is **rêg-**, which you get by dropping off the **-is** genitive ending of the third declension from the form **regis** which the dictionary gives. Now decline this noun: **corpus, corporis**, *n.* (Wheelock 43-4).

	Singular	**Plural**
N/V.	corpus	corpora
Gen.	corporis	corporum
Dat.	corporī	corporibus
Acc.	corpus	corpora
Abl.	corporе	corporibus

One of the difficulties beginning students have with third declension nouns is that dictionaries only abbreviate the second entry, where you're given the stem of the noun, and it's often puzzling to see just what the stem is. Look over this list of typical abbreviations. After a very short time, they'll cause you no problem.

Entry	**Stem**	**Entry**	**Stem**
vêritâs, -tâtis, *f.*	vêritât-	ôrâtiô, -ônis, *f.*	ôrâtiôn-
homô, -inis, *m.*	homin-	finis, -is, *f.*	fin-
labor, -ôris, *m.*	labôr-	lîbertâs, -tâtis, *f.*	lîbertât-
tempus, -oris, *n.*	tempor-	senectûs, -tûtis, *f.*	senectût-
virgô, -inis, *m.*	virgin-	amor, -ôris, *m.*	amôr-

Now you try it. Write down the stems of these words by looking at the abbreviation in the genitive entry.

Entry	**Stem**	**Entry**	**Stem**
corpus, -oris, *n.*	corpor-	honor, -ôris, *m.*	honōr-
hûmânitâs, -tâtis, *f.*	hūmānitāt-	frâter, -tris, *m.*	frātr-
mûtâtiô, -ônis, *f.*	mūtātiōn-	pater, -tris, *m.*	patr-
pestis, -is, *f.*	pest-	scrîptor, -ôris, *m*	scrīptōr-
valêtûdô, -inis, *f.*	valētūdin-	cupiditâs, -tâtis, *f.*	cupiditāt-
uxor, -ôris, *f.*	uxōr-	môs, môris, *m.*	mōr-
nômen, -inis, *n.*	nōmin-	carmen, -inis, *n.*	carmin-

MODIFYING THIRD DECLENSION NOUNS

Modifying a third declension noun is done the same way you modify a first and second declension noun: put the adjective in the same number, gender, and case as the target noun, and away you go. What causes beginners in Latin some discomfort is that they can't quite bring themselves to modify a third declension noun with an adjective which uses first and second declension endings. They suppose that an adjective must use third declension endings to modify a third declension noun. That's not true.

Let's go through this step by step. Suppose you want to modify the noun **virtûs, -tûtis**, f. with the adjective **vêrus, -a, -um**. You want to say *true virtue*. You know that **virtûs** is nominative, feminine, and singular. So for the adjective **vêrus, -a, -um** to agree with it, it must also be nominative, feminine, and singular. Look at the adjective's listing closely. How does **vêrus, -a, -um** become feminine? From the second entry, you see that it uses endings from the first declension to modify a feminine noun. Since **virtûs** is feminine, **vêrus** will use first declension endings. You now select the nominative singular ending from the first declension—**-a**—and add it to the stem of the adjective. The result: **vêra virtûs**. Now decline it.

	Singular		Plural	
	vêra	**virtûs**	**vêrae**	**virtûtês**
N/V.	vēra	virtus	vērae	virtūtēs
Gen.	vērae	virtūtis	vērārum	virtūtum
Dat.	vērae	virtūtī	vērīs	virtūtibus
Acc.	vēram	virtūtem	vērās	virtūtēs
Abl.	vērā	virtūte	vērīs	virtūtibus

Stare at these forms a while. You have to get used to seeing that agreement between adjective and noun does not mean identical forms or even the same declensional endings. It means having grammatically equivalent, not visually equivalent forms.

VOCABULARY PUZZLES

môs, môris, m. In the plural, **môs** takes on a new meaning. In the singular it means *habit*, but in the plural it means *character*. This isn't hard to understand. What a person does regularly to the point of being a habit eventually becomes what he is: it becomes his character.

littera, -ae, f. Like **môs, môris**, in the plural **littera** takes on an extended meaning. In the singular it means *a letter of the alphabet*; in the plural it means either *a letter*, like something you get in the mail, as in *Hey Mister Postman, look and see/if there's a letter, a letter for me*—or *literature*: **Graecae litterae**, *Greek literature*.

If a Roman needed to talk about more than one letter (things you get in the mail), a different word was used in the plural: **epistula, -ae** *f.*

post + acc. Means *after,* but it is only a preposition in Latin, and cannot be used as a conjunction. **Post** is not a correct translation of the English *after* in this sentence: *After I went to the zoo, I went to the movies.* That *after* is a conjunction, not a preposition.

sub + acc./abl. This preposition, like a few others you'll see, can be followed by the accusative or the ablative case. When it takes the accusative case, it means motion to and under something; when it takes the ablative it means *position under. She walked under the tree*—in the sense that she was not beneath the tree at first but walked there—would be **sub** + accusative in Latin. *She sat under the tree* would be **sub** + ablative.

8

Beginning the Third Conjugation

PRESENT INFINITIVE AND PRESENT TENSE

If you remember what happens to the short -e- in Latin, you'll have very little trouble with this chapter. If you don't, you will, so I'll remind you. You remember that Latin verbs are divided into groups called *conjugations*, and the conjugations are distinguished from one another by their thematic vowels. The thematic vowel of the first conjugation is **-â-**. The thematic vowel of the second is **-ê-**. You can tell what the stem vowel (its thematic vowel) of a verb is—and thereby its conjugation—by dropping the **-re** ending from the infinitive, which is given to you in the dictionary.

laudô, laudâre, stem: laudâ-, 1st conjugation

moneô, monêre, stem: monê-, 2nd conjugation

Now look at the dictionary entry for the verb *to lead* in Latin: **dûcô, dûcere**. Simply by looking at the first entry, you might think that this verb is going to be a first conjugation verb—it looks like **laudô**. But the next entry looks something like a second. Find the stem: it's **dûce-**. Look closely. The **-e-** of the stem is short. This is the characteristic vowel of the third conjugation: short **-e-**. Even if you're not watching the long marks, you can still tell a second conjugation verb in the dictionary from a third. The first entry for a second conjugation verb will always end in **-eô**,[16] and then the second entry will end **-êre**. The first dictionary entry of a third conjugation verb ends simply with **-ô** and then the second entry is **-ere**. So if the first entry of a verb looks like a first conjugation verb in the first person singular and if the infinitive looks like a second conjugation verb, then you have a third conjugation verb. Identify the conjugations of the following verbs.

Entry	Conjugation	Entry	Conjugation
doceô, docêre	2	audeô, audêre	2
amô, amâre	1	tolerô, tolerâre	1
dûcô, dûcere	3	valeô, valêre	2
scrîbô, scrîbere	3	agô, agere	3

---

[16]The first entry in a dictionary for a verb is the first person singular, and the first person singular of all second conjugation verbs ends in **-eô**.

We'll use **agô** as our example (paradigm) of third conjugation verbs. First we'll see about conjugating a third conjugation verb in the present tense. You remember the formula for all verbs in Latin in the present tense: it's just the stem plus the personal endings **-ô, -s, -t**, etc. Fill out the following table, except for the conjugated form.

Present tense of agô, agere

	Stem	Personal Endings	Conjugated Form
1st	age	ō	agō
2nd	age	s	agis
3rd	age	t	agit
Plural			
1st	age	mus	agimus
2nd	age	tis	agitis
3rd	age	nt	agunt

What we need to know is what happens to the stem vowel when you start attaching the personal endings. In the first and second conjugations, this presented no problem, because the stem vowels are long and strongly pronounced. But short vowels always cause difficulties in languages and are subject to changes. You already have experience with what happens to the short **-e-** before personal endings. Do you remember how you form the future tense of first and second conjugation verbs? You insert the tense sign **-bĕ-** in between the stem and the personal endings. And then the short **-e-** changes. Watch:

laudâbĕô	→	laudâbô	laudâbĕmus	→	laudâbimus
laudâbĕs	→	laudâbis	laudâbĕtis	→	laudâbitis
laudâbĕt	→	laudâbit	laudâbĕnt	→	laudâbunt

In a third conjugation verb, then, what is going to happen to the short **-e-** of its stem? It will undergo precisely the same changes.[17] Now go back to the table and fill out the conjugated forms of **agô** (Wheelock 49).

FUTURE TENSE

Third conjugation verbs form the future tense in a way entirely different from that of the first and second conjugations. First and second conjugation verbs insert a tense sign, **-be-**, between the stem and the personal endings. By contrast, third conjugation verbs do two things:

---

[17] Those of you wondering why the infinitive is **agere** instead of **agîre**, read on. The rule is that a short **-e-** stays a short **-e-** if it is followed by an **-r-** which was originally an **-s-**. The **-re** infinitive ending, as you recall, was originally **-se**, but the **-s-** became an **-r-** because it was intervocalic. Hence, the short **-e-** stays short **-e-** because the **-r-** was originally an **-s-**.

(1) For the first person singular, they replace the stem vowel with an **-a-** and use the alternate personal ending **-m**—instead of **-ô**.

(2) For all the other forms, they lengthen the short **-e-** of the stem to long **-ê-**. Since the **-ê-** is now long, it no longer goes through any of the changes it went through in the present tense. It simply stays **-ê-**. (Except, of course, where long vowels normally become short: before **-t**, and **-nt**.)

Fill out the future tense of the verb **agô** (Wheelock 49).

	Stem	Tense Sign	Personal Endings	Conjugated Form
1st	age	a	m	agam
2nd	age	ē	s	agēs
3rd	age	ē	t	aget
Plural				
1st	age	ē	mus	agēmus
2nd	age	ē	tis	agētis
3rd	age	ē	nt	agent

FUTURE OF THIRD CONJUGATION VS. PRESENT OF SECOND

The way a third conjugation verb forms its future presents an interesting problem. Write out the *present* tense of the second conjugation verb **moneô, monêre**, and next to it write out the future of the third conjugation verb **mittô, mittere**, *to send*.

	Singular		Plural	
	moneô	**mittô**	**moneô**	**mittô**
1st	moneō	mittam	monēmus	mittēmus
2nd	monēs	mittēs	monētis	mittētis
3rd	monet	mittet	monent	mittent

As you can see, except for the first person singular, the endings of both these verbs look the same: the personal endings in both these verbs are preceded by an -ê-. This could cause you some problems when you're reading and translating. I'll explain.

Suppose that you see a form like this in a text you're reading: **legent**. What do you do with it? First you recognize the **-nt** as an ending that's attached to verbs, so the word you're looking at is a verb. You want to look up this verb in the dictionary, so you must simplify it to its basic form, which is the first person singular. You remember that a verb is conjugated by adding personal endings; so to reduce this form, you drop off the **-nt**. This leaves you with **lege-**.

The next thing you have to consider is the **-e-**. Is it the stem vowel of a second conjugation verb, or is it the tense sign of the future for a third conjugation verb? That is, is this a present tense form of a second conjugation verb (stem + personal endings), or is it a future of a third (stem + **-ê-** + personal endings)?

What do you do next to find out? You've gone as far as you can with your preliminary analysis of the form. Now you have to proceed provisionally.

Suppose that the verb is a second conjugation. What will the dictionary entry look like? The first entry is the first person singular, the second is the infinitive. So, if this is a second conjugation verb, the entry will be **legeô, legêre**. Right? Because all second conjugation verbs end in **-eô** in the first person singular, and the infinitive will show the vowel **-ê-** before the infinitive ending **-re**. So you've reduced the conjugated form **legent** to a form you can look up.

The next step is to look it up—but look for exactly what you've supposed the form to be. Look for *both* **legeô**, and then **legêre** right after it. So look it up. You didn't find it, did you? If your analysis was correct, **legeô** *must* be there. But it's not. What does that tell you? It tells you that **legent** is not a form of a second conjugation verb. If it were, you would have found **legeô** in the dictionary, but you didn't.

Go back to the other possibility: **legent** could be the future of a third conjugation verb, where the **-e-** is the sign of the future. So if this is correct, what will the dictionary entry be? It'll be **legô, legere**. Check it out. This time you found what you were looking for: **legô** means *to read*. So how do you translate **legent**: **leg** (*read*) **e** (*will*) **nt** (*they*), or *they will read*.

The moral of this is that your life used to be fairly simple. An **-e-** before the personal endings always used to indicate a present tense of a second conjugation verb. Now it could mean a future of a third conjugation verb as well. You have to proceed cautiously now; and make sure you have thoroughly mastered your grammar before you start reading. You'll also have to use the dictionary more deliberately and intelligently than you had to before. And that means thinking your forms through *before* you turn to the dictionary.

IMPERFECT TENSE

This shouldn't be too difficult. The imperfect tense is simply the stem of the verb plus the tense sign **-ba-** plus the personal endings. Right? Right. So here's the table. Fill out everything except the conjugated form for now.

	Stem	Tense Sign	Personal Endings	Conjugated Form
1st	age	ba	m	agēbam
2nd	age	ba	s	agēbas
3rd	age	ba	t	agēbat

	Stem	Tense Sign	Personal Endings	Conjugated Form
Plural				
1st	age	bā	mus	agēbamus
2nd	age	bā	tis	agēbatis
3rd	age	bā	nt	agēbant

It's all going to fall into place very nicely, with one exception: the vowel that's attached to the end of the stem, the short **-e**. You'd think, given what you know about how much that vowel changes, that it might become a short **-i-** or something. You might think you'd end up with a form like **dûcibam**. That's not what happens. Instead, the stem vowel lengthens to **-ê-**, and as such it doesn't undergo any further change. Okay. Go back and fill in the conjugated forms. Check what you've come up with against Wheelock, page 50.

IMPERATIVE

Do you remember the formulae you followed for forming the imperative of first and second conjugation verbs? It was this:

Singular.	stem	+	—
Plural:	stem	+	te

And so you came up with forms like this: **laudâ, laudâte, monê, monête**, etc. Third conjugation verbs follow the same formulae, but don't forget that pesky short **-e-** stem vowel. If there is something added to it, it changes, sometimes to an **-i-**, sometimes to a **-u-** and sometimes it disappears completely—before the first person singular ending **-ô**. But if there is nothing added to it, it stays short **-e-**. So how are you going to form the imperative of the verb **mittô**? Think.

Singular	mitte	+	—	→	mitte
Plural	mitte	+	te	→	mittite

Did you write down **mittite** for the second person plural? If you didn't, do you understand why your answer was incorrect? So, this is how all third conjugation verbs will form their imperatives—except for four very common verbs. The verb **dûcô** and three other verbs you'll get later form their singular imperatives by dropping the stem vowel altogether: **dûc** not **dûce**. But the plural imperative is quite regular: **dûcite**.

VOCABULARY PUZZLES

scrîbô, -ere One aid to memorizing the conjugation of verbs is to learn them with the proper accentuation. A second conjugation verb is accented on the stem vowel in the infinitive, while a third conjugation is accented on the syllable before the stem vowel. So the second conjugation infinitive **monêre** is pronouned *moh NEH reh.* The third conjugation infinitive **scrîbere** is pronounced *SCREE beh reh.*

côpia, -ae, *f.* Here's another one of those words which have a different meaning in the plural! In the singular, **côpia** means *abundance;* in the plural—**côpiae, -ârum**, *f.*—it means *supplies, troops, forces.*

ad + acc. This preposition means, among a few other things, *to* and *toward*, always with a sense of *movement to.* Students often confuse **ad** + acc. with the dative case of indirect object, which we can often translate into English with the preposition *to.* Contrast these two examples: *I am giving you a dollar* (*you* would be dative case) and *I am running to you* (*you* would be in the accusative case governed by **ad**).

ex, ê + abl. Students sometimes get hung up on when to use **ex** or **e**. It's really not very important in the grand scheme of things, but use **ex** before any word you like, but use **ê** only before words which start with a consonant. If you wish, use **ex** only. That way, you'll always be right!

agô, agere An idiom with this verb which Wheelock is going to use a lot is **agô vîtam**, which means *to live, to lead a life.* Another is **agô grâtiâs** + dative, which means *to thank.* The person being thanked is in the dative case: **Populus hominibus grâtiâs aget**, *the people will thank the men.* Literally: *the people will make thanks to the men.*

dûcô, dûcere It means *to lead*, but can also mean *to think.* This extension is logical: we want our leaders to be thinkers too, don't we?

9

Demonstratives

THIS, THESE; THAT, THOSE IN ENGLISH

This is going to be a difficult chapter, not because it introduces you to new and bizarre concepts, but because there are a lot of little details coming at you at the same time. Let's begin. Consider the following expressions: *this car, that car; these cars, those cars.* The words *this, these, that,* and *those* are obviously telling you a little something more about *car* or *cars.* They're indicating the relative spacial location *car* or cars have to the speaker. When we say *this car* or the plural *these cars,* we are referring to the car or cars which are nearby: *this car right here; these cars right here.* For the most part, when we say *that car* or *those cars,* we mean cars which are some distance from us: *that car over there; those cars over there.* It would sound odd for someone to say *that car right here* or *these cars way over there.* So the words *this, these, that,* and *those* are telling us more about the words they're attached to, than they are qualifying or modifying their nouns. And we call words that modify nouns *adjectives.* So our words *this, these, that, those* are adjectives.

As you know, English adjectives hardly ever change their form to *agree* with the thing they're modifying: *tall tree* and *tall trees; bad boys* and *bad girls.* This is different from Latin adjectives, which must change their endings to show the different numbers, genders, and cases of the nouns they modify. But look again at the adjectives *this* and *that.* When the nouns they modify become plural, the adjectives themselves change form: from *this* to *these;* from *that* to *those.* These two are the only adjectives in English that actually change their forms to match a grammatical feature of the nouns they're modifying. They have slightly different forms to indicate a change in number of the nouns they modify.

These words are adjectives, since they qualify nouns, and since their main purpose is to *point out* the nouns, we call them *demonstrative adjectives* because they *point out* or *point to* (Latin **dêmônstrâre**) something. This is very important to remember: these words are *demonstrative **adjectives**.*

THE LATIN DEMONSTRATIVES: ILLE, HIC, ISTE
<u>Ille</u>

Latin also has demonstrative adjectives roughly equivalent to our *this* and *that.* Now remember, since these words are adjectives in Latin, they must be able to agree with the nouns they're modifying. Therefore, these demonstrative adjectives must be able to decline to agree with all three different genders. For the most part, the Latin demonstrative adjectives decline just like the adjectives you've seen so far. That is, they add the first and second declension endings to their stems. But there are some unexpected irregularities which you simply must memorize:

(1) The nominative singulars are irregular.

(2) The genitive singular for all genders is **-îus**.

(3) The dative singular for all genders is **-î**.

Keep these irregularities in mind and decline the demonstrative adjective *that*. Its dictionary listing includes all the nominatives—just as an adjective like **magnus, -a, -um** does—so that you can see its declension pattern. The adjective for *that* is **ille, illa, illud** (Wheelock 55).

STEM: ill-

	Masculine	**Feminine**	**Neuter**
N/V.	ille	illa	illud
Gen.	illīus	illīus	illīus
Dat.	illī	illī	illī
Acc.	illum	illam	illud
Abl.	illō	illā	illō
Plural			
N/V.	illī	illae	illa
Gen.	illōrum	illārum	illōrum
Dat.	illīs	illīs	illīs
Acc.	illōs	illās	illa
Abl.	illīs	illīs	illīs

As you can see, the inflection of the demonstrative adjective **ille** is quite recognizable after the nominative, genitive, and dative singulars. With some more time, you'll become well-acquainted with the irregular forms **-îus** and **-î** of genitive and dative singulars. All the demonstrative adjectives and pronouns in Latin use these alternative genitive and dative singular endings, as do some adjectives. You can think of this declensional pattern as a hybrid declension because it seems to be borrowing the genitive and dative singular forms from somewhere else.

Hic

Let's turn now to the Latin demonstrative adjective that corresponds to our word *this*. The stem is **h-**, and it follows the pattern set by **ille**: unusual nominatives, alternative endings for the genitive and dative singulars. But there are four additional things to note about its declension:

(1) In the genitive and dative singulars, the stem lengthens from **h-** to **hu-**.

(2) In all the singular cases and genders, and in the neuter plural nominative and accusative, the particle **-c** is added to the end of case endings for a little extra emphasis: like *this here* in English. We call the **-c** an *epideictic* (*eh peh DAY tick*) particle, from the Greek word that means *to point out*.

(3) When the epideictic particle **-c** is added to a case ending that ends in an **-m**, the **-m** becomes an **-n**.

(4) The neuter nominative and accusative plural endings are **-ae**, not **-a**, as you might expect from the second declension.

This is quite a list of oddities, and students have some difficulty mastering this demonstrative adjective. Keep your mind on this list of irregularities and try to decline the Latin demonstrative *this*: **hic, haec, hoc** (Wheelock 55).

STEM: h- (or hu-)

	Masculine	Feminine	Neuter
N/V.	hic	haec	hoc
Gen.	huius	huius	huius
Dat.	huic	huic	huic
Acc.	hunc	hanc	hoc
Abl.	hōc	hāc	hōc
Plural			
N/V.	hī	hae	haec
Gen.	hōrum	hārum	hōrum
Dat.	hīs	hīs	hīs
Acc.	hōs	hās	haec
Abl.	hīs	hīs	hīs

Iste

Finally, there exists in Latin a demonstrative adjective that has no real translation into English, though we can readily recognize its meaning. It can only be rendered into English by an inflection of the voice, one implying contempt, disdain, or outrage. Read this exchange:

X: *What book is Professor de Vine using in Calculus 201?*

Y: *"Calculus for Geniuses."*

X: *Oh, Lord no! Not **that** book!!*

The final *that* in this dialogue corresponds to the Latin demonstrative adjective **iste, ista, istud**.[18] There is nothing complicated about the declension of **iste**; It uses the alternative genitive and dative singular endings **-îus** and **-î**, and the neuter nominative and accusative singular is **-ud** (like **illud**). Aside from that, it uses the standard first and second declension endings.

---

[18]Although there's some sense in it, Wheelock's suggested translation *that of yours* is unhelpful. Forget Wheelock on this for now. It causes beginning students more problems than it's worth.

STEM: ist-

	Masculine	Feminine	Neuter
N/V.	iste	ista	istud
Gen.	istīus	istīus	istīus
Dat.	istī	istī	istī
Acc.	istum	istam	istud
Abl.	istō	istā	istō
Plural			
N/V.	istī	istae	ista
Gen.	istōrum	istārum	istōrum
Dat.	istīs	istīs	istīs
Acc.	istōs	istā	ista
Abl.	istīs	istīs	istīs

LEARNING TO LOVE THE HYBRID DECLENSION

As irritating as it may be to have to memorize more endings, the hybrid declension has a nice advantage. It can often help you establish the case of a noun. Like this. What case is the word **cônsiliô** from the noun **cônsilium, -iî**, *n*. You can't be sure because it can be either the dative or ablative case singular. But if it's modified by a demonstrative adjective, you can tell immediately which of the two it is: **huîc cônsiliô**, *dative*; **hôc cônsiliô**, *ablative*. That's because **huîc** is dative only. Write out the number, gender, and case the following nouns are in.

	Number	Gender	Case
illae cîvitâtês	pl.	F	Nom.
illâs cîvitâtês	pl.	F	Ac.
istî puerô	sg.	M	Dat
istô puerô	sg.	M	Ab.
illî amôrês	pl.	M	Nom
illôs amôrês	pl.	M	Ac.
hae puellae	pl.	F	N
huic puellae	sg.	F	D

ADJECTIVES IN -IUS AND -I

As I mentioned, there are some adjectives in Latin which use the alternative genitive and dative endings. Aside from that, however, these adjectives follow the normal declensional patterns. There are very few of them, but they are important adjectives which get a lot of use. You've got to know them. Beginning with the 5th edition of Wheelock, there's a very helpful memory aid for this. The expression **ûnus nauta** spells out an acronym for the adjectives that follow this declension:

U	ûnus, -a, -um	one		N	nûllus, -a, -um	no, none
N	neuter, -a, -um	neither		A	alter, -a, -um	the other
U	uter, -a, -um	either		U	ûllus, -a, -um	any
S	sôlus, -a, -um	sole, alone		T	tôtus, -a, -um	whole; entire
				A	alius, -a, -ud	other

Judged by their dictionary entries alone, these adjectives look deceptively normal. They appear to be the standard variety adjectives of the first and second declensions. But their genitive and dative singulars are not the standard kind. Watch this declension of the expression *the other man alone*:

Nom.	alter	vir	sôlus
Gen.	alterîus	virî	sôlîus
Dat.	alterî	virô	sôlî
Acc.	alterum	virum	sôlum
Abl.	alterô	virô	sôlô

ALIUS AND ALTER

Alius, alia, aliud is the adjective that means *other*, and it's one of those adjectives which follow the hybrid declension: **-îus** and **-î** for the genitive and dative singulars. For a totally mysterious reason, Latin tends to replace the genitive singular of **alius** with the genitive singular of **alter**. Hence, we find **alterîus** in place of the expected **aliîus** in the declension of **alius**. After that oddity, the declension of **alius** regains its sanity.

	Masculine	Feminine	Neuter
N/V.	alius	alia	aliud
Gen.	*alterîus*	*alterîus*	*alterîus*
Dat.	aliî	aliî	aliî
Acc.	alium	aliam	aliud
Abl.	aliô	aliâ	aliô

THE DEMONSTRATIVE AS A PRONOUN

So far, so good. The demonstrative adjectives **hic, ille**, and **iste** modify nouns and point them out. Essentially, this is their nature. They are demonstrative *adjectives*. But they have a very common extended use. They are frequently used as *demonstrative pronouns*. So what does this mean—demonstrative pronoun? The demonstrative part of it you understand: it means something that points out or gives emphasis. But what is a pronoun? Without getting overly ambitious about setting down an eternally unassailable definition, let's just say for now that a pronoun is a word that takes the place of another word in a sentence. Here are some examples of pronouns in English:

It just missed **her**.

She has a most interesting way of speaking.

Does **he** have **it**?

As you can see, the underlined words are referring you to something or someone that has already been mentioned sometime before; so to recall them we only have to use a sign marker or abbreviation. The word or idea which the pronoun is replacing is called the *antecedent (an teh CEE dent)*.[19] In addition to replacing their antecedents, pronouns also tell you a little something about the nature of the antecedent. For example, in the first sentence, you can tell that the antecedent of *it* is singular and inanimate; the antecedent of *her* is singular and feminine and animate. This is an important rule to remember about pronouns: *Pronouns get their number and gender from their antecedents.*

Let's look again at the English third person pronouns. We divide the third person pronoun into two groups—those that refer to animate objects (mainly humans) and those that refer to inanimate objects. Our third person pronouns observe the distinction between the masculine and feminine genders of animate things in the singular;[20] in the plural, however, they make no distinctions among gender or animate and inanimate.

	Masculine	Feminine	Neuter	Masc./Fem./Neuter
Subj.	he	she	it	they
Pos.	his	her	its	their
Obj.	him	her	it	them

Latin pronouns are much more observant of the gender of their antecedents—as they would likely be, because of the importance of grammatical gender in Latin. Consequently, by looking at the forms of the demonstrative pronouns **hic, ille**, or **iste**, you can tell much more about their antecedents. This makes constructions in Latin much more flexible.

---

[19]From the Latin **ante + cêdô**, *to go before.*

[20]For poetic or sentimental effect, we sometimes use the pronoun *she* to refer to ships or cars.

Look at this sentence: **Nôn poteram haec vidêre**. How would you translate the **haec?** You can tell that it is neuter, accusative plural from its form and from the way it's being used in the sentence. (It's the direct object of the verb **vidêre**.) Its antecedent is neuter in gender, and plural. So what's our plural, accusative third person pronoun? It's *them*. This sentence would be translated *I was not able to see **them***.

In English, you see, this sentence could mean that I am looking at men, women, or rocks, since the pronoun only tells us that the antecedent is plural. But Latin also tells us the gender of the antecedent; so it can be much more specific. Now let's look at a pronoun with a little more context. **Urbs est magna, sed nôn possum hanc vidêre**, *the city is large, but I can't see it*.

Remember that a pronoun gets its number and gender from its antecedent, but it gets its case from the way it's being used grammatically in the sentence. The antecedent of **hanc** is **urbs**; they are both singular and feminine. But **hanc** is accusative because of the way it's being used: it's the direct object of the verb **vidêre**.

We would translate this into English: *The city is large, but I don't see **it***. Notice that even though the pronoun in Latin is feminine in gender—**hanc**—we don't translate it *her*, because we use *she*, *her*, and *her* most of the time only for things that are biologically female. Unlike Latin, our nouns don't have grammatical gender.

Now try this: **Est bona femina, et hanc amâmus**, *She is a good woman, and we love her*. This time, since the antecedent *is* biologically feminine, we would translate **hanc** with our feminine pronoun: *She is a kind woman and we love **her***. You'll have to take a little care when you translate the pronouns into English. You'll use our pronouns *he* and *she*, and so on, only when the antecedents of the Latin pronouns are biologically masculine or feminine. Otherwise, you'll use our neuter *it*, *its*, *it*, and *them*, even if the Latin demonstrative is feminine or masculine.

VOCABULARY PUZZLES

locus, -î, *m.* Something a little unusual happens to **locus** in the plural. In the singular, **locus** means either a physical place or a place in a book (a passage in literature). In the plural, **locî,** it means only passages in literature. To say *places* as in physical places (regions), Latin uses a neuter derivative from **locus: loca, -ôrum,** *n.* So **locus** actually has two different forms in the plural, each with different meanings: **locî** means *passages*; **loca** means *regions*.

enim Like **igitur, enim** is postpositive.

in + acc./abl. Like **sub** + accusative or ablative, **in** will take its noun either in the accusative or the ablative case. When it takes the accusative **in** means *motion into*; with the ablative it shows only position, with no motion into involved. You can keep these two straight by translating **in** + accusative always as *into*. Say *in* for **in** + ablative.

alter It can only mean *the other* of two things. E.g., *I have two pencils you can choose from. Do you want this one or the other [**alter**] one.* For this reason, in strict English, an *alternative* is one choice of two possibilities and only two possibilities. Never say *we have many alternatives.* You may have many options, but you can never have more than one alternative.

nunc It's the temporal *now,* not the logical *now.* **Nunc** would be a translation for *it's raining now,* not for *now, what were we talking about again?*

10

Fourth Conjugation
and -iô Verbs of the Third

REVIEW OF VERBS

Just as the title says, this chapter introduces you to yet another—and the last—conjugation. If you understand the concept of a conjugation, all you'll be dealing with is more details. Just in case you're still a little spongy on that, we'll start with a review.

You already know the present and future tenses of the first three conjugations, and you know how to form their imperatives and infinitives. Let's have a fast look at what you know so far about these verbs:

(1) To form the *present tense* of verbs of all conjugations, you simply take the stem of the verb (which includes its stem vowel) and add the personal endings.

(2) To form the *future tense* of all conjugations, you start with the stem of the verb, add on a tense sign for the future, and then add the personal endings (for first and second conjugation verbs, the tense sign of the future is **-be-**,[21] and for the third conjugation, the tense sign is **-a-/-ê-**).

(3) To form the *imperfect tense* of all conjugations, you start with the stem of the verb, add the tense sign **-bâ-**, and then the personal endings (using **-m** for the first person singular.

(4) To form the *imperative mood* in the singular, you use just the stem (without any additional ending), and for the plural you add the ending **-te** to the stem.

(5) The *infinitive* is just the stem plus the ending **-re** for all conjugations. Just for review, conjugate the paradigm for each of the three conjugations in all the forms you know so far. I know, it seems like a bother, but do it anyway.

Refreshing your memory on these points will really help with your study of the last conjugation. Check your work at Wheelock, page 452.

---

[21]Remember how the short **-e-** changes when you start putting endings on it: **-bô, -bis, -bit, -bimus, -bitis, -bunt**.

First Conjugation: laudô, -âre

	Present	Future	Imperfect	Imperative	Infinitive
1st	laudō	laudābō	laudābam	laudā	laudāre
2nd	laudās	laudābis	laudābās		
3rd	laudat	laudābit	laudābat		
Plural					
1st	laudāmus	laudābimus	laudābāmus	laudāte	laudāre
2nd	laudātis	laudābitis	laudābātis		
3rd	laudant	laudābunt	laudābant		

Second Conjugation: moneô, -êre

	Present	Future	Imperfect	Imperative	Infinitive
1st	moneō	monēbō	monēbam	monē	monēre
2nd	monēs	monēbis	monēbās		
3rd	monet	monēbit	monēbat		
Plural					
1st	monēmus	monēbimus	monēbāmus	monēte	monēre
2nd	monētis	monēbitis	monēbātis		
3rd	monent	monēbunt	monēbant		

Third Conjugation: dûcô, -ere

	Present	Future	Imperfect	Imperative	Infinitive
1st	dūcō	dūcam	dūcēbam	dūc	dūcere
2nd	dūcis	dūcēs	dūcēbās		
3rd	dūcit	dūcet	dūcēbat		
Plural					
1st	dūcimus	dūcēmus	dūcēbāmus	dūcite	dūcere
2nd	dūcitis	dūcētis	dūcēbātis		
3rd	dūcunt	dūcent	dūcēbant		

FOURTH CONJUGATION

This is going to be easy. Look at the entry for the Latin verb to hear: **audiô, -îre**. Take a close look. What's the stem vowel? Remember, you discover the stem of a verb by dropping the **-re** infinitive ending. What's left is the stem (including the stem vowel). So the stem of the verb *to hear* is **audî-**. And it's to this stem that you add the various tense signs, personal endings, and so on to conjugate the verb.

Fourth conjugation verbs are verbs whose stem ends in a *long* **-î-**. So how are you going to form the present tense of this verb? As you know already, the formula of the present tense is: stem plus personal endings. (There is no intervening tense sign for the present tense). In other words, fourth conjugation verbs are verbs having an **-î-** for their stem vowel, and they follow precisely the same rules as the other conjugations for forming the present tense, with the one exception that: in the third person plural, an extra **-u-** is inserted between the stem vowel **-i-** and the **-nt** personal ending.

How about the future tense? The fourth conjugation uses the same tense sign as the third conjugation for the future tense, inserting the letters **-a/ê-** between the stem and the personal endings. Because the **-î-** is long it *survives* the addition of endings. How about the imperfect? It's the stem plus the tense sign **-bâ-** and then the personal endings. How about the present imperative? It's just like the other conjugations: the stem alone in the singular, and the stem plus **-te** for the plural. And, finally, the present infinitive? The stem plus **-re**.

So you can see that the principal difference between the fourth conjugation and the others you've seen so far is the quality of the stem vowel. Conjugate the fourth conjugation verb *to come*, **veniô, -îre**.

Fourth Conjugation veniô, -îre

	Present	Future	Imperfect	Imperative	Infinitive
1st	veniō	veniam	veniēbam	venī	venīre
2nd	venīs	veniēs	veniēbās		
3rd	venit	veniet	veniēbat		
Plural					
1st	venīmus	veniēmus	veniēbāmus	venīte	venīre
2nd	venītis	veniētis	veniēbātis		
3rd	veniunt	venient	veniēbant		

THIRD CONJUGATION I-STEM

The third conjugation contains a subset of verbs, called *i-stems*, that seem to imitate the fourth conjugation. The third conjugation, as you know, contains verbs whose stem vowel is short **-e-**. The short **-e-** is almost entirely hidden in the conjugation of the verbs because it changes to a short **-i-** or short **-u-** before the personal endings in the present tense. Still, it follows all the same rules as the other verbs when deriving its different forms. Both the i-stem and non-i-stem third conjugation verbs have the stem vowel short -e-, that's why they're both third conjugation verbs.

But the *i-stem* third conjugation verbs insert an extra -i- in some places in their conjugation. These places are really quite easy to remember, if you know fourth conjugation verbs: a third conjugation *i-stem* verb inserts an extra -i- everywhere a fourth conjugation verb has an -i-. In fact, you might want to think of a third conjugation *i-stem* verb as a failed fourth conjugation verb—as a verb that *wants* to be a fourth. Here's the dictionary entry for many third conjugation i-stem verbs. Notice the extra -i- in the first entry, and the short -e- of the infinitive in the second:

capiô	capere	cupiô	cupere
rapiô	rapere	faciô	facere

Let's have a closer look at all this. Write out the present tense of the following verbs. Remember, a third i-stem verb has an extra -i- everywhere there's an -i- in the fourth conjugation (Wheelock 62-3).

	Third (non-i-stem)	Fourth	Third i-stem
	mittô, -ere	veniô, -ire	capiô, -ere
1st	mittō	veniō	capiō
2nd	mittis	venīs	capis
3rd	mittit	venit	capit
Plural			
1st	mittimus	venīmus	capimus
2nd	mittitis	venītis	capitis
3rd	mittunt	veniunt	capiunt

As you can see, the fourth and third i-stem verbs look identical. But there is a difference. Go back and put in the long marks over the stem vowel long -î- of **veniô**. The -î- is long in the second person singular and plural, and in the first person plural. *Now* compare the forms of **veniô** with those of **capiô**—you can see the differences. The -î- of a fourth conjugation verb is long by nature and *wants* to stay long wherever it can. The stem vowel of a third conjugation verb is short -e-, which turns into short -i- or -u-. But it will never become long -î- regardless of what ending is added to it.

Now, the difference between a short and long vowel may seem rather subtle to us, but look again. In Latin pronunciation, the accent of a word falls on the second to the last syllable if the vowel in the syllable is long. If it is short, then the accent goes back to the third to the last syllable. So, what's the difference in the way these forms would have been pronounced? **Capimus** is pronounced *CAH peh muhs*; **audîmus** is pronounced *owh DEE muhs*. Similarly, **capitis** is pronounced *CAH peh tis*; **audîtis** is pronounced *owh DEE tis*. So the difference for a Roman between these verbs in some of the forms would have been quite striking.

What about the future tense of the third conjugation i-stem verbs? They look just like the fourth conjugation verbs: stem (**i**) + **a/e** + personal endings.

	Third (non-i-stem)	Fourth	Third i-stem
	mittô, -ere	veniô, -ire	capiô, -ere
1st	mittam	veniam	capiam
2nd	mittēs	veniēs	capiēs
3rd	mittet	veniet	capiet
Plural			
1st	mittēmus	veniēmus	capiēmus
2nd	mittētis	veniētis	capiētis
3rd	mittent	venient	capient

Next, write out the imperfect tenses of all three verbs. Remember, the third conjugation i-stem wants to look just like a fourth conjugation.

	Third (non-i-stem)	Fourth	Third i-stem
	mittô, -ere	veniô, -ire	capiô, -ere
1st	mittēbam	veniēbam	capiēbam
2nd	mittēbās	veniēbās	capiēbās
3rd	mittēbat	veniēbat	capiēbat
Plural			
1st	mittēbāmus	veniēbāmus	capiēbāmus
2nd	mittēbātis	veniēbātis	capiēbātis
3rd	mittēbant	veniēbant	capiēbant

Did you remember to lengthen the stem of **capiô**? The stem to which you add the tense sign is not **capê-**, which is what you might expect from a third conjugation verb. It's **capiê-**. Do you know why?

Now let's consider the imperative mood. In this case, there is no difference at all between the third i-stem verbs and the third non-i-stems. And why should there be? They both have the same stem vowel: short **-e-**.

	Third (non-i-stem)	Fourth	Third i-stem
	mittô, -ere	veniô, -ire	capiô, -ere
Singular	mitte	venī	cape
Plural	mittite	venīte	capite

VOCABULARY PUZZLES

-ficiô, -cipiô The short **-a-** of the verbs **faciô** and **capiô** changes (or *grades*) to short **-i-** in compound forms of the verb; i.e., when a prefix is attached. It will save you a lot of time if you learn this fact, particularly when you're looking at verbs like **perficiô, conficiô, interficiô, incipiô, dêcipiô,** and so on.

11

Personal Pronouns

THE ENGLISH PRONOUNS

You know what a pronoun is. It's a word that takes the place of a noun in a sentence. The word it's replacing is called the *antecedent*. So we can ask, *What is the antecedent of this pronoun*, whenever we see a pronoun in a sentence. That is, we are asking, *To what noun is this pronoun pointing?* If it weren't for pronouns, you'd have to repeat every noun and every name each time you wanted to refer to them, no matter how obvious the reference was. Pronouns are useful and ubiquitous. In this paragraph, you saw all kinds of pronouns in all kinds of shapes and varieties, referring to different antecedents and performing different grammatical tasks in their sentences. Let's review what you've learned so far about pronouns.

First of all, every pronoun is going to imply person. Not *a* person, but grammatical person: 1st, 2nd, or 3rd. And why should that be? You might remember that in language there is a speaker, the audience, and the thing the speaker is talking about. If the speaker is referring to him/herself or to a group of people of which he/she considers him/herself to be a part, he/she uses the first person pronoun. In English, the first person pronoun has three forms to indicate different cases (grammatical function).

Case	Singular	Plural
Subjective	I	we
Possessive	my	our
Objective	me	us

If the speaker is referring to the person or people to whom he/she is directly talking, he/she uses the second person pronoun. (Notice that the cases are not so clearly visible in the morphology of this pronoun. Notice, also, that English makes no distinction between second person pronouns in the singular and plural.)

Case	Singular	Plural
Subjective	you	you
Possessive	your	your
Objective	you	you

Let's stop here for a minute and take a close look at these pronouns. What *don't* they tell you about their antecedents? You can see the difference in number in the first person pronoun, but you can't in the second. What else don't you know about the antecedents? Do you know their genders? Do you know simply by looking at the form of, say, *me* whether the person referred to is male or female? No. In English (as well as in Latin), the first and second person pronouns make no distinction in the forms among the possible genders of their antecedents. Think about this for a moment. Why should the languages have evolved this way? Why is it *not* important for a speaker to be able to indicate differences in gender in the first and second persons? Try to figure it out.

Here's why. Let's take a step backwards for a moment: what is the first person? It's the speaker or speakers of the sentence, right? And what is the second person? It's the person or people whom the speaker(s) is (are) directly addressing. Should it be necessary for someone who's speaking to indicate his or her own gender to the listener(s)? Look, I surely know what gender I am; so there's no reason to indicate in the grammar of my sentence my gender. Furthermore, the psychology of language is such that there is an assumed (or real) audience to whom I am directing my thoughts. There is always an implied second person in everything spoken or written. If I'm standing directly in front of you, talking to *you*, you should have no doubt about my gender, because you can see me. Therefore, it would be superfluous for me to add special gender markings to my first person pronouns to tell you what gender I am. That is plainly visible. For this reason, then, the first person pronouns make no distinctions among the genders of their antecedents.

Can you guess now why the second person pronoun makes no distinctions among the genders, either? Right, because if I (the first person) am directly addressing you (the second person), then I should be able to tell your gender, too. You know my gender, and I know your gender, because we're standing in front of each other. As the first person in our conversation, I don't need to remind you, my audience, of your own gender, do I? (Obviously, written language creates a problem. It's possible for the speaker and the audience never to have met and hence not to know one another's gender. But languages were first spoken, not written, and its grammar is rooted in the oral experience.)

Now let's look at the first and second person pronouns in Latin. They'll make distinctions in number. And, to be useful in Latin, they'll have to decline through all the cases just like Latin nouns. Write out what's listed in Wheelock, pages 67-8.

	Singular		Plural	
	1st Person	**2nd Person**	**1st Person**	**2nd Person**
N/V.	ego	tū	nōs	vōs
Gen.[22]	meī	tuī	nostrum	vestrum
Dat.	mihi	tibi	nōbīs	vōbīs
Acc.	mē	tē	nōs	vōs
Abl.	mē	tē	nōbīs	nōbīs

[22]Despite what you may think, the genitive of the first and second person pronouns is *never* used to show possession. If you need to say *my book*, or *our book*, or *your book*, etc., Latin uses the possessive adjectives instead of the pronouns in the genitive case: **meus liber, noster liber, tuus liber,** or **vester liber.** You won't see **liber meī,** or **liber vestrī.** In fact, you won't really be using the genitive of the first and second person pronouns much at all in the first year of Latin. For now, just bracket them off. You'll come back to them when you need them.

Look at the following examples. You'll see how useful these pronouns are:

Mittam ad vôs fîlium meum, *I will send my son to you.*

Ego[23] scrîbô hâs litterâs, *I write this letter.*

Ego vôs videô, atque vôs mê vidêtis, *I see you, and **you** see me.*

THE WEAK DEMONSTRATIVE IS, EA, ID

So what about the third person pronouns? Here there's a problem, one which plagued, and continues to plague, the Romance languages derived from Latin. First off, the third person pronoun is going to have to tell you more about its antecedents than the first and second person pronouns did. If I (the first person) am talking to you (the second person) directly, I certainly know what gender you are. But if I am talking to you about something else (which is the third person) or if I am talking to you about several things, it would be nice if I could refer to the gender of these things to help keep them distinct. Look at the following passage:

I've got to tell you a story. Yesterday I saw Betty and Steve. *He* asked *her* for an apple. *She* told *him* that *she* didn't have any. When *he* asked *her* again, *she* told *him* to go buy *his* own apples.

Let's look at this little narrative more closely. The first *he*—how do you know that it's referring to Steve and not to Betty? That's easy; it's because *he* is masculine and not feminine. If the antecedent had been Betty, then you would have had *she* in place of *he*. Another thing *he* tells you about the antecedent is that the antecedent is singular. If the antecedent had been plural, then *he* would have been *they*. Right? One last thing. Look at the antecedent for *he*. What case is it in? It's in the objective (or accusative) case because it's the direct object of the verb *saw*. Now look at the pronoun *he*. What case is it in? It's in the nominative case. Why? Because in its sentence it's the subject of the verb *asked*. Now look at the pronoun *his* in the last line. What case is it in? This time the pronoun is in the possessive (or genitive) case; again because the grammar of the sentence it's in requires it to be in the genitive case. Even though all these pronouns are pointing to the same antecedent, they are all in different cases in their own sentences. Here is a rule you must remember: A pronoun gets its number and gender from its antecedent, but it gets its case from the way it (the pronoun) is being used grammatically.

Remember that. You'll need it very soon. So here's what the Latin third person pronoun must do: it must be able to show the number *and gender* of its antecedent, and it must be able to inflect through the entire case system.

Let's look once more at the English third person pronoun, so that you can see how unbelievably feeble and corrupted it is in comparison to the majestic power of the Latin third person pronoun.

---

[23]You'll only see the nominative of these pronouns used if there is some special emphasis attached to the subject; otherwise Latin shows person of the verb simply by the personal ending.

	Singular			Plural
	Masculine	**Feminine**	**Neuter**	**Masc./Fem./Neuter**
Subj.	he	she	it	they
Pos.	his	her	its	their
Obj.	him	her	it	them

As you can see, the English third person pronoun is so feeble it's hardly worth learning. In the singular, some of the case forms are identical; and in the plural it makes no distinction among the genders: *they* can refer to a group of men, women, or rocks. So it's not very useful. But look at the Latin third person pronoun. The third person pronoun starts its life as a weak demonstrative *adjective*. It means something like *the* and it agrees with the noun to which it's attached. Then, like the other demonstratives you've seen—**ille**, **hic**, and **iste**—it can be used independently as a pronoun. Let's see how it works.

First the morphology. The stem is **e-** and basically it's declined just like the other demonstratives you've seen before. Do you remember the hybrid declension, which has the irregular **-īus** and **-ī** for the genitive and dative singulars? Try to fill in the declension. Don't forget, now, the stem of the demonstrative is **e-** to which the case endings are going to be added. Except for the genitive and dative singular, it will use the standard first and second declension endings which all standard adjectives use (Wheelock 68).

	Masculine	**Feminine**	**Neuter**
N/V.	is	ea	id
Gen.	eius	eius	eius
Dat.	eī	eī	eī
Acc.	eum	eam	id
Abl.	eō	eā	eō
Plural			
N/V.	iī, or eī	eae	ea
Gen.	eōrum	eārum	eōrum
Dat.	eīs	eīs	eīs
Acc.	eōs	eās	eōs
Abl.	eīs	eīs	eīs

First let's see how the weak demonstrative **is, ea, id** works as an *adjective*. Don't forget that as with the demonstratives **ille**, **hic**, and **iste**, **is** can be used both as an adjective and as a pronoun. When used as a demonstrative adjective, **is** has about the same force as our article the; although, as you'll see, Latin doesn't use **is, ea, id** in some places where we would use our *the*. Briefly, we may say this: Latin uses **is, ea, id** as a demonstrative adjective to give a little emphasis to something that has already been talked about. Like this:

I have a book.

Well, then, give me *the* book.

The book is on the table.

Okay, thanks. I'll get *the* book myself.

The underscored *the's* are candidates for the Latin **is, ea, id**, because the book the two are talking about has already been identified; and the speakers are calling just a little attention to it. Can you see also how **is, ea, id** differs from the strong demonstrative adjectives **ille** and **hic**? Can you feel the difference between saying *Give me the book* and *Give me **that** book* or *Give me **this** book here?* In English we have a weak *this* that corresponds nicely to the Latin **is, ea, id** used as an adjective. We can say, for example, *I like this book*, without placing much emphasis on the *this*. That is, we're not saying *I like **this** book [and not **that** one over there]*.

Here are some examples of **is, ea, id** used as weak demonstrative adjectives. Of course, without a context it may be a little difficult to see precisely the shades of feeling; but at least you can see the grammar involved.

Eôs librôs vôbîs dâbimus, *we will give the (or these) books to you.*

Eâs litterâs ad mê mittet, *he will send the (or this) letter to me.*

Eî librî sunt bonî, *the (or these) books are good.*

Animî eârum fêminârum valent, *the courage of the (or of these) women is strong.*

Nûlla cîvitâs ea bella tolerâre poterat, *no city was able to endure the (or these) wars.*

IS, EA, ID AS A PRONOUN

Remember the demonstrative adjectives **ille**, **hic**, and **iste**? You remember that they can be used as adjectives, to add emphasis to the noun they're modifying:

Ille liber est bonus, *that book is good.*

Hic vir est malus, *this man is evil.*

Cicerô videt istâs însidiâs, *Cicero sees that plot.*

Possum superâre vitia illa, *I can overcome those faults.*

Habeô pecûniam illârum fêminârum, *I have the money of those women.*

That's all fine and good. But you also remember that the demonstrative adjective can be used, just like all other adjectives, without a noun explicitly stated, but only implied. In order to supply the correct noun, you must do two things: (1) you must examine the form of the demonstrative and (2) you must examine the context. Watch: **Illae fêminae sunt ibi, sed illâs vidêre nôn possum**.

How do you translate the **illâs**? Well, **illâs** is feminine, accusative plural, right? It's in the accusative because it's the direct object of the verb **vidêre**. But why is it feminine and plural? Because the noun which has been left out—that is, the things to which **illâs** is referring—is feminine and plural. And what is that? Look at the context. **Fêminae** is feminine and plural. So you'd translate it, *those women are there, but I can't see those women* (or, more idiomatically in English, *but I can't see them*).[24]

When the demonstratives are used without a noun, then they are taking the place of a noun. And words that take the place of a noun are called pronouns. Hence the metamorphosis from demonstrative adjective to demonstrative pronoun is complete.

Now let's take a look at the weak demonstrative adjective **is, ea, id**. It will undergo the same process from adjective to pronoun. Because there is only a weak demonstrative force attached to **is, ea, id**, we can translate it into English simply as our third person pronoun: *he, she, it,* etc. **Vidêtisne meôs amîcôs? Videô eôs,**[25] *do you see my friends? I see them.*

All you have to do when you see the weak demonstrative adjective in a sentence without a noun is to treat it just like a third person pronoun: check the antecedent and find the appropriate English equivalent. Read these sentences (go very, very slowly and be reasonable):

Cicerô amat Rômam, et in **eâ** beâtam vîtam agit. Ego quoque cîvitâtem **eius**[26] amô. Tôtî amîcî **eius** sunt Rômânî. Vîtae **eôrum** sunt beâtae, et **eâs** magnâ cum sapientiâ agunt. **Eî** igitur sunt beâtî. Cicerô **eôs** amat, et **eî** eum amant. Ôlim cîvitâs **eôrum** in perîculis magnîs erat, sed **ea** superâre poterat, quoniam vîrôs multôs bonôrum môrum invenîre poterat.

Cicero loves Rome, and he is leading a happy life in it. I also love his city. All his friends are Romans. Their lives are happy, and they are leading them (they are leading their lives) with great wisdom. They are therefore happy. Cicero loves them, and they love him. Formerly their city was in great danger, but it was able to overcome them (the dangers), since he was able to find many men of good character.

---

[24] As you can see, English doesn't really have fully developed demonstrative pronouns like the Latin **ille, hic,** and **iste**. We have them in some instances; but we can't use them in as many places as Latin uses theirs: *Give me some of those, please. Some of these? Yes, some of those.* But we can't quite say, *I see those* when we mean *I see those women,* but Latin can: **videô illâs**.

[25] Don't forget now. The **eôs** in the second sentence is accusative because it is the direct object of the verb *in its own sentence,* not because the word it is standing in for, **amîcôs,** is accusative. A pronoun gets its number and gender from its antecedent, but it gets its case from the way it's being used in its own sentence or clause.

[26] Don't panic with this one. Start at the beginning. It's the genitive singular of **is, ea, id,** right? And it could be any one of the three genders. But it has no noun to go with it, correct? So you have to treat it as if it were a third person pronoun. What, in English, are the genitive singular forms of the third person pronoun: *his, her,* or *its.* Now, look around. Which do you think is more appropriate here? One last point to notice. In the first and second persons, Latin *does not* use the genitive case of the pronouns to show possession, but in the third person it does.

THE DEMONSTRATIVE ÎDEM, EADEM, IDEM

This is simple. Latin adds an indeclinable suffix to the end of the inflected forms of the demonstrative **is, ea, id** and comes out with *the same*. Like the demonstrative **is, ea, id**, the resulting form can be used either as an adjective—**eadem fêmina**, *the same woman*—or as a full-blown pronoun—**videô eâsdem**, *I see the same (feminine) things*. Remember, the syntactically important information comes *before* the **dem** suffix: **e***is***dem**, **e***a***edem**, etc.

The addition of the suffix causes some distortion of the spelling of **is, ea, id**. First, in the nominative singular masculine, the **s** of **is** collides with the **d** of -**dem** and disappears; but the **i** of **is** becomes long as a result. In the nominative singular neuter, instead of **iddem** we get **idem**. No big surprise here. Finally, and this isn't much of a surprise either, wherever the case ending of **is, ea, id** ends in an **m**, the addition of **dem** changes the **m** to an **n**.[27] Decline **îdem, eadem, idem** (Wheelock 449).

	Masculine	Feminine	Neuter
N/V.	īdem	eadem	idem
Gen.	eiusdem		
Dat.	eīdem		
Acc.	eundem	eandem	idem
Abl.	eōdem	eãdem	eōdem
Plural			
N/V.	eīdem	eaedem	eadem
Gen.	eōrundem	eārundem	eōrundem
Dat.	eīsdem		
Acc.	eōsdem	eāsdem	eadem
Abl.	eīsdem		

VOCABULARY PUZZLES

nêmô The pronoun for *nobody* has more than its share of oddities: (1) The stem of the word is **nêmin-**. (2) It uses the third declension endings; (3) It's potentially masculine or feminine—*no man* or *no woman*; (4) Like the English *nobody*, it's only singular; (5) It uses the genitive singular of the adjective **nûllus, -a, -um** instead of its expected form of **nêminis**; (6) In the ablative singular it uses **nûllô**, *m.* and *n.*, or **nûllâ**, *f.* instead of the expected **nêmine**. (Consequently, the only place *nobody* in Latin make any distinction in gender is in the ablative. Why that should be I haven't the foggiest idea.)

---

[27]You saw something like this in the forms of **hic, haec, hoc**. Remember **hanc** and **hunc**?

12

The Perfect Active System

VERBS: PRINCIPAL PARTS

Let's pretend you're a native French speaker learning English, and you want to look up the English equivalent of the French verbs **voir**, **avoir**, **prendre**, and **regarder**. You turn to your French-English dictionary and you find this:

voir	*to see,*	pret. *saw,*	pt. *seen*
avoir	*to have,*	pret. *had,*	pt. *had*
prendre	*to take,*	pret. *took,*	pt. *taken*
regarder	*to look*		

What's all this about? Why are there three entries for the first three verbs? Wouldn't it have been enough for the dictionary just to have listed the infinitive *to see* for **voir**, *to have* for **avoir**, etc.? Of course not; and why not? Consider our verb *to see*? What tenses of the verb are formed from the stem indicated in the infinitive *to see*? Let's list a few: Present Simple, *see*; Present Progressive, *I am seeing*; Present Emphatic, *I do see*; Imperative, *See*; Future Simple, *I will see*; Future Progressive, *I will be seeing*; Imperfect, *I was seeing*.

You can see that if you know a few basic tricks, you can use the infinitive form *to see* as the base for several tenses and moods in English. *To see* provides the raw material. But there are tenses English uses that are not formed from the infinitive *to see*. How about the preterit (*PREH tuh reht),* the simple past tense? Can you form the simple past from *to see*? No, English uses another form of the verb to form this tense; and unless you know what that form is, you can't use the verb *to see* in the preterit tense. Therefore, the dictionary must give you the form English uses: *saw.* So, the second entry in the dictionary for the English verb *to see* is the preterit form. Look at the second entries for *to have* and *to take.* Their preterits are *had* and *took*, respectively. Do we get any other tenses from this form of the verb? No, just one: the preterit tense.

Look at the third entry, *seen.* For what tenses, voices and moods does English use this form? A lot of them. Here are some: Present Passive, *I am seen*; Perfect Active, *I have seen*; Pluperfect Active, *I had seen*; Perfect Passive *I have been seen*; Future Perfect Active, *I will have seen*, and so on.

With the three forms given in the dictionary, you have all the raw material from which to build every possible tense, mood, voice, and number of the verb *to see.* Therefore, to know an English verb thoroughly, and to be able to use it in all its possible applications, you must know all three of its basic forms. Once you know them, you simply apply the rules for the formation of the different tenses, voices, and moods. We call these three forms the *principal parts* of the verb. English verbs have three principal parts, which we call the infinitive, the preterit, and the perfect participle.

Fine, now look at the verb *to look*. Why aren't there two more principal parts listed after the infinitive? Well, what are the next two principal parts? The verb goes: *to look, looked,* and *looked.* As you can see, the second and third principal parts are derivable from the first principal part: you simply add *-ed* to the *look.* There are hundreds of verbs in English that work this way. Their second and third principal parts are simply the first principal part with the suffix *-ed.* Verbs that operate like this are called *regular* (or *weak*). If a verb is regular, you don't need to be given the second and third entries separately. That is, once you know the first principal part, you know the next two, and thus have all the basic material you need to form all the possible tenses, moods, and voices of the verb. On the other hand, verbs whose principal parts are not readily derivable from the first principal part are called *irregular* (or *strong*) verbs.

What have I convinced you of so far? All possible tenses, voices, and moods of an English verb are reducible to three different principal parts. If a verb is irregular (strong), you must learn the principal parts by memory; but if it is regular (weak), you can easily derive the second two principal parts from the first by applying the rule of added *-ed* to the first principal part.

LATIN VERBS: PRINCIPAL PARTS

Latin verbs have three principal parts (three different stems), but for reasons I'll explain soon, we say that they have four.[28] Up to this chapter, I've been misleading you slightly by calling the basic verb form of the present, imperfect, and future tenses the *stem.* That was justifiable when, so far as you knew, there was only one stem for verbs. But now you must realize that the word *stem* is no longer limited to just one possible part of the verb. The stem with which you are so familiar is really only the first principal part. Let's look again at the first principal part. What tenses do we get from the first principal part? You know three of them already. The first principal part is the stem from which Latin forms the present, future, and the imperfect tenses. And remember, you use the infinitive—the second principal part—to tell you what the stem of the first principal part is.

This, then, is the big picture of the sum total of your knowledge of Latin verbs. All the tenses and moods you know are based on the first principal part of the verb—the first entry you see in the dictionary. For reasons which you needn't worry about yet, we call all the tenses derived from the first principal part of the verb the tenses of the *present system.* So we say that the first principal part is the root of the present system of the Latin verbs. Now on to some new territory.

---

[28]This is because the second principal part, the present infinitive, really only tells you something more about the first principal part—namely, the stem vowel of the first principal part. Still, we say first and second principal parts of the present first person singular and of the present infinitive, even though there are no tenses, moods, or voices that are derived from the present infinitive.

THE PERFECT SYSTEM OF LATIN VERBS

As you saw, English verbs have three roots from which different voices, moods, and tenses are derived. A Latin verb uses its first principal part to form the present system: the present, future, and imperfect tenses. And this would have suited the Romans just fine, if their language had had only three tenses, but it has six (one less than English). We divide the tenses into two major systems: the present system (which you know) and the perfect system (which you are about to learn). The perfect system uses the remaining two principal parts—the third and the fourth—as its base. In this chapter, we're going to be concerned only with the tenses formed off the third principal part. The perfect system is composed of three tenses: the perfect; the pluperfect, and the future perfect:

(1) The perfect tense is used in Latin just as we use our preterit and our perfect tenses: I *saw* or I *have seen*.[29]

(2) The pluperfect tense is used to talk about an action which has taken place before another action in the past. In English, we use the preterit of the auxiliary verb *to have* with the past participle (the third principal part) of the verb: I *had seen*. E.g., *Before you came to the door, I **had** already **seen** you pull up in the driveway.*

(3) The future perfect tense is used to talk about an action which will have taken place *before* another event in the future. In English, we use the future of the auxiliary verb *to have* with the past participle of the verb: I *will have seen*. E.g., *Before you come back, **I'll have cleaned** this mess all up.*

The perfect, pluperfect, and future perfect tenses in the *active voice only* are formed from the third principal part. The perfect system passive, as you will see in a few chapters, uses the fourth principal part, not the third. Let's look first at the perfect tense active.

The perfect tense is formed exactly according to the formula for the formation of the tenses you already know. It's made up of personal endings that are added to a stem. The differences are (1) the perfect tense uses the third principal part in place of the first and (2) the perfect tense uses a different set of personal endings. Write down the perfect personal endings (Wheelock 77).

	Singular	Plural
1st	-ī	-imus
2nd	-istī	-istis
3rd	-it	-ērunt, -ēre

Okay, so where are we now? To form the perfect tense, Latin uses these perfect personal endings and puts them onto the third principal part of the verb. Let's have a look at the third principal parts of verbs.

---

[29]We'll refine the distinction between these two tenses later. For now, use the Latin perfect tense as either the English preterit or the perfect. Use whichever English tense feels more natural.

This may sound like a small consolation, but in the perfect system, the distinctions between the different conjugations melt away. You undoubtedly remember all the differences between the conjugations in the present system: each conjugation has a different stem vowel and, what's even worse, the first and second conjugations form their futures differently from the third and fourth conjugations. But in the perfect system, once you get to the verb's third and fourth principal parts, you needn't worry any longer whether the verb is a first, second, third, third-i stem, or fourth conjugation. The fourth conjugation will not form, say, its future perfect differently from verbs of the first or second conjugations. All the conjugations obey exactly the same rules in the perfect system. But getting to the third principal part is the first thing you've got to think about. Let's make all this a little more real by looking at some actual forms. Let's look at the perfect tense of a first conjugation verb. First we have to get to its third principal part.

The First Conjugation

Remember the verb *to look* in English? *To look* is a regular verb in English, which means that its second and third principal parts are formed by adding *-ed* to the first principal part: *to look, looked,* and *looked.* Because it's regular, the English dictionary didn't list the second and third principal parts separately. Anybody with any business looking up English verbs in the first place should at least know how regular verbs work. Like a regular verb in English, the first conjugation in Latin forms its principal parts by predictable and regular modification of the first principal part.[30] Like this:

I	II	III
laudô	laudâre	laudâvî

Let's go slowly. First off, the dictionary lists the first principal part in the first person singular. So you see **laudô** instead of **laudâ-**. To see the stem vowel, and hence to see the conjugation, you must look to the second principal part, where the stem vowel is revealed by dropping off the infinitive ending **-re**. In the same way, the third principal part is listed in the dictionary in the first person singular perfect tense; that is, with the **-î** of the first person singular. To see the stem, you must drop off the **-î**. So the true stem of the third principal part is **laudâv-**. As you can see from this example, the third principal part of the verb **laudô** is just the stem of the first principal part—**laudâ-** plus **v**. And nearly *all* first conjugation verbs form the third principal part in just this way: the first principal part (i.e., the stem) plus a **-v-**. Write out the second and third principal parts of some of the first conjugation verbs you already know:

---

[30]Don't worry about the fourth principal parts for now; Wheelock includes them only for the sake of completeness here. Briefly, the fourth principal part is a participle—a verbal adjective—so it must have adjectival endings. That's why you see **-us, -a, -um** tacked onto the end. These endings are often abbreviated either as the neuter **-um** or the masculine **-us**.

First	Second	Third
amô	amāre	amāvī
cogitô	cōgitāre	cōgitāvī
tolerô	tolerāre	tolerāvī
superô	superāre	superāvī
laudô	laudāre	laudāvī

As you can see, there's really nothing to this. Once you know that a verb is first conjugation, you can easily derive its principal parts. For this reason, a dictionary need tell you only a verb is first conjugation, and from there you'll be able to derive the other parts on your own. Given the first part, you know the other two (provided that you remember your grammar!). A Latin dictionary tells you that a verb is first conjugation by simply putting a [1] (or [I]) directly after the first entry. For example, **certô** (1). This tells you the verb is first conjugation; and with that knowledge alone, you know the rest of the principal parts: **certāre, certâvî**.

Now let's put the third principal part to work. And remember, these are the rules that will govern the use of the third principal parts of *all* the conjugations, first through fourth. Use the first conjugation verb **laudô** (1) as your paradigm.

PERFECT TENSE

Remember that to form the perfect tense of a verb you use the stem of the third principal part (what's left after you drop the -**î**), to which you add the perfect personal endings (Wheelock 77).

	3rd Pr. Part	+	Personal Ending	→	Conjugated Form
1st	laudāv	+	ī	→	laudāvī
2nd	laudāv	+	istī	→	laudāvistī
3rd	laudāv	+	it	→	laudāvit
Plural					
1st	laudāv	+	imus	→	laudāvimus
2nd	laudāv	+	istis	→	laudāvistis
3rd	laudāv	+	ērunt	→	laudāvērunt

PLUPERFECT TENSE

Another tense of the perfect system of tenses (tenses that use the third and fourth principal parts of the verb) is the pluperfect tense. To form the pluperfect tense, you use the imperfect tense of the verb **sum** for the personal endings, which are attached to the third principal part.

	3rd Pr. Part	+	Personal Ending	→	Conjugated Form
1st	laudāv	+	eram	→	laudāveram
2nd	laudāv	+	erās	→	laudāverās
3rd	laudāv	+	erat	→	laudāverat
Plural					
1st	laudāv	+	erāmus	→	laudāverāmus
2nd	laudāv	+	erātis	→	laudāverātis
3rd	laudāv	+	erant	→	laudāverant

FUTURE PERFECT TENSE

The future perfect uses the future of the verb **sum** for the personal endings (with the exception of the third person plural where it is **-erint** instead of the normal future form **-erunt**).

	3rd Pr. Part	+	Personal Ending	→	Conjugated Form
1st	laudāv	+	erō	→	laudāverō
2nd	laudāv	+	eris	→	laudāveris
3rd	laudāv	+	erit	→	laudāverit
Plural					
1st	laudāv	+	erimus	→	laudāverimus
2nd	laudāv	+	eritis	→	laudāveritis
3rd	laudāv	+	erint	→	laudāverint

Now you have it. You know all the rules for forming the entire perfect active system of any Latin verb. Once you know the third principal part, you simply apply these formulae and away you go.

The Second Conjugation

Please remember, the rules for forming the tenses of the perfect system don't change from one conjugation to the next. You're still going to use the third principal part of the verb plus the endings we just went through. What we're doing now is having a look at how verbs form their third principal part. Many, very many, second conjugation verbs form their third principal part regularly off the first principal part. Like this:

I	II	III
moneô	monêre	monuî
doceô	docêre	docuî
timeô	timêre	timuî
terreô	terrêre	terruî

If we look into this more closely, what really is going on is that the third principal part of these verbs is formed simply by adding **-v-** to the stem of the first principal part, just as it's done for first conjugation verbs. But when the **-v-** of the third principal part comes up against the **-ê-** of the stem of a second conjugation verb, the result is one, solitary **-u-**. So for the verb **moneô**, the third principal part is **monêvî** which becomes **monuî**. So, also, with many second conjugation verbs.

Now, as I said, many second conjugation verbs form their principal parts just this way; and if you remember this, you won't be confronted with such a daunting list of forms to memorize. There is some order to it. But there are enough verbs differing from this regular pattern that you can't take for granted that you can deduce the principal parts from the first for *every* second conjugation verb. The dictionary can't simply put a *(2)* next to the first entry and leave it up to you to derive the rest of the parts. The dictionary must give you the parts as separate entries. Here are the second conjugation verbs you've had so far. You can see that the rules work fairly well, but there are deviations.

I	II	III
dêbeô	dêbêre	dêbuî
habeô	habêre	habuî
remaneô	remanêre	remansî
videô	vidêre	vidî
valeô	valêre	valuî

DRILLS

Let's consolidate our ground now by doing a few exercises. Produce the following forms, and try to do it from memory at first.

1.	They will have had.	Habuerint
2.	I had seen.	Vīderam
3.	You (*pl.*) remained.	Remānsistis
4.	We will have called.	Vocāverimus
5.	She will be strong.	~~Valuerit~~ Valēbit
6.	You (*s.*) have tolerated.	Tolerāvistī
7.	They had taught.	Docuerant
8.	You (*pl.*) had had.	Habuerātis
9.	We have loved.	Amāvimus
10.	They thought.	Cōgitāvērunt

The Third Conjugation (Including the I-stems)

Now you have to batten down the hatches; the third conjugation is where irregularity is the norm. You must simply learn the principal parts of third conjugation verbs outright. But, as I will try to show you, reason isn't completely banished from the third conjugation. Our minds can impose some order here too. Some classifiable things happen to third conjugation verbs as they form their principal parts. Here's a list of things that often happen to the first principal part when it becomes a third principal part.

(1) Reduplication of Initial Consonant

Often the third principal part of a third conjugation verb will begin by doubling the initial consonant of the first principal part and putting an -e- or -i- in between the two of them:

I	II	III
pellô	pellere	*pe*pulî
discô	discere	*di*dicî
dô	dare	*de*dî[31]

(2) The Sigmatic (or -S) Perfect

Many verbs add an -s- to the end of the first principal part to produce the third principal part. Often the -s- is hidden in an -x- or another consonant which comes about from the collision between the -s- and the consonant at the end of the verb. If the first principal part ends in a -t-, the -t- may disappear completely. A final -b- changes slightly to a -p-. Can you hear an -s- sound at the end of each of these three principal parts?

I	II	III
mittô	mittere	mîsî
dicô	dicere	dîxî
scrîbô	scrîbere	scrîpsî
vîvô	vîvere	vîxî

(3) Change in the Medial Vowel; Loss of Stem Nasal

Very often a vowel in the first principal part that is near the end of the verb will change in the third principal part: it will lengthen from a short to a long vowel; or it will grade, often from an original -a- to a long -ê-. Nasals, -m- or -n-, in the first principal part may also be dropped in the third principal part.

---

[31] If you look closely at the stem vowel of **dô, dare**, you'll see that the -a- is short, not long. So it's not really a full-fledged first conjugation verb after all. Its third principal part betrays it.

I	II	III
agô	agere	êgî
faciô	facere	fêcî
fugiô	fugere	fûgî
vincô	vincere	vîcî

By now you must be wondering why I'm troubling you will all these patterns. Isn't it enough to have to memorize the principal parts without being burdened with all this? Well, yes, you are going to have to memorize the principal parts of the verbs you're given in the vocabulary, that's true. But, there are more words out there in Latin than you can easily memorize before you begin to read Latin. For much of your reading, you're going to have to rely not on pre-memorized vocabulary items, but on your powers of deduction. Suppose you see this form in your text: **recêperant**.

Okay, you recognize the **-erant** ending as the third person plural pluperfect. From this realization you can make another deduction. If you're in the perfect system, then the **-erant** was attached to the third principal part of the verb; and you know that the first entry in a dictionary is the first principal part, not the third. This could be a problem. Can you look up *been* in the dictionary in English? No, of course not. That's because *been* is a principal part of *to be* and it'll be listed under *to be*. So how are you going to look up **recêp-**? You'll never find it just like that in a dictionary. You must recreate the first principal part of the verb to look it up. What are you going to do?

Think a little. What else can you deduce about this verb? For one, it's not a first conjugation verb. They all look like **-âv-** in the third principal part. So you won't find it under **recêpô, -âre**. It could be a second conjugation verb, even though most of those have third principal parts ending in **-u-**: like **habuî** and **docuî** from **habeô** and **doceô**. Still, it might be worth a shot. So you look up **recêpeô**, expecting to see **recêpêre** and **recêpî** listed as its principal parts after it. (Don't forget, what you're looking for is a verb whose third principal part is **recêpî**.) But there is no **recêpeô, -êre, -cêpî**. Then, in bitter frustration, you forget my stern warning not to go window-shopping in the dictionary; and you look at all the entries beginning with **recêp-** hoping to find that third principal part **recêpî**. But you fail.

Now you start thinking to yourself. Suppose this is a third conjugation verb? Sometimes strange things happen to verbs as they go from the first to the third principal part. Is there any evidence of reduplication? No. Any hidden **-s-** sound at the end that's throwing off my search? No. What's left? Grote once said something about the medial vowel changing, so I'll try that. I look up **r-e-c-?-p-**. Because that **-ê-** could have been something else in the first principal part, I'll stay flexible on it: the verb could be **recap-** or **recip-**.

Leave yourself some intelligently limited flexibility. Now you find it, **recipiô, -ere, -cêpî**. You see, this works sometimes. That's why I showed you the major patterns of variations.

Fourth Conjugation

The formation of the third and fourth principal parts of a fourth conjugation verb is quite straightforward. There are enough irregular forms to warrant separate listing in the dictionary—they aren't all regular derivatives from the first principal part as in the first conjugation—but many verbs do have regular principal parts. Here are a few fourth conjugation verbs:

I	II	III
sentiô	sentîre	sensî
veniô	venîre	vênî
inveniô	invenîre	invênî
audiô	audîre	audîvî

DRILLS: TENSES

Conjugate the perfect system of the verb dûcô, -ere, dûxî

		Perfect	Pluperfect	Future Perfect
1st		dūxī	dūxeram	dūxerō
2nd		dūxistī	dūxerās	dūxeris
3rd		dūxit	dūxerat	dūxerit
Plural				
1st		dūximus	dūxerāmus	dūxerimus
2nd		dūxistis	dūxerātis	dūxeritis
3rd		dūxērunt	dūxerant	dūxerint

Translate into Latin

1.	I came.	vēnī
2.	I saw.	vīdī
3.	I conquered.	vīcī
4.	I will have begun.	incēperō
5.	She had taught.	docuerat
6.	They lived.	vīxērunt
7.	We had.	Habuimus
8.	You (pl.) have written.	~~scrīpserātis~~ scrīpsistis
9.	They sent.	mīsērunt

10.	They have been.	*fuērunt*
11.	We have found.	*invēnimus*
12.	He had fled.	*fūgerat*
13.	You couldn't see us.[32]	*nōs nōn potuistī vidēre*
14.	You (s.) had seen.	*vīderās*
15.	They came.	~~*vēnimus*~~ *vēnērunt*

VOCABULARY PUZZLES

deus, -î (m) The short **-e-** of the stem causes the word some grief in the plural: **dî**, (instead of **deî**); **deôrum**; **dîs** (instead of **deîs**); **deôs**; **dîs** (instead of **deîs**).

---

[32]Fill in the blank: *Today I can't see you, but yesterday I _____. Could* is our normal preterit tense of the verb *can.*

13

More Pronouns

FIRST AND SECOND PERSON REFLEXIVE PRONOUNS

In Chapter 11 you studied the first, second, and third person pronouns. Here's what you should remember about them. The first and second person pronouns don't show any gender; there aren't three forms, for example, for the word *I*: one that's feminine, one that's masculine, and another that's neuter. The first and second person don't have to indicate different gender for reasons that are grounded psychologically in the nature of language itself. Another thing is that Latin uses the weak demonstrative adjective **is, ea, id** as its third person pronoun. Here, making distinctions among the three genders is very important, so the third person pronoun has thirty possible forms—five cases in three genders in both the singular and the plural. Remember all that? Let's go on. Look at these English sentences:

We saw you there.

You saw me there.

You saw us there.

We are coming with you.

You are giving it to us.

If you had to, you could put each of these sentences into Latin, using the appropriate number and case of the first and second person pronouns. But I have something else in mind. As you can see, in each of these sentences the person of the pronoun of the subject is different from the pronoun that appears in the predicate. In the sentence *we saw you there*, the subject pronoun is first and the pronoun in the predicate is second. And similarly for the rest of the sentences. This is because in each of these sentences someone is doing something to or with someone else.

Now look at these sentences. They're not in standard English, but I'm going to make a point: *You saw you; I saw me; I bought me an apple; We like us.* In these sentences, unlike the first batch, the person of the subject pronoun is the same as the pronoun in the predicate. In *You saw you*, both the subject and the predicate pronouns are second person. In the second and third sentence, they're both first person singular. In the fourth sentence, they're both in the first person plural. Now, I warned you, these sentences are not in standard English. But suppose a foreigner who's just learning English had said them. Is there any question in these sentences about who's doing what to whom? No. In *I saw me*, the speaker is obviously trying to say that he saw himself. He's trying to say that the subject of the verb is performing an action on itself, not on something or someone else. So even though they don't qualify as good English, these sentences can be understood. The subject of the verb is performing an action that affects the subject itself; and because the person of the pronouns in the subject and the predicate is the same, you can see that.

When the subject of a sentence performs an action that affects itself, then the pronouns in the predicate are called *reflexive* (from the Latin words that mean *to bend back*). That's because they *bend* you *back* through the verb to the subject. So here you go: a reflexive pronoun is a pronoun in the predicate of the sentence that refers you to the subject.

That's the easy part. Now the hard part. In the first and second persons, this task could be easily accomplished by using pronouns that have the same person. It's really not necessary to have separate forms in the first and second person for non-reflexive pronouns on the one hand and reflexive pronouns on the other. *I saw me* can only mean that the subject saw itself. Similarly, *You saw you* can only mean that the subject is acting on itself. One set of forms can do double duty. English, how-ever, does have separate forms. We use a form of the pronoun with the suffix *-self*.

	First Person	Second Person
Singular	myself	yourself
Plural	ourselves	yourselves

So we don't say *I saw me*. Instead, we say *I saw **myself***. It's not *You saw you*, but *You saw **yourself***.

Latin, however, being the wise and economical language it is, has no separate forms for reflexive and non-reflexive pronouns in the first and second persons. It simply uses the personal pronouns you've already seen:

Videô mê, *I see myself.*

Vidêmus nôs, *we see ourselves.*

Vidêtis vôs, *you see yourselves.*

Vidês tê, *you see yourself.*

In the first and second persons, if the pronoun in the predicate is the same per-son as the subject pronoun, the pronoun in the predicate is referring to the subject and is therefore *de facto* reflexive.

There is one interesting feature worthy of comment. Will a reflexive pronoun ever be in the nominative case? Think about it. When a pronoun is nominative, it is the subject of the sentence. But a reflexive pronoun by definition is in the predicate and is receiving in some way the action which the subject of the sentence is per-forming. So a reflexive pronoun will never be in the nominative case. That's why you see Wheelock listing the reflexive pronouns like this:

	1st Sg.	2nd Sg.	1st Pl.	2nd Pl.
Nom.	_____	_____	_____	_____
Gen.	[meî]	[tuî][33]	[nostrî/nostrum]	[vestrî/vestrum]
Dat.	mihi	tibi	nôbîs	vôbîs
Acc.	mê	tê	nôs	vôs
Abl.	mê	tê	nôbîs	vôbîs

These forms ought to look pretty familiar. They are nothing more than the regular, non-reflexive pronouns you got in Chapter 11. But there are no nominatives, for the reason we just went through. Actually, a better way to say this would be that Latin has no separate forms for the reflexive pronoun in the first and second persons at all; it simply uses the existing pronouns reflexively.

THIRD PERSON REFLEXIVE PRONOUN

In the third person things are a little more complicated. You remember that the third person pronoun needs to show gender because, unlike the first and second persons, the gender of the topic of conversation may not be obvious. The same kind of ambiguity is possible in the third person with regard to reflexive and non-reflexive pronouns. It may be possible that the third person subject is performing an action that is affecting another third person. Consider these sentences: *He saw him; They saw them; She saw her.*

Here the person of the pronouns is the same in each of these sentences. In the first and second persons, that would have been enough to tell you that the subject is acting upon itself. But that's not going to work in the third person. You can't tell whether the *her*, for example, in the predicate of the third sentence is the same female as the subject of the sentence. *She* could be seeing another female. The third person must have one form for the reflexive pronoun and another for the non-reflexive pronoun, since the possibility of ambiguity is real if the forms were the same. In English, we use the old stand-by: the suffix *-self* for the reflexive: *He saw him**self**; They saw them**selves**; She saw her**self**.*

The standard third person pronoun **is, ea, id** won't do for this in Latin; different forms are required for the third person reflexive pronoun—that is, for a pronoun that will refer you to the subject of the sentence and not to some other third person. Latin does, indeed, have separate forms, but unlike the barbarous prolixity of English, Latin keeps its forms to a bare minimum.

Look at it this way. All the third person reflexive pronoun has to do is to refer you to the subject of the sentence. The pronoun itself does *not* have to tell you the gender or the number of the subject of the sentence. The subject itself can tell you that. The reflexive pronoun only has to point you back to the subject, and if you remember the subject of the sentence you're reading or listening to, you can mentally bring forward the number and gender.

---

[33]Remember that you're not going to see these used to show possession.

Try it this way. Suppose in English the sign * is the reflexive third person pronoun. It tells you to go back to the subject of the sentence; so every time you see it, you plug in the words *the subject*:

She saw *.	→	She saw (*the subject*).
They saw *.	→	They saw (*the subject*).
He bought it for *.	→	He bought it for (*the subject*).

Do you see? In all three sentences you get a full understanding of what's going on without having to be told by the reflexive pronoun what the gender and number of the subject are. But in English we'd have to say: *She saw **herself**; They saw **themselves**; He bought it for **himself***.

In the first sentence, we don't need to be told again by the reflexive pronoun that the subject is feminine and singular. Yet this is precisely what English does. Similarly for the other two. Does the speaker of the English sentence really think our attention spans are so short that we have to be reminded after a second or two what the subject of the sentence is? Evidently.

In Latin, no such forgetfulness is impugned to us the audience. The Latin third person reflexive pronoun is simply a sign that directs us back to the subject of the sentence. It declines, of course, because it may be used in the different cases (not the nominative); but it tells us nothing about the number or gender of the subject. It just tells us, *no matter what the subject of this sentence was, think of it again*. Here's Latin's reflexive third person pronoun:

	Singular and Plural
Nom.	————
Gen.	[suî][34]
Dat.	sibi
Acc.	sê
Abl.	sê

Do you see? There are no gender indications in this pronoun, and there is no distinction in number. The forms are the same for the singular and the plural. That's because all this pronoun does is to refer you to the subject of the sentence. It doesn't matter to the pronoun whether the subject is singular or plural, masculine, feminine or neuter. Think of it kind of like a mirror in the predicate, that reflects whatever is true about the subject—everything except the case. How do we translate this into English? Remember that the English third person reflexive pronoun does contain the number and gender of the subject. So when we bring a Latin third person reflexive pronoun over into English, we have to reinsert subject's

---

[34]Again, not used to show possession.

number and gender. Like this: **Ea sê videt.** To a Roman ear it means, *she sees (the subject).* For us, we have to repeat the gender and number in the reflexive pronoun. We would say, *she sees herself.* Let's try a few more:

Hominês sê vidêrunt, *the men saw (**sê** = the subject) themselves.*

Feminae sê vident, *the women see (**sê** = the subject) themselves.*

Vir sê videt, *the man sees (**sê** = the subject) himself.*

Puellae litterâs ad sê mittent, *the girls will send a letter to (**sê** = the subject) themselves.*

Cîvitâs sibi pecûniam conservat, *the state is saving the money for (**sibi** = the subject) itself.*

Of course, in the sentences Wheelock gives you, it may be impossible to say precisely what the gender of the third person subject is if it isn't explicitly stated, as in the examples above. For example, **Sê videt** could be translated as *he sees himself, she sees herself,* or *it sees itself.* Without a context, it's impossible to decide. Choose whichever you prefer.

So let's collect ourselves. Here's what we've covered so far. In the first and second persons in Latin, there are no new forms for the reflexive pronouns. If a pronoun in the predicate is the same person as the subject, then the pronoun is reflexive. This is because the reflexive pronoun in the predicate must be referring to the subject of the sentence. Additionally, for this reason, the reflexive pronoun will never be in the nominative case. If it were in the nominative case it would be the subject of the verb and, hence, not in the predicate; and all reflexive pronouns must be in the predicate.

Despite this inherent simplicity of reflexive pronouns in the first and second persons, English nevertheless adds *-self* or *-selves* to the end of the non-reflexive pronouns to form the reflexive pronouns. Strictly speaking, it's not necessary to distinguish formally the non-reflexive from the reflexive pronouns in the first and second persons; context could do that for you. The third person reflexive pronoun must differ in form from the third person non-reflexive pronoun. But all the third person reflexive pronoun need do is point you back to the subject of the sentence.

Because you remember the subject of the sentence, it's not really necessary for the reflexive pronoun itself to remind you of the gender and the number of the subject. The Latin third person reflexive pronoun, therefore, does not in itself make any distinctions in number and gender. It simply works as a sign pointing you back to the subject. To translate the Latin reflexive pronoun properly in English, however, you must resupply the gender and number to the pronoun.

REFLEXIVE AND NON-REFLEXIVE POSSESSION

On to new business. Read this English sentence: *I see my daughter.* Now is there any question whose daughter this is? It's the daughter of the subject of the sentence. And how do you know that? Because the possessive *my* is first person and the subject of the sentence is first person. So the subject of the sentence is being recalled in the predicate because the subject owns the direct object of the verb. We can call this relationship between *I* and *my* **reflexive possession**. The subject of the verb is possessing something in the predicate. You can see that to show reflexive possession no new form of the possessive pronoun is needed. *My* does just fine.

Do you have **your** money? (*reflexive possession*)

Do you have **my** money? (*non-reflexive*)

Have you seen **our** friend? (*non-reflexive*)

Hey, we can see **our** car from here. (*reflexive possession*)

I haven't found **my** book yet. (*reflexive possession*)

Latin has no different forms for reflexive and non-reflexive possession in the first and second persons. There's no need. Latin simply uses the existing possessive adjectives:

First Person	Second Person
meus, -a, -um	tuus, -a, -um
noster, -tra, -trum	vester, -tra, -trum

If the person of the possessive adjective in the predicate is the same as the person of the subject, then the possessive is reflexive. Simple.

Vidêtis amîcôs vestrôs. (*reflexive possession*)

Vidêtis amîcôs meôs. (*non-reflexive possession*)

Let's look just a little more closely at these possessive adjectives. They consist of two parts. There are the stem and the adjectival ending. The stems tell you about the possessor, not about what the possessor is possessing. The stem **me-** of the adjective **meus, -a, -um** tells you that the possessor is singular and in the first person. It doesn't, however, tell you what gender the possessor is. The adjectival ending agrees in number, gender, and case with the object possessed. Got that? So even though the stem **me-** is first person singular, the adjectival ending can be plural, if the noun it's agreeing with is plural. So also with the other possessive adjectives of the first and second persons. The stem has number fixed in it, but the adjectival ending takes its number from the noun it's modifying. Notice.

Habeô meum librum, *I have my book.*	Habeô meôs librôs, *I have my books.*
Habêmus nostrum librum, *we have our book.*	Habêmus nostrôs librôs, *we have our books.*
Habês tuum librum, *you have your book.*	Habês tuôs librôs, *you have your books.*
Habêtis vestrum librum, *you have your book.*	Habêtis vestrôs librôs, *you have your books.*

Now let's get on with the third person. The simple rule that worked so well in the first and second persons isn't going to work here. Look at this sentence: *She had her ticket.* The possessive pronoun *her* is the same person as the subject—third person—but can you tell from this sentence whether *she* has her own ticket or the ticket of some other female? No, you can't. There is a real ambiguity here, and often in English we have to ask for further information: *Whose ticket does she have?* If the speaker hasn't made it clear, an additional *own* can be used to help out: *She has her **own** ticket.* Normally, we rely on context to clear up any possible ambiguities, but sometimes it's really not clear who's owning what: *They have their books* (Their own or some other peoples' books?). The only thing the possessive pronoun *their* tells you about the possessors is that there is more than one of them. But you can't tell whether these people are the same folks indicated by subject pronoun *they.*

In Latin, the same possibility for ambiguity exists, so some solution to the problem is in order. First off, how does Latin show *non-reflexive* possession in the third person? It uses the genitive of the third person pronoun **is, ea, id**.[35] Watch:

Eius librum habuit, *he/she had his/her book (not his/her own).*

Eius gladium invênit, *he/she found his/her sword (not his/her own).*

Servâvit patriam eius, *he/she saved his/her fatherland (someone else's).*

Servâvêrunt patriam eôrum, *they saved their (other peoples') fatherland.*

A couple of things to notice. First, unlike the first and second person possessive adjectives, the possessive in the third person is *not* an adjective. It does *not* agree with the thing being possessed. In the third person, the possessive *pronoun* only tells you about who's doing the possessing; it tells you absolutely nothing about the object possessed.

Secondly, the genitive of **is, ea, id** is used to show only *non*-reflexive possession. **Eius librum habuit** could not possibly mean *he had his own book.* It can only mean *he has his (another person's) book.* In English, the possessive *his* can be used to show reflexive or non-reflexive possession, but the Latin **eius** and **eôrum, eârum** can only be used non-reflexively. So what does Latin use to show reflexive possession in the third person? How does it say *his own, her own, its own* and *their own?*

To show reflexive possession in the third person, Latin uses the *reflexive possessive **adjective*: **suus, -a, -um**. This adjective has a couple of interesting features. First, it's an adjective, so it must agree with the object which is being possessed. Second, unlike the first and second persons, the third person reflexive possessive adjective doesn't have two stems, one for the singular and another for the plural.

Like this: the **-us, -a, -um** part of the adjective agrees with the object possessed; the **su-** part tells you to go back to the subject of the sentence. And that's all it tells you. Like the reflexive pronoun **suî, sibi, sê, sê**, the possessive adjective only tells you that the subject of the sentence owns something that's in the predicate.

Habuêrunt suôs librôs, *they had (the subjects') books.*

Habuit suôs librôs, *he had (the subject's) books.*

Puella habuit suôs librôs, *the girl had (the subject's) books.*

---

[35]This is important to remember. Although the first and second persons never use the genitive of their personal pronouns to show possession, the third person does. But only when the possession is not of the reflexive type. That is, when the subject of the verb is third person and is not the one doing the possessing.

But to translate this into English, we have to reinstate the number and gender (when the subject is singular) of the subject in the predicate.

Habuêrunt suôs librôs, *they had (the subject's) their own books.*

Habuit suôs librôs, *he had (the subject's) his own books.*

Puella habuit suôs librôs, *the girl had (the subject's) her own books.*

Do you see? The stem of the Latin adjective **suus, -a, -um** isn't changing, but our English rendition does, because in English we repeat the gender and number of the subject of the sentence in the reflexive possessive pronoun. Latin doesn't, and there's really no reason it should. The **su-** part of the possessive says, *Go back to the subject.* And that's all it has to say to get the message across.

SELF VERSUS SELF VERSUS SELF

One thing about this chapter that really baffles students is a complication that doesn't come from Latin but from English. Our little suffix -*self* really means three different things: it can signify a reflexive relationship, such as we studied in this chapter; it can signify an emphatic adjective; it can also mean *alone.* In Latin, however, these three constructions are each different from one another. Watch.

	English	**Latin**
Reflexive	She saw herself.	Vidit sê.
	We love ourselves.	Nôs amâmus.
Emphatic	The teacher herself said this.	Magistra ipsa haec dîxit.
	I saw Caesar himself.	Caesarem ipsum vidî.
Alone	I saved Rome by myself.	Sôlus Rôman conservâvî.
	The Romans conquered Greece by themselves.	Sôlî Rômânî Graeciam vîcêrunt.

VOCABULARY PUZZLES

ipse, ipsa, ipsum This pronoun always causes some confusion because of its English translation. It's an emphatic adjective or pronoun, and we translate it with our *him-, her-, it-* or *them- self (selves).* Because it's the same form we use for our reflexive pronoun, students often mistranslate it. **Ipse** underlines or emphasizes the noun it's modifying or the noun it's replacing. **Ipse id fêcit** would mean *He himself did it,* not *He did it himself,* which means he did it all by himself, or *He did it to himself.* **Ipsa id fêcit** would mean *She herself did it.* **Vidî ipsôs virôs** would mean *I saw the very men themselves.* You'll have to practice with this demonstrative some.

ante + acc. or adv. The preposition means *before* as in **ante bellum**, *before the war.* As with **post** + acc., however, **ante** can't be used as a conjunction. No: *George left before you arrived.* Yes: *He came before noon.* Wheelock also warns you not to confuse it with **anti**, which is a Greek word meaning *against* or *instead of.*

14

More about the Third Declension; What To Do with Ablatives?

THIRD DECLENSION NOUNS (AGAIN)

As you learned in Chapter 7, the thematic vowel of the third declension case endings tends to be a short **-e-**. You also saw that the short **-e-** has a habit of turning into an **-i-**. Let's take a look at the third declension endings again. Remember, part of the problem of nouns that belong to the third declension is that their stem—that is, the root to which the case endings are added—may be a little different from the nominative singular. You must look at the dictionary listing for the genitive singular to get the true stem of the noun. (And don't forget the laws of the neuter nouns: (1) the accusative is always the same as the nominative; and (2) the nominative plural ending is a short **-a-**.) Decline the following nouns (Check your work at Wheelock 446).

	homô, -inis, *m.*	virtûs, -tûtis, *f.*	tempus, -oris, *n.*
N/V.	homō	virtūs	tempus
Gen.	hominis	virtūtis	temporis
Dat.	hominī	virtūtī	temporī
Acc.	hominem	virtūtem	tempus
Abl.	homine	virtūte	tempore
Plural			
N/V.	hominēs	virtūtēs	tempora
Gen.	hominum	virtūtum	temporum
Dat.	hominibus	virtūtibus	temporibus
Acc.	hominēs	virtūtēs	tempora
Abl.	hominibus	virtūtibus	temporibus

As you can see, masculine, feminine, and neuter nouns of the third declension use the same case endings. The only exceptions are the accusative singular and the nominative and accusative plural of neuter nouns. But that's to be expected because neuter nouns always do this, no matter what declension they belong to. Now the new material.

THIRD DECLENSION I-STEM NOUNS

There is a class of nouns in the third declension that has a couple of different case endings. We call this class of third declension nouns the *i-stems* because an **-i-** turns up in some unexpected places. What is more, i-stem masculine and feminine nouns don't behave the same way neuter i-stem nouns behave. So you're going to have to learn three things in this chapter:

(1)   How to recognize whether a third declension noun is an i-stem noun.

(2)   How to decline masculine and feminine i-stem nouns.

(3)   How to decline neuter i-stem nouns.

First off, how can you tell whether a noun is an i-stem noun of the third declension? The dictionary doesn't tell you explicitly whether a noun is i-stem or not because there are ways to tell simply by looking at the normal dictionary entries for a noun: the nominative case, the genitive case (including the stem), and the gender.

NEUTER I-STEMS

Let's start with the easiest: The rule for detecting neuter i-stem nouns is: (1) if a third declension noun is neuter, and (2) if its nominative case ends in **-al**, **-ar**, or **-e**, then the noun is a neuter i-stem.

This is fairly easy. You look up the word *animal*, and the Latin dictionary shows you this: **animal, -is**, *n.* **Animal** is the nominative case. The next entry tells you the genitive, from which you spot any stem changes and learn the declension of the noun. The **-is** entry tells you there are no stem changes and that the noun is third declension (since **-is** is the genitive ending in the third declension). The final entry is, of course, the gender; and for **animal**, it's neuter. Therefore, you have a neuter noun of the third declension whose nominative ends in **-al**. So the noun is an i-stem. Simple.

And how do neuter i-stems decline? They differ from non-i-stem nouns in four places:

(1)   The ablative singular is a long **-î** instead of the normal short **-e**.

(2,3)   The nominative (and therefore the accusative) plural is **-ia** instead of just plain **-a**.

(4)   The genitive plural is **-ium** instead of **-um**.

Let's have a look. First decline the neuter noun that's not an i-stem, **corpus, -oris**, *n.*, and then next to it decline the neuter noun **mare, -is,** *n.*, which is an i-stem (Wheelock 446). So really, the neuter nouns of the third declension use the same endings as third declension masculine and feminine nouns. The only differences are where neuter nouns are obeying their own peculiar laws.

	corpus, -oris	**mare, -is**
N/V.	corpus	mare
Gen.	corporis	maris
Dat.	corporī	marī
Acc.	corpus	mare
Abl.	corpore	marī
Plural		
N/V.	corpora	maria
Gen.	corporum	marium
Dat.	corporibus	maribus
Acc.	corpora	maria
Abl.	corporibus	maribus

MASCULINE AND FEMININE I-STEMS

Masculine and feminine i-stems are both easier and more complicated at the same time. On the one hand, there is only one place where the masculine and feminine i-stems differ from the regular non-i-stems. On the other hand, the detection process is more exquisite. First the detection.

There are two different rules for establishing whether a masculine or feminine third declension noun is an i-stem by studying its dictionary entry. Here are the two rules:

The Parisyllabic Rule (the Equal Syllable Rule)

(1) If a masculine or feminine noun ends in an **-is** or an **-ês** in the nominative singular, and

(2) if the full genitive singular form has the same number of syllables as the nominative, then the noun is an i-stem of the masculine and feminine type.

The Double Consonant Rule

(1) If a masculine or feminine noun ends in an **-s** or an **-x** in the nominative, and

(2) if its stem ends with two consonants, *then* the noun is an i-stem of the masculine and feminine type.

Let's look at an example of both these rules. Here's the first: **cîvis, cîvis**, *m*. Is it an i-stem? Well, it's a masculine noun of the third declension. It's not neuter, so you don't have to worry about whether the nominative ends in an **-al**, **-ar**, or **-e**. But you do have to run it through the two rules for masculine and feminine nouns. (The parisyllabic and the double consonant rules apply *only* to masculine and feminine nouns.) The nominative ends in an -s, so you have to pursue the double consonant rule a little further. Look at the stem: it's **cîv-**. Does its stem end with two consonants? No, so **cîvis** fails the second provision of the double consonant rule.

Now try to run it through the parisyllabic rule. The nominative ends in **-is**, which is the first provision of the rule, so you have to go on. Provision (2) of the parisyllabic rule also applies to **cîvis**, since the nominative and the genitive cases have the same number of syllables. So, according to the parisyllabic rule, **cîvis** is an i-stem noun of the masculine and feminine type.

Another noun: **ars, artis**, *m.* Follow the steps carefully. Is this an i-stem? Why or why not? Of course it is. It ends in **-s** or **-x** in the nominative (provision 1 of the double consonant rule) and its stem, **art-**, ends in a double consonant. It fulfills both provisions of the double consonant rule, so it is an i-stem.

How do masculine and feminine i-stem nouns decline? The only case where they differ from the non-i-stem nouns is in the genitive plural, where the i-stems insert an **-i-** before the normal **-um** ending of the third declension. And that's it. Decline one just for fun: **urbs, -is**, *f.*

	Singular	Plural
N/V.	urbs	urbēs
Gen.	urbis	urbium
Dat.	urbī	urbibus
Acc.	urbem	urbēs
Abl.	urbe	urbibus

This may seem like a lot to remember (and it probably is), but try to work slowly through these drills; be deliberate and logical. You'll be surprised at how quickly these rules stick. Which of these nouns are i-stems? If any is an i-stem, indicate which rule applies to it.

	i-stem (yes/no)	Relevant Rule
ignis, ignis, *m.*	y	Parisyllabic
dêns, dentis, *m.*	y	x2 Consonant
cîvitâs, -tâtis, *f.*	n	
rêx, rêgis, *m.*	n	
opus, operis, *n.*	n	
tempus, -oris, *n.*	n	
nox, noctis, *f.*	y	x2 Consonant
môlês, môlis, *f.*	y	Parisyllabic
urbs, urbis, *f.*	y	x2 Consonant
sôl, sôlis, *m.*	n	
hostis, hostis, *m.*	y	Parisyllabic

	i-stem (yes/no)	Relevant Rule
dux, ducis, *m.*	n	
ôrâtor, -tôris, *m.*	n	
fînis, fînis, *m.*	y	Parasyllabic
gêns, gentis, *f.*	y	x2 Consonant
laus, laudis, *f.*	n	
genus, generis, *n.*	n	
vêritâs, -tâtis, *f.*	n	
aetâs, -tâtis, *f.*	n	

USES OF THE ABLATIVE: MANNER, ACCOMPANIMENT, MEANS

Way back when, I promised you that we'd someday have to start cleaning up the ablative case. Today is that day, but this is going to be just a start, and just a review. As you've seen, the ablative case can be used either with a governing preposition or without one. If the ablative case completes the meaning of a preposition, then the ablative itself poses no real problem as far as the translation goes. You simply translate the preposition and then the noun: **dê vêritâte**, *about truth*; **ê cîvitâte**, *from the city*; **sub marî**, *under the sea*; **in Graeciâ**, *in Greece*; **cum meô fîliô**, *with my son*. In other words, the fact that the noun itself is in the ablative case has nothing to do with the translation. It's in the ablative case because that is the case required by the preposition which is governing it.

A noun can be in the ablative case, however, without a preposition. When it is, the noun takes on a special meaning that is derived from the ablative case itself. As the weeks go by you'll be collecting a list of the uses of the prepositionless ablative case. Up to this point, you have only one use of the ablative case without a preposition: it's the instrumental ablative (also called the *ablative of means*). Do you remember this one: **Vêritâtem *oculîs* animî vidêre possumus**. Here you have the noun **oculîs** in the ablative plural without a preposition. So you have to do something with it to translate it, you have to add something. Since this must be an instrumental ablative (or ablative of means),[36] we can say:

We can see truth *with* the eyes of the soul.

We can see truth *by* the eyes of the soul.

We can see truth *by means of* the eyes of the soul.

We can see truth *through* the eyes of the soul.

---

[36]Be on your guard. I'll probably use these two terms interchangeably. There is no difference between the two (as far as you're concerned).

Although each of these translations in English has its own feel and association of meanings, they are all legitimate translations of the Latin instrumental ablative. Use your own native English sense to tell you which translation to use, but remember the essential meaning of the Latin instrumental ablative: it shows with what thing the action of the verb is performed.

ABLATIVE OF MANNER VERSUS ACCOMPANIMENT

One use of the ablative with a preposition needs a little further examination. You probably remember that the preposition **cum** + ablative means *with* in the sense of accompaniment. This use of the ablative is fairly straightforward, because it works like English:

Veniam cum amîcîs meîs ad nostram pâtriam, *I will come to our fatherland with my friends.*

Inveniêtis eum ibi cum nostrô fîliô, *you will find him there with our son.*

Magister erat sub arbore cum dûcibus, *the teacher was under the tree with the leaders.*

But **cum** + ablative can also mean something that borders on our adverbs. We'll call it the *ablative of manner*, because it gives you some information about *how* or in what manner the action was completed. Now let's pause a second. Don't get this confused with the ablative of means. The ablative of means will answer the question *with what* the action is performed; the ablative of manner tells you *in what manner* the action is being performed. Study these examples. Where would the English be representing a Latin ablative of manner, where an ablative of means, where an ablative of accompaniment?

She saw the fire *with her binoculars.*(Means)

Dogs run *with their legs.* (Means)

He drove the nail in *with his hammer.* (Means)

He drove the nail in *with great haste.* (Manner)

He drove the nail in *with indifference.* (Manner)

So how does the ablative of manner approach the adverb? What is another way to say *with great haste*? We could say *very hastily;* and *hastily* is an adverb. How about *with indifference*? *Indifferently.* But some of the ablatives of manner have no nice one-word adverbial equivalent. For example, what would the adverb for *with great speed* be? The ablative of manner affords the writer the opportunity to elaborate on the manner in which the action is being performed in a way a simple adverb does not.

VOCABULARY PUZZLES

vîs, vîs, *f.* In the singular it means *power;* in the plural it means *strength.* A very strange noun, with a very strange declension. As you can tell it's third declension and it's an i-stem noun (the parisyllabic rule). In the singular it's odd but somewhat predictable. In the plural, it changes stems: from **v-** to **vîr-**. Pay attention, though; it's easy to mix up the plural of **vîs** with the second declension noun **vir, -î**, *m* . Look it over, and write down the plural of **vir** next to **vîs** in the plural. Even though, as you can see, none of the forms of the two words is identical, students always confuse them. Believe me: you must work a little to keep the two straight.

	Singular	Plural	Plural of vir, -î
N/V.	vîs	vîrês	virî
Gen.	vîs	vîrium	virôrum
Dat.	____	vîribus	virîs
Acc.	vim	vîrês	virôs
Abl.	vî	vîribus	virîs

15 _____

Numbers and Their Constructions

CARDINAL AND ORDINAL NUMBERS

What's the difference in English between the word *one* and *first*? Well, the word *one* is just a number, a counting number, whereas the word *first* means that you're identifying a particular place something holds in a sequence of things. *One, two, three, four*... you're just counting; *first, second, third, fourth*... you're arranging, or ordering. What this means is there are two numbering systems in English. The first group of numbers are called the *cardinal* numbers. The word *cardinal* comes from the Latin **cardo, -inis**, m., *the hinge of a door*, and we call them *cardinal* numbers because they are the most important, fundamental numbers. The other kind of numbers are called *ordinal* numbers, because they *order* things.

Let's take a look at several English cardinal and ordinal numbers. You'll notice that nearly all ordinal numbers are derivatives of the basic, cardinal numbers:

Cardinal	Ordinal	Cardinal	Ordinal
one	first	five	fif*th*
two	second	six	six*th*
three	third	twenty	twentie*th*
four	four*th*	fifty-six	fifty-six*th*

ROMAN NUMERALS

You might very well be wondering why we are going to learn the Latin numbers. Didn't the Romans use Roman numerals? Of course they did, just as we might be tempted to write *1,000* in a text instead of *one thousand*. But we might not. The same is true for the Romans, so you'll need to know both to work your way through a Latin text. Wheelock doesn't explain the conventions for Roman numerals in the text—perhaps because he thought them so obvious and simple that no study was required—but if you'd like a quick look at how they work, read on. It'll take about ten minutes.

Latin Roman numerals are arranged around several pivot points which they count up to and away from: **I** (1), **V** (5), **X** (10), **L** (50), **C** (100), **D** (500), and **M** (1000).[37] In effect, they use these symbols to count like this: one (**I**), one-one (**II**), one-one-one (**III**), one-from-five (**IV**), five (**V**), five-one (**VI**), five-one-one (**VII**), five-one-one-one (**VIII**), one-from-ten (**IX**), ten (**X**), ten-one (**XI**), ten-two (**XII**), ten-three (**XIII**),

---

[37]Obviously, there are conventions for Roman numerals extending beyond this. If you're curious about how the Romans would have written 565,231, you should consult any standard grammar.

ten-one-from-five (**XIV**), ten-five (**XV**), ten-five-one (**XVI**), and so on. Do you see what they're doing? They count up to the number just before one of these marks and three after it. Look at a few more, this time with their symbols:

English	Latin Thinking	Roman Numeral
3	one and one and one	III
8	five and one and one and one	VIII
9	one-from-ten	IX
14	ten and one-from-five	XIV
19	ten and one-from-ten	XIX
24	ten and ten and one-from-five	XXIV
46	ten-from-fifty and five-one	XLVI
947	hundred-from-thousand and ten-from-fifty and five and one-one	CMXLVII
1999	thousand and one hundred-from-one-thousand ten-from-one-hundred and one-from-ten	MCMXCIX

It can get to be a real mess, can't it? But there is some logic to it, and with practice you can develop some fluency with them. Here's how I approach a cluster of Roman numerals. Start from the left and read to the right—the larger symbols are on the right. If, however, you see a smaller symbol to the left of a larger symbol, you know that this is meant to be subtracted from the symbol immediately to its right. Like this: **CM** (100-1000 900); **MMMCM** (1000 1000 1000 100-1000 → 3,900). Then, as you keep reading left to right, just add up the emerging total in your head. Try a few drills.

	Roman	English		Roman	English
1.	XL	40	6.	XXXIV	34
2.	XXIV	24	7.	LXXVIII	78
3.	LXXIV	74	8.	CDXLIII	443
4.	DCCXLVIII	748	9.	MMMDCCLXXXIV	3,784
5.	MMCMLX	2960	10.	CMXCI	991

LATIN CARDINALS

Because Latin is an inflected language, you can expect some complications in its numbers. After all, in the expression *one horse*, the word *one* is modifying, hence agreeing with, the noun *horse*. In a way, *one* is an adjective and should be expected to decline to agree in number, gender, and case with the noun it's describing. Therefore, in theory at least, *all* Latin cardinal numbers could be declinable. In practice, however, only the first three cardinal numbers decline to agree with their noun. After that up to one hundred, Latin numbers are all indeclinable.

The number *one* is **ûnus, -a, -um**, and you've already been working with it. You can tell by the dictionary entry that it's an adjective of the first and second declensions, but what you can't tell is that it's a hybrid—using **-ius** for the genitive singular and **-î** for the dative singular. That's something you simply have to memorize.

The number *two*, for obvious reasons, has no singular forms; in the plural its declension is sort of a mixture of first and second declension endings, with a temporary loan of the dative and ablative plurals from the third declensions. It's declined for you at Wheelock 97. Take a look at it. The number *three* is a perfectly normal adjective of the third declension—with the natural exception that there are no singular forms. The cardinal numbers after that up to 100 don't decline. After ten, however, Latin and English begin to vary.

We have distinct words for the two numbers after *ten*; we say *eleven*, and then we say *twelve*. But Latin says *one-ten* and then *two-ten*. After *twelve*, however, our numbers are composites, just like Latin's: *thirteen* (three-ten), *fourteen* (four-ten), *fifteen* (five-ten) and so on up to twenty. But when Latin comes to within two of the next ten marker, it begins to count backwards. So in place of *eight-ten*, Latin says *two-from-twenty*; in place of *nine-ten*, Latin says *one-from-twenty*.

We could spend hours reviewing the Roman counting system, but for our immediate purpose—to get you started reading Latin prose—it's probably necessary for you to be familiar only with the first twenty-five Latin cardinals. And this is really more a matter of recognition than theoretical understanding. You'll be helped along if you try to detect English derivatives from them. Write out the Latin cardinals from one to ten. As you do so, try to think of English derivatives (Wheelock 451).

English	Latin	English	Latin
1	ûnus	6	sex
2	duo	7	septem
3	três	8	octô
4	quattour	9	novem
5	quînque	10	decem

The remaining cardinals to twenty-five are fairly transparent composites from numbers you'll have already studied. Take a moment and write down the Latin equivalents for these English numbers. Pay attention to what you're writing, and try to think out what the Latin is doing. For example, the Latin number for 19 isn't *ten-nine*, but rather *one-from-twenty* (Wheelock 451).

English	Latin	English	Latin
11	ūndecim	19	ūndevīgintī
12	duodecim	20	vīgintī
13	tredecim	21	vīgintī ūnus [38]
14	quattourdecim	22	vīgintī duo
15	quīndecim	23	vīgintī trēs
16	sēdecim	24	vīgintī quattour
17	septendecim	25	vīgintī quīnque
18	duodēvīgintī		

THE HUNDREDS AND THOUSAND (MÎLLE, MÎLIA)

Although you probably won't have to memorize the words for *one hundred*, *two hundred*, *three hundred*, and so on, you should be able to recognize them when you see them. They aren't difficult, since you can well imagine they'd be mainly composites made up of *one*, *two*, *three*, and so on plus the word for *hundred*—just like English. Notice carefully that whereas the word for *hundred* is indeclinable, the words for *two hundred*, *three hundred*, and so on to *nine hundred* are adjectives:

100, centum

200, ducentî, -ae, -a (duo + centum)

300, trecentî, -ae, -a (três + centum)

400, quadringentî, -ae, -a[39] (quattuor + centum)

500, quîngentî, -ae, -a (quînque + centum)

600, sêscentî, -ae, -a (sêx + centum)

700, septingentî, -ae, -a (septem + centum)

800, octingentî, -ae, -a (octô + centum)

900, nongentî, -ae, -a (novem + centum)

The word for *one thousand* is **mîlle**, an indeclinable adjective. It would seem to follow that the word for *two thousand* would be a combination of **duo** and **mîlle**, and would also be an adjective and possibly indeclinable as well. But this is not so. The word **mîlle** is an indeclinable adjective, but the word *thousand***s** is a neuter i-stem noun of the third declension: **mîlia, -ium (n)**. So if it's a noun, how would you write *two thousand horses* in Latin? Latin thinks of it this way: *two thousands **of** horses*. And so it writes **duo mîlia equôrum**[40]; for *three thousand*

---

[38]Despite their appearance, the ordinals **vîgintî ûnus, vîgintî duo, vîgintî três** do *not* decline. *Twenty-one horses* would be **vîgintî ûnus equî**, and not **vîgintî ûnî equî**.

[39]The change from **c** to **g**, from **cent-** to **gent-**, isn't really too surprising. The hard *c* sound and the hard *g* sound are quite similar. Pronounce them a couple of times and you'll see.

[40]**Duo** here is neuter nominative plural to agree with **mîlia**.

horses, **tria mîlia equôrum**; *four thousand horses*; and so on. Let's pause a moment to review all this material. Study these examples and then try your hand at a few simple compositions.

Sunt três equî in agrô, there are three horses in the field.

The word for three is a declinable adjective, so since **equî** is nominative plural masculine, the correct form is **três**. Look at some other examples of sentences with **três, tria. Videô três equôs in agrô**, *I see three horses in the field*; **Vênêrunt cum tribus equîs**, *they came with three horses*; **Erant tria animâlia in agrô**, *there were three animals in the field*.

Sunt duodecim equî in agrô, there are twelve horses in the field.

Since it's *not* declined to agree with the noun it's modifying, **duodecim** will not change its form. Watch: **Videô duodecim equôs in agrîs, Vênêrunt cum duodecim equîs, Erant duodecim animâlia in agrô**.

Sunt centum equî in agrô, there are one hundred horses in the field.

Like **duodecim, centum** is not declined. **Videô centum equôs in agrîs, Vênêrunt cum centum equîs, Erant centum animâlia in agrô**.

Sunt ducentî equî in agrô, there are two hundred horses in the field.

Ducentî, -ae, -a *is* declined. **Videô ducentôs equôs in agrîs, Vênêrunt cum ducentîs equîs, Erant ducenta animâlia in agrô**.

Sunt mîlle equî in agrô, there are a thousand horses in the field.

Mîlle is not declined. **Videô mîlle equôs in agrîs, Vênêrunt cum mîlle equîs, Erant mîlle animâlia in agrô**.

Sunt tria mîlia equôrum in agrô, there are three thousand horses in the field.

Mîlia is a noun and will inflect as needed by its use in the sentence. The dependent genitive, of course, will *not* be affected by the case of **mîlia. Videô tria mîlia equôrum in agrîs, Vênêrunt cum tribus mîlibus equôrum, Erant tria mîlia animâlium in agrô**.

ORDINAL NUMBERS

As you know, the ordinal numbers are those which arrange things in sequence: *first, second, third*, and so on. If you look closely at the English ordinals, you'll notice that with the exception of the the first two, they are simple derivatives from the cardinal numbers: *one, first; two, second; three, third; four, fourth; five, fifth; ten, tenth; thousand, thousandth*. In Latin, the ordinal numbers are *all* first and second declension *adjectives* and they are derived from the cardinals—again with exception of the first two. As you might have suspected, however, sometimes the base cardinal is modified just a little bit. Cover up the list of ordinals and try to guess what they'll be based on the cardinals. Warning: don't try to memorize all these words. It will drive you batty, and take up entirely too much time. Your goal for now is simply to be able to recognize them when you see them. That is, you know that 7 is **septem**, and 10 is **decem**. That's because you can see English words in them: September and decade. From that, you should be able to see through the Latin word **septendecim**. It's 17. Once again, the rule is *think*! Study each of these words.

Cardinal	Ordinal	Cardinal	Ordinal
ûnus, -a, -um	prîmus, -a, -um	quattuordecim	quârtus decimus
duo, -ae, -o	secundus, -a, -um	quîndecim	quîntus decimus
três, tria	tertius, -a, -um	sêdecim	sextus decimus
quattuor	quârtus, -a, -um	septendecim	septimus decimus
quînque	quîntus, -a, -um	duodêvîgintî	duodêvîcêsimus, -a, -um
sêx	sextus, -a, -um	ûndêvîgintî	ûndêvîcêsimus, -a, -um
septem	septimus, -a, -um	vîgintî	vîcêsimus, -a, -um
octô	octâvus, -a, -um	vîgintî ûnus	vîcêsimus prîmus
novem	nônus, -a, -um	vîgintî duo	vîcêsimus secundus
decem	decimus, -a, -um	vîgintî três	vîcêsimus teritus
ûndecim	ûndecimus, -a, -um	vîgintî quattuor	vîcêsimus quârtus
duodecim	duodecimus, -a, -um	vîgintî quînque	vîcêsimus quîntus
tredecim	tertius decimus		

GENITIVE OF THE WHOLE

This is a use of the genitive which you could probably intuit very easily. In this expression *some of the people*, *of the people* is in the genitive case, obviously, but it doesn't show possession. Instead, it's identifying a group, part of which has been isolated for further discussion.

*Some **of the people** in this room haven't paid their membership fees yet.*

*Very few **of you** will ever have your taxes audited.*

*None **of them** knows up from down.*

*All **of us** are in big trouble now.*

*All **of me**, why not take all **of me**?*

This use of the genitive case is also called the partitive genitive because you're specifying a *part* of a larger group or whole.

Some applications of the genitive of the whole, or the partitive genitive, are fairly obvious—like the examples I just ran through: **Superâvit partem urbis**, *he conquered part of the city*; **Nôs omnium înfêlîcissimî sumus**, *we are the most unfortunate of all*. Sometimes, however, Latin uses the genitive of the whole in ways that aren't so obvious to us.

Do you remember the vocabulary word **satis**? It means *enough* and, contrary to our English expectations, it is a noun and takes the genitive case. So Latin doesn't think *enough money*, but *enough of money*. **satis pecuniae**. The partitive genitive frequently is used after neuter nouns or pronouns specifying quantity. Like this: **multum mali**, *much of evil*, or *much evil*; **plûs sapientiae**, *more of wisdom*, or *more wisdom*.

The noun for *thousands*, **mîlia, -ium, (n)** which we just looked at is an example of a neuter noun of quantity taking the genitive of the whole: **novem mîlia mîlitum**, *nine thousands of troops*. Wheelock gives you a list of expressions of this sort on page 98. You should have a look at them now.

Often, however, the genitive of the whole is expressed with the preposition **dê** or **ex** plus the ablative case. With numbers other than **mîlia**, this is the regular construction. Latin does *not* write **sêx hôrum mîlitum**, *six of these soldiers*. Instead it uses the preposition **e, ex** + ablative: **sêx ex hîs mîlitibus**, *six from these soldiers*.

Ûnus ê fîliîs tuîs in illâ urbe habitat, *one of your sons lives in that city*.

Multî amîcôrum meôrum in illâ urbe habitant, *many of my friends live in that city*.

Sunt ducentî mîlitês in illâ urbe, *there are two hundred soldiers in that city*.

Sunt duo mîlia mîlitum in illâ urbe, *there are two thousands soldiers [two thousands of soldiers] in that city*.

Magnus numerus ê vestrîs in illâ urbe est, *a great number of your [men] are in that city*.

Quantum voluptâtis in pecûniâ est, *how much [of] pleasure is there in money?*

Quid novî, *what of new what's new?*

Cum duobus mîlibus mîlitum veniet, *he will come with two thousand soldiers [two thousands of soldiers]*.

Ûndecimâ hôrâ ad urbem pervênêrunt, *they arrived at the city on the eleventh hour*.

Pars meî[41] mortem vincet, *part of me will conquer death*.

ABLATIVE OF TIME: WHEN AND WITHIN WHICH

As you saw in the last chapter, the ablative case can either be used with a governing preposition or by itself. When there is a preposition, the ablative poses no special problems *per se*. You simply translate the preposition and then the noun. The meaning of the preposition overrides any special senses attached to the ablative case. (The one preposition, however, you need to watch out for is **cum**, which can either mean *with* in the sense of accompaniment or *with* in the sense of manner.)

---

[41]This is the genitive of the first person pronoun **ego**. Do you remember when you first studied the personal pronouns? You learned then *not* to use their genitive forms to show possession. Now you see that the genitive of these pronouns is used for the partitive genitive: **pars meî/nostrum, tuî/vestrum, suî**.

The only use of the ablative case *without* a preposition you know so far is the instrumental ablative or ablative of means.

Another prepositionless use of the ablative case is called the ablative of time. You can easily spot such a use in Latin. If you see a noun in the ablative case which is not governed by a preposition, and if the noun is some unit of time, then you have an ablative of time. But what makes this use of the ablative beastly difficult for English-speaking students is not the Latin, but the variety of English translations we can use to represent the Latin expression of time.

You see, Latin has one construction—a noun expressing a unit of time in the ablative case—and English has two ways of translating it; and they mean something quite different. We call the construction in Latin the *ablative of time when* or *time within which*, not because *Latin* has two different constructions, but because *English* does. When we translate the Latin construction into English, we have to choose which of the two English constructions best fits the context. Let's start by looking at some English expressions of time that use prepositions:

1. They'll be here *in an hour.*
2. They came *on Tuesday.*
3. *In less than five minutes* they were all gone.
4. Snow never falls *in the summer.*
5. It'll be snowing *in a couple of months.*
6. *At that time in human history,* there were no alarm clocks.
7. *Within a couple of years,* all Gaul was at Caesar's feet.
8. *In the Middle Ages,* things were different.

I don't doubt that you had no trouble understanding these sentences and recognizing, in particular, the meaning of the expressions of time. You don't have to scratch your heads and puzzle over them because their exact meanings are embedded unconsciously in your linguistic repertoire. But to translate the Latin ablative of time, you must force yourself to understand consciously what these different expressions of time are telling you. So let's look at the Latin.

Consider the following Latin sentences. Try to decide how best to translate the expression of time into English: **Paucîs hôrîs Caesar in Asiam vênit.** Which would be best: *within a few hours* or *at, on, or in*[42] *a few hours*? Undoubtedly *within (or in) a few hours* is the better here. Not *At a few hours, Caesar went into Asia,* but *In (or within) a few hours, Caesar went into Asia.* Next: **Aestâte puerî lûdêbant** (**lûdô,** *to play*). *Within the summer* or *in the summer*? The latter, obviously, since it can be thought to answer the question *time when,* not *time within which.* One last example: **Ûnâ hôrâ Asiam tôtam vicî.** Is this telling time *within which* or *time when*? Certainly *time within which* because there's a sense of duration of time with a terminus of the action in mind: *I conquered all Asia within (or in) one hour.* I know that some of these distinctions can be rather hair-splitting. You just have to work with them a lot and keep your mind in high gear at all times.

---

[42]The English *in* can mean both time when, *in December,* or time within which, *in a week.*

VOCABULARY PUZZLES

miser, -a, -um You haven't seen an adjective like this for a while. It uses the case endings of the first and second declensions, but in place of the **-us** ending for the masculine nominative singular, it uses the other ending **-er**. Is the **-e-** or **-er** part of the stem?

iaciô There is nothing terribly unusual about this verb. It's a normal third conjugation i-stem. The tricky part comes in recognizing it in a compound verb (when a prefix is attached to it). The first principal part loses the vowel **-a-** altogether: **ê + iaciô êiciô**, which is pronounced *eh YI ki oh*. In the third principal part, the vowel returns; but this time as the long **-ê-**, which is the normal vowel for the third principal part: **ê + iêcî êiêcî**, pronounced *eh YEAH kee*.

inter + acc. It means either *among or between*, so we need to fret over which is the best English translation. Do you remember when standard English calls for *among* and when *between*? Use *between* with two objects; *among* for three or more. *This is a secret just between you and me. This is a secret we keep among the family members only.*

16

Adjectives of the Third Declension

ADJECTIVES

Wheelock assures you that there isn't much new material to learn in this chapter. In a way, he's right. You know what adjectives are, and you know the case endings of the third declension. In this chapter, you're going to see that a class of adjectives uses the third declension endings to form the different numbers, genders, and cases. Even though these adjectives use the third declension endings, they may modify nouns of *all* the declensions; i.e., third declension adjectives are not restricted to modifying only third declension nouns. But that's nothing conceptually new. You've seen adjectives of the first and second declensions modifying nouns of the third declension. So, as you can see, Wheelock is right to say that this chapter doesn't really confront you with a mass of new material to memorize.

First, let's take stock of what you know. You know that adjectives are words that modify nouns, and that they *agree* in number, gender, and case with the nouns they are modifying. To agree with nouns, which may be in all the possible cases, numbers, and genders, adjectives must be able to decline. The adjectives you're familiar with decline in the first and second declensions: they use first declension case endings to modify nouns that are feminine, second declension endings to modify nouns that are masculine and neuter. The dictionary entry for such adjectives looks like this: **magnus, -a, -um; miser, -a, -um; bonus, -a, -um; pulcher, -chra, -chrum; bellus, -a, -um; noster, -tra, -trum.** Things to notice are:

(1) Adjectives have no inherent gender fixed in the stem, so the dictionary doesn't list a gender for them.[43]

(2) Sometimes the true stem of the adjective is not identical with the masculine, nominative singular, so you must scan the other listings for stem changes (e.g. the **-e-** of **pulcher** and **noster** is not a part of the true stem).

(3) First and second declension adjectives can modify nouns of any of the other declensions, not just those of the first and second declensions.

ADJECTIVES OF THE THIRD DECLENSION

The name speaks for itself. Some adjectives get their case endings from the third declension. So you have two things to consider:

(1) What are the case endings?

(2) How does the dictionary distinguish a third declension adjective from one of the first and second declensions; i.e., how can you tell where the adjective

---

[43]In fact, this is the surest sign that a word you've looked up in the dictionary is an adjective: it has case endings listed with no gender specified.

is going to get its case endings simply by looking at the dictionary entries?

Let's take up the first point by reviewing the third declension endings for nouns. Decline the following third declension nouns; and don't forget to check whether the nouns are i-stems: **homô, -inis**, *m.;* **tempus, -oris**, *n.;* **urbs, -is**, *f.;* **mare, -ris**, *n.* (Check the endings at Wheelock 446.)

	man	time	city	sea
N/V.	homō	tempus	urbs	mare
Gen.	hominis	temporis	urbis	maris
Dat.	hominī	temporī	urbī	marī
Acc.	hominem	tempus	urbem	mare
Abl.	homine	tempore	urbe	marī
Plural				
N/V.	hominēs	tempora	urbēs	maria
Gen.	hominum	temporum	urbium	marium
Dat.	hominibus	temporibus	urbibus	maribus
Acc.	hominēs	tempora	urbēs	maria
Abl.	hominibus	temporibus	urbibus	maribus

Here are the things to remember about the third declension case endings:

(1) The third declension endings are divided into two groups: the non-i-stem endings and the i-stem endings.

(2) The nominative singular has many different appearances.

(3) Basically the case endings are the same for non-i-stem nouns of all three genders. The apparent exception is with the neuter nouns, where the neuter nouns are following their own peculiar set of laws: nominative and accusative cases are always the same, and the nominative (hence also accusative) plural ending is short **-a**.

(4) With i-stem nouns, however, the endings used by masculine and feminine nouns are slightly different from those used by neuter nouns.

So what endings does a third declension adjective use? An adjective needs to be able to modify nouns of all three genders, so a third declension adjective will have to be able to be masculine, feminine, and neuter. To do this, a third declension adjective uses the pattern of the i-stem endings, with one further refinement: the ablative singular of the masculine and feminine is long **-î**, not short **-e**. Cover up the two columns of endings below and try to write down the endings third declension adjectives are going to use. Check your work against the answers given in the two right columns.

Case Endings for Third Declension Adjectives

	Masc./Fem.	Neuter	Masc./Fem.	Neuter
N/V.	_____	_____	_____	_____
Gen.			-is	-is
Dat.			-î	-î
Acc.			-em	_____
Abl.			-î	-î
Plural				
N/V.			-ês	-ia
Gen.			-ium	-ium
Dat.			-ibus	-ibus
Acc.			-ês	-ia
Abl.			-ibus	-ibus

These are the variable case endings that are going to be attached to the stem of third declension adjectives. The endings are almost identical to those of the third declension nouns. So, as Wheelock himself put it, there's nothing much new to be learned.

STEMS OF THIRD DECLENSION ADJECTIVES

You've seen that adjectives of the third declension follow the analogy of first and second declension adjectives: stem + case endings. And you've studied their case endings. Now let's look at the stems of these adjectives and see how they're going to be listed in the dictionary.

But before I show you that (do you get the feeling I'm trying to put this off?) let me give you some good news. There are only two kinds of adjectives in the Latin language: those of the first and second declensions, and those of the third. There are no other possibilities. Either an adjective uses the **-us (-er), -a, -um** endings or those of the third declension. So if you see an adjective in the dictionary and the adjective is not of the first and second declensions, then it must be a third declension adjective. There are no adjectives of the fourth and fifth declensions. That's the good news.

Now the bad news. There are three different types of adjectives of the third declension, *but* the difference is *only* in the nominative singular. All three adjectival types of the third declension use the case endings you studied above for all the cases except the nominative singular. We need to focus now on the nominative singulars of these three types of adjectives. They are:

(1) Adjectives of two terminations.

(2) Adjectives of one termination.

(3) Adjectives of three terminations.[44]

The distinguishing feature among these declensions is how many different endings are possible in the nominative singular. Type (1) adjectives have one ending in the nominative singular for the masculine and feminine genders, and one ending for the neuter gender. That makes two endings, hence the name, *adjective of two terminations*. Type (2) has only one ending in the nominative singular for all three genders: hence, *adjective of one termination*. Finally, obviously, type (3) has one ending in the nominative singular for the masculine gender, one for the feminine, and another for the neuter; that makes three endings. Hence, *adjective of three terminations*.

ADJECTIVES OF TWO TERMINATIONS

The dictionary entry for adjectives typically does not include the genitive singular; it instead moves across the genders in the nominative case. What does this mean for our third declension adjectives? *All* adjectives of two terminations look like this: *stem*-**is, -e**. E.g.

omnis, -e, *all; each, every*

fortis, -e, *strong*

dulcis, -e, *sweet*

difficilis, -e, *difficult*

brevis, -e, *short [in time]; swift*

Now think. I told you that adjectives typically will move across the genders in the nominative case; and here you have only two different forms indicated. This means that two of the genders will have identical forms in the nominative. For adjectives listed like this, the **-is** ending is used both for the masculine and feminine genders; the **-e** is used for the neuter in the nominative singular. And, as you can see, the stem does not change. It's evident in the nominative singular of the masculine and feminine genders. You just drop off the **-is**.

ADJECTIVES OF ONE TERMINATION

These adjectives have only one form in the nominative singular for all three genders. This creates an interesting problem. What will its dictionary entry look like? Most adjectives, remember, simply move across the nominative entries. But an adjective of only one termination in the nominative singular has ... only one form in the nominative singular! So, the dictionary must give you the information you

---

[44] If you're wondering why I listed them like this—two, one, three terminations—instead of the more rational way—one, two, three terminations—it's that type (1) is much more common than type (2), and type (2) is much more common than type (3). Most adjectives of the third declension are adjectives of two terminations; some are adjectives of one termination; and fewer are of three terminations.

need about it—stem changes and declension—by beginning its declension. Just like a noun, the second entry for an adjective of one termination is the genitive singular. You drop off the genitive singular ending **-is** to find the stem. Except in the nominative singular, adjectives of one termination operate just like all the other adjectives of the third declension; they all use the same case endings and obey the same laws. *Hint:* don't forget the laws of the neuter!

ADJECTIVES OF THREE TERMINATIONS

As the name tells you, these are third declension adjectives which have three nominative singular endings, one ending for each gender. But there is an added twist. These adjectives end in **-er** in the masculine singular; and you know what that means. It means that the **-e-** of the **-er** may or may not be part of the true stem. Remember this problem with first and second declension adjectives like **miser, -a, -um** and **noster, -tra, trum**? Look at these two entries for third declension adjectives of three terminations: **celer, celeris, celere**, *swift*; **âcer, âcris, âcre**, *keen; fierce*.

Do you see what the dictionary is telling you? The first listing is the masculine nominative singular. The second is the feminine nominative singular, and it's here you need to look for stem changes. As you can see, the stem of **celer** is **celer-**; the stem of **âcer**, however, is **âcr-**. In all its forms except the masculine, nominative singular, therefore, the root of **âcer** to which the case endings will be added is **âcr-**. The final entry is the neuter nominative singular. Don't forget, the only place where these adjectives have different forms for the three genders is right here, in the nominative singular. After the nominative singular, these adjectives use the normal endings of third declension adjectives.

DRILLS

After you've studied the forms of the adjectives in the Wheelock text, you'll come to see that the third declension adjectives can often help you out of some problems. As you'll see once you start reading, one of the main difficulties with Latin is that it has too few discrete case endings, not too many. The case endings overlap in so many places that it's often difficult to tell what case a noun is in. Having yet another set of endings helps you identify the case of the nouns these adjectives are modifying.

For example, look at the form **sapientiae**. What case is **sapientiae**? Well, it could be (1) genitive singular, (2) dative singular, or (3) nominative plural. The **-ae** ending in the first declension is used for three different cases. But suppose you see a third declension adjective next to it with an ending **-ês**. The **-ês** ending in the third declension can only be nominative or accusative plural. So, if a third declension adjective ending in **-ês** is agreeing with **sapientiae**, **sapientiae** must be nominative plural, since that's the only number, gender, and case the two words have in common. Write out the possible case(s) of the following nouns.

Latin	Case(s)
omnium puerôrum	gen. pl.
celerem puellam	acc. sg.
potentî rêgî	dat. sg.
potentibus virîs	dat. pl., abl. pl.
fortês fêminae	nom pl.
fortis fêminae	gen. sg.
fortî fêminae	dat. sg.
acrês mortês	nom pl, acc pl
acrî memoriâ	abl. sg.
acrî bellô	dat. sg, abl. sg.

VOCABULARY PUZZLES

adiuvô Despite its appearance, the verb is not a regular first conjugation. Look carefully at its principal parts: **adiuvô, -âre, -iûvî, -iûtus**.

quam This adverb is used to emphasize an adjective. It doesn't mean *how* as in *in what way*. It's used to modify adjectives, and means *how* as in *How sweet it is!* or *How tall that young man is!*

17

The Relative Pronoun

THE CLAUSE: WHAT IS IT?

You remember the junior high school definition of a sentence: it's a complete thought. And by that we mean a thought that includes a noun, either expressed or implied, and a verb, either expressed or implied. That is, a complete thought must involve something which is doing something or which is being held up for description: *The road is blocked; The tree fell down;* and so on.

Now, the human mind is a wonderful thing. It reasons and perceives dozens of different kinds of relationships among events, things, and ideas. It arranges events and facts logically and temporally, and in levels of priority. That is to say, it takes two or more things, things that are separate ideas, separate visions, and weaves them together conceptually and linguistically into what we call *reasoning*. The way this reasoning is expressed in language is called *syntax*, which literally means *arranging together*—putting together events and things and facts.

For example, the two separate ideas or visions—*the road is blocked* and *the tree fell down*—might have a causal relationship, which the mind instantly recognizes and expresses linguistically with an appropriate conjunction: *The road is blocked **because** the tree fell down.* The conjunction *because* in this example is spelling out the relationship the speaker perceives between the two ideas. It's arranging them into a cause and effect relationship: that the tree fell down is a fact, and because of that fact, the road is now blocked.

Each thought, idea, or event, when it is expressed in language, is called a *clause.* Hence, the sentence *The road is blocked because the tree fell* contains two *clauses:* the fact that the tree fell is expressed in one clause, and the fact that the road is blocked forms another clause. We can classify sentences based on how clauses are used.

Simple Sentence

It's possible for a sentence to contain only one clause, as in *Roses are red.* When that's the case, we call the sentence a *simple* sentence.

Compound Sentence

A compound sentence contains two or more clauses which are presented as equally important. That is, no clause is dependent upon, or put there to tell you more about, another clause. The practical result of this is that you can take the clause out of the sentence and turn it into a complete sentence without adding anything. A couple of examples will make this clear: *The tree is tall and it fell down. We came by last night, but no one was there.* We call clauses like this *coordinate* and the words that join them *coordinating conjunctions.*

Complex Sentence

Here's an example of a complex sentence: *The tree fell down because the wind was blowing so hard.* The main idea of the sentence is contained in the clause *the tree fell down.* The clause *the wind was blowing so hard* is there to give more information about it, and it's introduced with a conjunction that tells you what kind of information you're going to get. In this case, it's a causal relationship. The clause in a complex sentence that's the main idea is called the *main clause* and the clause that's giving you more information is classed a *dependent* or *subordinate clause.* Hence, a definition of a complex sentence might be a sentence with one or more subordinate clauses. Words that begin subordinate clauses are called *subordinating conjunctions* or *adverbs.* As you'll see in a moment, a sentence with a relative clause is a complex sentence, and the relative clause is a subordinate clause.

ENGLISH RELATIVE CLAUSES

Here's a bare bones definition of a relative clause: *A relative clause is a subordinate clause that acts like an adjective by providing additional information about a noun in another clause.* Now here's an example showing you what this means. Here are two clauses:

Clause 1: *The five o'clock train is never on time.*

Clause 2: *Hundreds of people take the five o'clock train.*

Now let's bring these two thoughts into the same sentence. There are many ways to do this. We'll begin by assuming that the most important fact the speaker wants to get across is contained in clause 1, and that clause 2 is going to be worked in only as *subordinate* material. How is this going to happen?

Step 1: Substitute *for the five o'clock train* in clause 2 the appropriate pronoun. The pronoun will refer the listener to the noun stated in clause 1.

Clause 1: *The five o'clock train is never on time.*

Clause 2: *Hundreds of people take **it**.*

Now hold on. Why did we choose *it* as the appropriate pronoun to reproduce *the five o'clock train* in clause 2? Well, the noun which the pronoun has to reproduce is singular in number and inanimate, so *it* is the correct choice. Next, what case is *it* in? It's acting as the object of the verb *take* in its clause; so *it* is in the objective (or accusative) case. (This was just a review. You already know that pronouns get their number and gender from their antecedents, but get their case from the way they're being used in their own clause.)

Step 2: Embed the subordinate clause in the main clause: *The five o'clock train—hundreds of people take it—is never on time.*

We could almost stop here. The two sentences have been merged into one; and clause 2 has been subordinated to the idea in clause 1. But English developed a further modification to work these two clauses into one sentence. It replaces the pronoun of the subordinate clause with a pronoun that indicates without a doubt that the clause coming up is dependent, or subordinate to, the clause that has just been interrupted. We replace the pronoun with the *relative* pronoun *who* or *which* in the proper case and move it to the beginning of the clause. Now the two clauses have been completely welded into one sentence.

Step 3: Replace and move the pronoun: *The five o'clock train,* **which** *hundreds of people take, is never on time.*

And there you have it. Clause 2 has been fully incorporated into the message of the first clause. As soon as you read the relative pronoun *which* in this sentence, your mind automatically understands two things:

(1) The clause coming up is not as important as the clause you've just left.

(2) The clause coming up is going to give you more information about something in the main clause.

So this sentence is saying something like this: *the five o'clock train—which, by the way, hundreds of people take—is never on time.* And one last pesky question: what case is *which* in? It's in the objective (or accusative) case because it is still the object of the verb in the relative clause: *take.* Remember, number and gender from the antecedent, but case from its clause. Now let's go back to the two clauses when they were independent thoughts.

Clause 1: *The five o'clock train is never on time.*

Clause 2: *Hundreds of people take the five o'clock train.*

It's also possible that the main idea the speaker wishes to get across is the fact contained in clause 2 and will have to subordinate clause 1 into clause 2; in which case, clause 2 will provide the basic architecture for the new sentence. Like this: *Hundreds of people take the five o'clock train, which is never on time.* Now what case is *which* in? Look at the relative clause. If that doesn't help, look at the sentence from which the relative clause evolved. It came from clause 1, where *the five o'clock train* was nominative. The *which* is simply standing in for it; so *which* must be nominative. And it is.

THE ENGLISH RELATIVE PRONOUN: CASE SYSTEM

We need to look at the English relative pronoun a little more closely. Like the other pronouns in English, the relative pronoun preserves three distinct case forms and even distinguishes between animate and inanimate. There is no distinction between the numbers.

	Animate	Inanimate
Subjective	who	which
Possessive	whose	whose
Objective	whom	which

Notes

(1) Obviously, since English has lost its grammatical gender, the relative pronouns *who, whose, and whom* are only going to be used for living beings, usually only human beings, though sometimes for animals.

(2) A lot of people sniff at *whom* as archaic and elitist. That's possible, but I look at it this way: you should know how and *when* to use *whom* properly. If you're in a situation where your audience will denounce your pretensions to aristocracy if you use *whom*, then don't use it. Don't go into a bar and say *Is this the same team whom the Packers beat last week?* On the other hand, if your listener will dismiss you as a bumpkin and ignoramus if you say *These are the actors who I'd admire*, then use *whom*. Knowing when to use *whom* correctly is like knowing the difference between a salad and an oyster fork. It's not knowledge that's useful every day of your life, but when you need it it's nice to have. In any case, never use *whom* when you should use *who*. You'll outrage everyone: those who know and those who don't know. If you're in doubt as to which to use, use *who*.

(3) The nominative and accusative case of the relative pronoun *who, which* has been almost entirely replaced in colloquial English by *that*: *The boy that I saw* ..., *The girl that plays basketball* ..., *The car that is in the garage* ...

(4) English also has the option of omitting the relative pronoun altogether, and often it does: *The boy whom I saw is six feet tall* becomes *The boy I saw is six feet tall*. Latin doesn't have this option. It must always use the relative pronoun.

THE LATIN RELATIVE PRONOUN

We've done all the difficult work. You understand what relative clauses are: (1) they are subordinate clauses; (2) they are introduced by relative pronouns; (3) the relative pronoun agrees in number and gender with its antecedent, but gets its case from the way it's being used in its own clause; and (4) they modify something in the main clause. Now you have only to learn the declensional system of the Latin relative pronoun and practice with it.

The Latin relative pronoun has a full declensional system. That is to say, it has 30 separate forms: five cases in three genders in both numbers. The stem is **qu-** and it follows basically the pattern set down by the pronouns **is, ea, id; ille, illa, illud**, etc. But there are some substantial variations. Look at page 110 in Wheelock as you go through the following discussion. Let's start the close-up examination by running down the masculine forms first.

(1) The nominative case singular is a little unusual: **quî**, but most of the demonstratives and pronouns are odd in the nominative singular.

(2) The genitive and dative singulars (of all the genders) use the predictable pronoun case endings **-îus** and **-î**, but the stem has changed from **qu-** to **cu-**.

(3) In the accusative singular you'd expect **quum** (**qu** + **um**); but no such luck: **quem** is the form. The **-em** looks as if it's *borrowed* from the third declension, doesn't it?

(4) Things calm down for a while, but the dative and ablative plurals use the **-ibus** ending which they evidently import from the third declension. Notice again that **quibus** is the form for all the genders in the dative and ablative plural.

Now let's have a look at the feminine.

(1) The nominative's odd: **quae** instead of **qua**. But so what?

(2) Genitive and dative singular: stem **cu-** + **-îus** and **-î**, like the masculine.

(3) Finally, the dative and ablative plurals aren't **quîs** but, like the masculine, **quibus**.

And then the neuter.

(1) After having seen the masculine and feminine forms of the relative pronoun, the only truly unexpected quirk of the neuter is the nominative (hence, also accusative) plural: you get **quae** instead of **qua**. Pay attention. The form **quae** can be any one of four possibilities: (1) feminine nominative singular; (2) feminine nominative plural; (3) neuter nominative plural; (4) neuter accusative plural. Context will be your only guide.

Now try to write out the forms yourself. Just think of these forms as trying to be a pronoun of the first and second declension endings. And then remember the exceptions.

	Singular			Plural		
	Masculine	**Feminine**	**Neuter**	**Masculine**	**Feminine**	**Neuter**
Nom.	quī	quae	quod	quī	quae	quae
Gen.	cuius	cuius	cuius	quōrum	quārum	quōrum
Dat.	cui	cui	cui	quibus	quibus	quibus
Acc.	quem	quam	quod	quōs	quās	quae
Abl.	quō	quā	quō	quibus	quibus	quibus

DRILLS

Okay, now let's take apart a couple of Latin sentences with relative clauses. Translate these sentences, and tell me the number, gender, and case of the relative pronouns. Try following these steps:

(1) Go slowly.

(2) First read the entire sentence and try to identify the main clause and the relative clause. The relative clause will begin with the relative pronoun and probably end with a verb.

(3) After you've isolated the relative clause, forget it for a moment, and concentrate on translating the main clause—the main clause is, after all, the most important thought in the sentence.

(4) Next, look at the relative pronoun and try to figure out its number and gender—forget about the case for now. You want to match up the relative pronoun with its antecedent, and the relative pronoun will agree with its antecedent in number and gender.

(5) After all that, then you're ready to translate the relative clause. For that you'll need to know the case of the relative pronoun. Look carefully. Use what you know about its gender and number to check off any multiple possibilities.

(6) The last step, then, after all the pieces of the sentence have been analyzed separately, is to put it all back together.

1.	Vîdî canem[quî ex Asiâ vênit](**canis, -is**, *m.*, *dog*)	
	Relative Pronoun:	quī; m sg. Nom.
	Translation:	I saw the dog which came from Asia.
2.	Vîdî canês[quôs amâs.]	
	Relative Pronoun:	quōs; m pl. Acc.
	Translation:	I saw the dogs which you love.
3.	Puellae, quârum pater est parvus, sunt magnae.	
	Relative Pronoun:	quārum; f. pl. gen.
	Translation:	The girls, whose father is small, are large.
4.	Vîdî puerôs[quibus librôs dedistis.]	
	Relative Pronoun:	quibus; m pl. dat.
	Translation:	I saw the boys to whom you gave the books.
5.	Vîdî puerôs cum [quibus vênistis]	
	Relative Pronoun:	quibus; m pl. abl.
	Translation:	I saw the boys with whom you came.
6.	Cîvem[quem mîserâtis]laudâvêrunt.	
	Relative Pronoun:	quem; m acc. sg.
	Translation:	They praised the citizen whom you sent.

Now let's do it the other way. Write down the correct form of the Latin relative pronoun needed to complete these sentences.

1.	Tyrannus urbês dêlêvit *from which* cîvês fûgerant.	*ex* quibus
2.	Vênistî cum cîvibus *to whom* vîtâs commîserant.	quibus
3.	Cîvês vîdî *with whom* fûgistî.	quibuscum
4.	Pecûniam habent *with which* urbem tyrannus cêpit.	quâcum
5.	Pater *whose* fîliî stultî erant ex Asiâ vênit.	cuius

VOCABULARY PUZZLES

aut . . . aut It is used like this: **aut** x **aut** y *either x or y.* The trouble is that the word **aut** by itself means just *or.* But if there's another **aut** corresponding to it, then the first one is translated *either.* You've seen this kind of thing happen before with   **et . . . et**, *both . . . and*, and **neque . . . neque**, *neither . . . nor.*

coepî, coepisse, coeptus The first entry for this verb is the perfect tense, first person singular. The second is the perfect infinitive, which you haven't studied yet, and the third entry is the fourth principal part, which you also haven't studied yet. The verb is listed this way because it has no first principal part—which means logically that **coepî** has no present system tenses: no present, future, or imperfect. Another way to list this verb would be: ———-, ———-, **coepî, coeptus**. Verbs that lack one or more principal part are called *defective verbs.* So you may be wondering: "If the verb *to begin* in Latin has no present system, then how does Latin say *I begin* or *I will begin* or *I was beginning?*" To say *I begin, I will begin*, or *I was beginning*, Latin uses the first principal part of another verb **incipiô, -ere, -cêpî, -ceptus**. Does this strike you as odd that a verb can be defective? It shouldn't. We have lots of defective verbs in English. Consider the verb *must.* What are its principal parts? *must, musted, musted?* Try putting it into the future: *Will must?* How about a past tense perfect: *I have musted, I had musted, I was musting?* You can't do it. This verb exists only in the present tense in English. If we want to express the idea of obligation in any of the other tenses, we simply switch over to another verb, like *need* or *should.* You see? Like the Latin verb **coepî**, the English verb is defective; it lacks one or more of its possible tense systems.

18

Starting the Passive Voice

VOICE

We need to talk. There's something I've been keeping from you. Do you remember the personal endings of the present system, the endings **-o, -s, -t, -mus, -tis, -nt**? I told you that they indicate which person the verb is in. We called them the *personal endings*. Well, that's still true. These endings do indicate person and number. But there's something else they're telling you. They tell you that the subject of the verb is the agent performing the action in the verb. For example, in the sentence **Puerî litterâs ad amîcôs suôs mittent**, the subject of the verb, **mittent**, is **puerî**, and it is the **puerî** who are actually performing the action.

You're probably wondering, "How could it be otherwise? What would it mean for the subject of the verb *not* to be performing the action of the verb?" I'm glad you asked. Think about this sentence for a minute: *the letter will be sent by the boys to their friends.* What's the subject: *letter.* And what's the verb: *will be sent.* So is the letter performing the action of the verb or not? No, of course it isn't. It's actually receiving the action of the verb. It's as if the subject of the verb is the object of the verb at the same time.

What this means is that there are two relationships the subject can have with respect to the action of the verb. It either can be performing the action, or it can be receiving the action. We call this relationship *voice.* When the subject is performing the action of the verb, we say that the verb is in the *active* voice. When the subject of the verb is receiving the action, we say that the verb is in the *passive voice.* So much for the theory. How does this work out in reality?

PASSIVE VOICE IN ENGLISH

In English, the formation of the passive voice is a little clumsy: we use the third principal part of the verb and use it as a passive participle; then we use the verb *to be* in an inflected form as the auxiliary. Here are the principal parts of the English verb *to see: see, saw, seen.* The third principal part, often called a *participle* for reasons I'll explain in a later chapter, is *seen.* Let's put it to work in the passive voice. Change the voice of the following from the active to the passive. Think, now. You're rewriting these sentences so that the subject will be receiving the action of the verb instead of initiating it.

Active Voice	Passive Voice
I see.	I *am* seen.
I will see.	I *will* *be* seen.
I saw.	I *was* seen.

You will have written *I am seen, I will be seen, I was seen.* Can you detect the pattern form of the passive voice in English? It's an inflected form for the verb *to be* plus the participle of the verb you're using.

THE PASSIVE VOICE OF THE PRESENT SYSTEM IN LATIN

How does Latin form the active and passive voices? There are actually two different sets of rules for the two different tense systems. There's one set of rules for the present system passive and one for the perfect system passive. In this chapter, you're going to study only the present system of tenses (present, future, and imperfect). You'll learn the passive voice of the perfect system in Chapter 19.

Which principal part of the verb do you think the passive voice in the present system will be built upon? If you guessed the first principal part, you did well. Remember, the Latin present, future, and imperfect tenses are formed off the first principal part, regardless of the voice. Next, the verb endings you're familiar with are the *active* voice personal endings for the present system. So the **-o** of the first person singular was telling you more than just that the verb was in the first person singular. It was also telling you that the verb was in the first person singular *active*, and, accordingly, that the subject of the verb was performing the action of the verb. Similarly with the other endings—including the infinitive ending **-re**. They were all telling you that the subject of the verb was performing the action of the verb. They were all *active voice* personal endings. Logically, therefore, it follows that there must be a set of *passive* personal endings. Write down the active personal endings, and next to them write the passive forms (Wheelock 116-7). Compare them with the active endings, and watch for similarities:

	Singular		Plural	
	Active	**Passive**	**Active**	**Passive**
1st	-ō/m	-r [45]	-mus	-mur
2nd	-s	-ris [46]	-tis	-minī
3rd	-t	-tur	-nt	-ntur

Do you detect the similarities? Only the second person singular and plural endings are totally different from their active counterparts. Now let's take a closer look at how all of this is going to come together.

---

[45] The ending is only **-r**, but the **-ō-** of the personal ending active is always inserted in the present tenses and often in future tenses of the first and second conjugations.

[46] The ending is in reality **-sis**; but, according to the ancient rule, when an **-s-** comes between two vowels (when it's *intervocalic*) it becomes an **-r-**. Hence, the personal endings **-ris** and **-re**, not **-sis** or **-se**. The **-re** alternative ending for the second person singular passive is actually a little more common than the **-ris**; but Wheelock tells you that only the **-ris** ending is going to be used in his book.

PRESENT TENSE PASSIVE FOR ALL CONJUGATIONS [47]

The present tense in the active voice is formed simply by adding personal endings to the first principal part. (And remember, this stem includes the stem vowel: an **-â-** for first conjugation verbs, **-ê-** for the second, **-e-** for the third, and **-î-** for the fourth.) To form the present tense passive, you simply replace the active personal endings with the passive endings.

The only apparently unusual form you're going to see in all this is the second person singular of third conjugation verbs. You remember that the stem vowel of a third conjugation verb is short **-e-** and that it changes when you start adding personal endings. It becomes **-i-** and **-u-**. But think back. The infinitive of third conjugation verbs isn't **-ire** but **-ere**. That's because when the short **-e-** is followed by an **-r-** it stays short **-e-**. So what's that going to mean for the second personal singular passive? The passive personal ending is **-ris**, so, since the ending starts with an **-r-**, the stem vowel will not change to **-i-** as you might expect, but it will remain short **-e-**. So the form will end in **-eris**, not **-iris**, as you might have expected. Write out the present tense passive of all four conjugations (Wheelock 453).

Present Tense

	laudô, -âre	**moneô, -êre**	**agô, -ere**	**capiô, -ere**	**audiô, -îre**
1st	laudor	moneor	agor	capior	audior
2nd	laudāris	monēris	ageris	caperis	audīris
3rd	laudātur	monētur	agitur	capitur	audītur
Plural					
1st	laudāmur	monēmur	agimur	capimur	audīmur
2nd	laudāminī	monēminī	agiminī	capiminī	audīminī
3rd	laudantur	monentur	~~agetur~~	capuntur	audiuntur

aguntur

FUTURE TENSE PASSIVE OF ALL CONJUGATIONS

To form the future tense passive, just as in the present tense, you simply replace the active personal endings with the passive personal endings. Form the future tense of each verb, without the personal endings first; then simply attach the passive personal endings. But be careful. In the second person singular of all conjugations except the fourth something odd is going to happen. Do you remember this rule of Latin phonetics? When a short **-e-** is followed by an **-r-** it remains short **-e-**: **laudâ + be + ris laudâberis**; **monê + be + ris monêberis**. Write out the future tense passive of the paradigm verbs, and don't forget that third and fourth conjugation verbs form the future tense differently from the first and second.

---

[47]Wheelock considers only the first and second conjugations in the passive voice in the chapter, a restriction I find unnecessary. In my notes I'll take up the passive voice for verbs of all conjugations to show you that they all follow the same rules. For now, you should probably concentrate mainly on the first two conjugations. We'll look at the third and fourth again in Chapter 21.

Future Tense

	laudô, -âre	moneô, -êre	dûcô, -ere	capiô, -ere	audiô, -îre
1st	laudābor	monēbor	dūcēbor	capiar	audiar
2nd	laudāberis	monēberis	dūcēberis	capiēris	audiēris
3rd	laudābitur	monēbitur	dūcēbitur	capiētur	audiētur
Plural					
1st	laudābimur	monēbimur	dūcēbimur	capiēmur	audiēmur
2nd	laudābiminī	monēbiminī	dūcēbiminī	capiēminī	audiēminī
3rd	laudābuntur	monēbuntur	dūcēbuntur	capientur	audientur

IMPERFECT TENSE PASSIVE OF LATIN VERBS

Follow the same procedure you followed with the present and future tenses passive. Construct the imperfect tense without the personal endings, then use the passive personal endings. The first person singular is **-bar**, where the personal ending **-r** is attached directly to the **-bâ-** tense sign of the imperfect, without inserting an **-o-** as you did in the present and future tenses. (Write small!)

Imperfect Tense

	laudô, -âre	moneô, -êre	dûcô, -ere	capiô, -ere	audiô, -îre
1st	laudābar	monēbar	dūcēbar	capiēbar	audiēbar
2nd	laudābāris	monēbāris	dūcēbāris	capiēbāris	audiēbāris
3rd	laudābātur	monēbātur	dūcēbātur	capiēbātur	audiēbātur
Plural					
1st	laudābāmur	monēbāmur	dūcēbāmur	capiēbāmur	audiēbāmur
2nd	laudābāminī	monēbāminī	dūcēbāminī	capiēbāminī	audiēbāminī
3rd	laudābantur	monēbantur	dūcēbantur	capiēbantur	audiēbantur

THE PASSIVE INFINITIVE

The present infinitive passive is a form which is also derived from the first principal part. To form the passive voice of the infinitive of first, second, and fourth conjugation verbs, you simply use the ending **-rî** instead of **-re**. In third conjugation verbs, you replace the stem vowel with **-î**.

	Stem		Ending	→	Form	Translation
1st	laudâ	+	rî	→	laudârî	*to be praised*
2nd	monê	+	rî	→	monêrî	*to be warned*
3rd	dûcœ	+	î	→	dûcî	*to be led*
3rd i-stem	capœ	+	î	→	capî	*to be captured*
4th	audî	+	rî	→	audîrî	*to be heard*

ABLATIVE OF PERSONAL AGENT: AB + ABLATIVE

In the passive voice construction in Latin, the agent of the action, if it is mentioned, is expressed by the preposition **ab** + the ablative case. Wheelock gives you a stern warning: the *ablative of personal agent* is not the *ablative of means* (or the *instrumental ablative*). The *ablative of means* expresses the instrument with which the agent accomplished the action of the verb; the *ablative of personal agent* expresses the agent itself in a passive construction. Watch:

Nûllî tyrannî **ab Rômânîs** laudâbantur, *no tyrants used to be praised by the Romans.*

Multae rôsae puellîs **ab poêtîs** dabuntur, *many roses will be given to the girls by the poets.*

Omnês **hîs perîculîs** terrentur, *everyone is frightened by these dangers.*

Multae urbês **vî** pecûniae capientur, *many cities will be captured by the force of money.*

Omnês **â malîs** terrentur, *everyone is frightened by the evil [men].*

Multae urbês **istîs tyrannîs** capientur, *many cities will be captured by those tyrants.*

PASSIVE VOICE LIMITED TO TRANSITIVE VERBS

There is one other item you'll have to observe. As Wheelock tells you, the passive construction is only possible with verbs which are truly transitive: that is, with verbs that take direct objects. This makes sense. When you change the voice of a verb from the active to passive, the original direct object accusative becomes the subject nominative. Since only transitive verbs take direct object accusatives, it follows that only verbs that are transitive can have a passive voice.

Active	Passive
Rômânî nûllôs tyrannôs laudâbant.	Nûllî tyrannî ab Rômânîs laudâbantur.
Poêtae multâs rôsâs puellîs dabunt.	Multae rôsae puellîs ab poêtis dabuntur.

DRILLS

Change the voice of the following sentences. Be careful. This will involve more than simply changing the voice of the verb. You'll also have to reverse the subject and object. I'll do one for you.

Illî librî nôs adiuvâbunt becomes **Illîs librîs adiuvâbimur**.

Did you get all that? The original sentence read, *those books will help us.* To make it passive, you want it to read *we will be helped by those books.* The original object becomes the subject, and remember you don't have to include the nominative personal pronoun unless you're attaching some emphasis to the subject. Then the original subject becomes the ablative of means. If the original subject had been a person, then you would have had to use the ablative of personal agent: **ab** + ablative. Now you try your hand at a couple.

1.	Haec perîcula vôs terrêbant.
	Hîs perîculîs terrêbâminî.
2.	Discipulî meî hôs librôs cum celeritâte legent.
	Hî librî ab discipulîs meîs cum celeritâte legentur.
3.	Tê in viâ vidêbô.
	Tu ab mē in viā ~~vidēbĭs~~ vidēberis.
4.	Magna îra cîvês movêbat.
	Cîvēs magnā īrā movēbantur.

VOCABULARY PUZZLES

videôr, -êrî, visus sum The passive voice of the verb **videô** takes on a special meaning; one that is not entirely predictable simply by knowing the rules of translating the Latin passive voice into English. To be sure, **videôr** can mean *I am seen,* but more often it comes to mean *I seem* or *I appear* and is often followed by an infinitive: **videôr legere,** *I seem to be reading.* For your future reference, the third person impersonal passive of **videô**—**vidêtur** does not equal our popular construction *it seems*; rather it means *it seems right.* Latin never says *it seems that George is sick*; it says *George seems to be sick.*

19

Perfect Passive System; Answers about Questions [48]

PERFECT PASSIVE SYSTEM

We've so far been dividing the Latin tenses into two systems. The present system, active and passive, uses the first principal part of the verb. It includes the present, future, and imperfect tenses. Notice, these tenses use the first principal part for both the active and passive voices. The only difference between the active and passive voices in the present system is the personal endings. You learned all about this in Chapter 18.

The perfect system *active* uses the third principal part of the verb and attaches different personal endings to get the three different tenses of the perfect system. To form the perfect system tense in the passive voice, Latin uses the fourth principal part of the verb. Since it uses a different principal part, the perfect system passive is considered to be a different category of tenses. Accordingly, there are three tense systems in Latin: (1) the present system active and passive; (2) the perfect system active; (3) the perfect system passive. There, that about sums it up. Now let's talk these things over.

THE PASSIVE VOICE IN ENGLISH

First, let's look at how English forms its passive voice again. As we saw in Chapter 18, English uses the third principal part of the verb with an inflected form of the verb *to be* as the auxiliary or helping verb. That is to say, the verb *to be* will indicate the tense, the number, and the mood of the verb, while the third principal part of the verb will define the specific action involved.

The third principal part of the English verb is called a *participle*. Now listen closely; this is going to be an important definition: A participle is a *verbal adjective*, that is, an adjective derived from a verb. In fact, that's why we call it a participle, because it *participates* in the essence of both a verb and of an adjective. In the constructions of the English passive voice, the participle *seen* is actually *modifying* the subject of the verb *to be*. I can say *Betty is tall* and *Betty is seen*, and these two sentences are analogous. In the predicate of both these sentences the subject is further modified, since it is linked to an adjective by the verb *to be*.

It may seem bizarre to be thinking of a verbal construction as being essentially adjectival, but watch how we can use participles where their adjectival force is

---

[48]Chapter 19 covers two entirely unrelated subjects, so don't be misled by the title into thinking that the interrogative pronouns and adjectives have some special connection with the perfect passive system. They don't.

quite obvious: the *written* text, the *spoken* word, the *destroyed* city, the *bewildered* students, the *harried* professor, etc. So don't forget this: a participle is a verbal adjective. If you remember this well, you'll be sparing yourself a lot of confusion in the future.

THE LATIN PERFECT PASSIVE PARTICIPLE

So where are we? You already know that Latin forms the passive voice of some of its tenses—those of the present system—simply by using special passive endings. The formation of the passive voice of the *perfect* system, however, doesn't work that way.

The Latin perfect passive system is perfectly analogous to the formation of the English passive voice. The perfect passive system in Latin uses the fourth principal part of the verb, which is its participle, which is then linked to the subject with an inflected form of the verb **sum**. The fourth principal part of a Latin verb is called the *perfect passive participle*. Let's zero in on all the parts of this description.

(1) We call it *perfect* because the action is considered to have been completed. This is an important difference with the English participle. In English, we might say *Betty is being seen*, and the participle doesn't force us to understand that the action is finished. The Latin perfect passive participle, by contrast, does have the past tense in it.

(2) We say *passive* since whatever the participle is going with had something done to it, rather than having performed some action. Again, the English participle can be used in conditions where the passive force is not so obvious. In the sentence *I have seen Betty*, the participle *seen* doesn't strike us as passive in force, but rather as a part of an active construction.

(3) We say *participle* because it is a *verbal adjective*; and, for Latin, this is going to have some hair-raising implications. The participle is an adjective, so it must agree in number, gender, and case with the noun it is modifying. And if it must agree with nouns, then the participle must be able to decline to get the different numbers, genders, and cases it needs. This is the feature of the perfect system passive that causes students the most trouble. It's difficult for them to realize that the passive voice in the perfect system is essentially adjectival: the verb **sum** linking the subject of the verb with a predicate adjective.

Now let's look at the fourth principal part of a verb. As you know, the dictionary must give you all the principal parts of the verb you're considering. The fourth entry is the perfect passive participle, which is used with the auxiliary verb **sum** in the formation of the perfect system passive. We've said that the perfect passive participle is a verbal adjective, so it must be able to decline, just like adjectives, in order to agree with the nouns it's modifying. The perfect passive participle of all verbs declines just like the first adjectives you learned: just like **magnus, -a, -um**. That is, it uses endings of the first declension to modify feminine nouns, endings of the second declension **-us** type to modify masculine nouns, and endings of the second declension **-um** type to modify neuter nouns. The dictionaries tell you this in a number of different ways; but they're all telling you the same thing. Some dictionaries write out all three nominatives endings **-us, -a, -um**, whereas others abbreviate it by using only the neuter **-um** or the masculine **-us**. So you may see the entry for the fourth principal part of **laudô**, for example, given in these three different ways: (1) **laudâtus, -a, -um**; (2) **laudâtum**; (3) **laudâtus**.

PERFECT TENSE PASSIVE

Let's put this participle to work. How would you translate this in Latin: *I was praised*. Well, the tense is obviously perfect—that is, the action was completed before it was reported—so we must use the perfect passive participle: **laudâtus, -a, -um**. The person is first and the number is singular. Let's assume that the *I* is male. What case is *I*? Obviously nominative—it's the subject of the verb—so the form of the participle will be **laudât*us***—masculine, nominative singular. Got that? The participle is going to agree with the subject of the verb. The subject of the verb is nominative, so the participle must be nominative, too. Now what form of the verb *sum* should we use? Of course, we'll use the first person singular, but what tense?

Did you guess **eram**—*I was*? If you did, that's one demerit. Look, the fourth principal part is the *perfect passive participle* and the word *perfect* tells you that the action is considered to have been already completed. That is, in the participle itself is the notion of a past event, so **laudâtus** could be translated as *having been praised*. Therefore you needn't repeat the idea of past completion in the auxiliary verb *to be*. The correct form of the auxiliary is the present tense: **sum**.

Think of it this way (and I admit this may seem clumsy): **Laudâtus sum** means *I am now in the condition of **having been praised***. We can bring this over into English as either *I was praised* or *I have been praised*. So to form the perfect tense passive in Latin, you use the perfect passive participle + the verb **sum** as the auxiliary *in the present tense*.

Now let's suppose that the subject *I* is feminine. What changes would this necessitate? Well, the participle is a verbal adjective, so it must agree in number, gender, and case with whatever it's modifying. If the subject of the verb is feminine, then the participle has to be feminine, nominative, singular to agree with it. So the participle will have be **laudâta**. Therefore, if a woman is speaking, you would say **Laudâta sum** for *I was praised*.

PLUPERFECT TENSE PASSIVE

How do you imagine Latin forms the passive of the pluperfect tense? Think. You're still going to use the perfect passive participle linked to the subject with a conjugated form of the verb **sum**. All perfect system passive tenses do that. What tense will the verb **sum** be in? Right! Now you use the auxiliary verb **sum** in the imperfect tense. What you're doing is adding an additional past idea in auxiliary to the past idea already implicit in the participle. Therefore **Laudâtus eram** means *I was in the condition of **having been praised** or I **had** been praised*. And if the subject were feminine: **Laudâta eram**.

FUTURE PERFECT TENSE PASSIVE

And the future perfect tense? Yes. You use the future of the verb **sum**, thus attaching a future idea to the past idea in the participle; and that's the definition of the future perfect tense. **Laudâtus erô** therefore means *I will be in the condition of having been praised*, which comes out *I **will have been** praised*. And if the subject were feminine **Laudâta erô**.

PERFECT SYSTEM PASSIVE SUMMARIZED

Let's look at all this. Conjugate in full the three tenses of the perfect system passive, using the verb **laudô** (Wheelock 454).

Participle	Perfect	Pluperfect	Future Perfect
laudâtus, -a, -um	sum	eram	erô
	es	erās	~~erat~~ eris
	est	erat	erit
Plural			
laudâtî, -ae, -a	sumus	erāmus	erimus
	estis	erātis	eritis
	sunt	erant	erunt

LEARNING THE FOURTH PRINCIPAL PART OF VERBS

In Chapter 12, you realized that you were going to have to memorize the third principal part of all your verbs if you wanted to be able to work with them in all their tense systems. Similarly, now you must go back and memorize the fourth principal part of your verbs if you want to work with them in the perfect system passive. As with the third principal parts, the formation of the fourth will follow some regular patterns, so the task of memorization will not be as tedious as it at first might seem.

First Conjugation Verbs

The vast majority of first conjugation verbs, as you know, are regular. This means that their principal parts are formed regularly using the first principal part as the stem. The third principal part, as you recall, is just the first principal part + **vî**. The fourth principal part also is a regular derivation from the first principal part: it's the first principal part + **t** plus the adjectival endings **-us, -a, -um**. So for **laudô**, the fourth principal part is **laudâtus, -a, -um** (**laudâ** + **t** + **us, -a, -um**) which is often abbreviated just as **laudâtus** or **laudâtum**. Here are all the first conjugation verbs you've had up to this chapter. Fill out the principal parts, and double check your work. You can use these lists to review from.

	II	III	IV
amô	amāre	amāvī	amātus
côgitô	cōgitāre	cōgitāvī	cōgitātus
cônservô	cōnservāre	cōnservāvī	cōnservātus
dô	dare	dedī	datus
errô	errāre	errāvī	errātus
exspectô	exspectāre	exspectāvī	exspectātus
iuvô	iuvāre	~~iuvāvī~~ iūvī	~~iuvātus~~ iūtum
laudô	laudāre	laudāvī	laudātus
lîberô	līberāre	līberāvī	līberātus
mûtô	mūtāre	mūtāvī	mūtātus
parô	parāre	parāvī	parātus
servô	servāre	servāvī	servātus
superô	superāre	superāvī	superātus
tolerô	tolerāre	tolerāvī	tolerātus
vocô	vocāre	vocāvī	vocātus

Second Conjugation Verbs

Although second conjugation verbs are slightly less regular than first conjugation verbs, they do tend to follow a pattern in their formation of the second, third, and fourth principal parts. But because there are occasional irregularities in second conjugation verbs, the dictionary will list all four principal parts of a second conjugation verb. Often the third principal part of a second conjugation verb is the first principal part + **vî**, which then becomes simplified from **-êvî** to just **-uî**. The fourth principal part very often ends **-itus, -a, -um**. So for the paradigm verb **moneô**, the principal parts are **moneô, monêre, monuî, monitus**. Again, here's a sampling of the second conjugation verbs you've had till now. I've left the principal parts of the regular verbs blank for you to fill in on your own. When a verb lacks one of the principal parts, I've left no blank. Some verbs have unusual principal parts, which would involve some explanation. Where verbs have principal parts which are outside our interest here, I've crossed out the space they would occupy. For now, they don't exist. Just memorize the principal parts the verbs do have.

	II	III	IV
dêbeô	dēbēre	dēbuī	dēbitus
dêleô	dēlēre	dêlêvî	dêlêtus
doceô	docēre	docuī	doctus
habeô	habēre	habuī	habitum

	II	III	IV
moneô	monēre	monuī	monitus
moveô	movēre	môvî	môtus
remaneô	remanēre	remânsî	remânsus
teneô	tenēre	tenuī	tentus
terreô	terrēre	terruī	territus
timeô	timēre	timuī	
valeô	valēre	valuī	
videô	vidēre	vîdî	vîsus

Third Conjugation Verbs

The third conjugation (-i-stem and non-i-stem) displays several different ways of forming third and fourth principal parts. Each verb is best treated individually as if it were irregular, but certain patterns are obvious. Additionally, a great many of our English derivations come from the fourth principal part of the original Latin verb. If you keep this in mind as you try to memorize these forms, you'll find they'll stick more readily.

	II	III	IV
agô	agere	ēgī	actus
capiô	capere	cēpī	captus
		coepî	coeptus[49]
committô	committere	commīsī	commissus
currô	currere	cucurrī	cursus
dîcô	dīcere	dīxī	dictus
dûcô	dūcere	dūxī	ductus
dîligô	dīligere	dīlēxī	dîlêctus
êiciô	ēicere	iēcī	êiectus
faciô	facere	fēcī	factus
fugiô	fugere	fūgī	————
gerô	gerere	gessī	gestus
iaciô	iacere	iēcī	iactus
incipiô	incipere	incēpī	inceptus
intellegô	intellegere	intellēxī	intellectus
iungô	iungere	iūnxī	iūnctus

[49]**coepî, coeptus** is a defective verb. It has no present system; hence, no first or second principal part.

	II	III	IV
legô	legere	lēgī	lêctus
mittô	mittere	mīsī	missus
neglegô	neglegere	neglēxī	neglêctus
scrîbô	scrībere	scrīpsī	scrîptus
trahô	trahere	trāxī	tractus
vincô	vincere	vīcī	victus
vîvô	vīvere	vīxī	vîctus

Fourth Conjugation Verbs

The fourth conjugation sometimes forms third and fourth principal parts regularly by adding **-vi** to the present stem for the third and by adding **-tus, -a, -um** for the fourth. But there are so many irregularities that fourth conjugation verbs are listed with all four principal parts. Here's a list of some of the fourth conjugation verbs for your study:

	II	III	IV
inveniô	invenīre	invēnī	inventus
sentiô	sentīre	sēnsī	sensus
veniô	venīre	vēnī	ventus

THE INTERROGATIVE PRONOUN

Do you remember how Latin asks a question? You've learned that the enclitic **-ne** is attached to the end of the first word of the sentence to indicate a question. Latin must do this because the word order is so flexible that no rearrangement of the words will indicate necessarily that a question is coming up. In English, we ask a simple question by inverting the subject of the verb with an auxiliary. The statement *You are walking the dog* becomes a question like this: *Are you walking the dog?* But Latin doesn't have all these handy auxiliary verbs; and besides, since Latin doesn't rely on word order much to tell you the syntax of the words in the sentence, inverting words won't help.

So Latin uses the enclitic, and the word the enclitic is attached to is the focus of the question. For example, in the question **Laudâtisne fîliôs huius virî?** the point of inquiry is whether you are performing the action of praising. But if we begin the sentence with *the sons*—**Fîliôsne huius virî laudâtis**—then the focus of the question changes: *Are you praising this man's <u>sons</u>?* We can accomplish this effect in English by inflecting our voice when we reach the word that is the point of the question. Now look more closely at each of these questions. Even though each has a different emphasis, all the questions are essentially asking one thing: *If I should turn this question into a statement, would it be true?* That is, the question is about the validity of the predication.

The question *Are you praising this man's sons,* is asking whether it is true to say *You are praising this man's sons.* We call this kind of question a simple question; it asks for no information that is not contained in its structure. Now look at these questions: *Why are you praising this man's sons, When were you praising this man's sons, How are you praising this man's sons.*

Here it is taken for granted that the predication is true—you *are* praising this man's sons—and the questions being asked are not whether you're praising the sons, but why, when, or how. These questions are calling for information that is not contained within the syntax of the question; they are asking for specific kinds of additional information. And the kind of information they're asking for is indicated in the words *why, when, and how.* We call words that ask for specific kinds of information *interrogatives.* Some more questions with another kind of interrogative: **Who**'s got the button, **What**'s that dog doing here, **Whose** hamburger is this, **Whom** do you despise.

In these questions, the predication is taken as true. The information the questions are asking for, however, is temporarily replaced with another word, and the hope is that soon the information will be plugged into the spot where its replacement now stands. What do we call words that take the place of another word or idea? Right! We call them pronouns; so these words are interrogative (because they're asking questions) and pronouns (because they're replacing other nouns or ideas): *interrogative pronouns.*

The English interrogative pronouns, as you can see in the examples above, have different cases and even genders. The gender is determined by what is being filled in for, but the case is determined by the way the pronoun is being used in the question.

	Masculine and Feminine	**Inanimate**
Nom.	who	what
Gen.	whose	whose
Acc.	whom	what

Do you see any similarity between the interrogative pronouns and the relative pronouns? Of course you do. *Who, whose, and whom* are all forms that can also be used as relative pronouns. Only the interrogative pronoun *what* has no use as a relative pronoun.

The Latin interrogative pronoun also resembles the Latin relative pronoun. In the plural, the forms of the interrogative pronoun are identical to those of the relative pronoun. In the singular, *many* of the forms of the interrogative pronouns overlap with those of the relative pronouns, but there are some differences:

(1) The forms for the masculine and feminine are the same. Consequently, there are only two forms for the nominative singular: one for the masculine and feminine genders, and one for the neuter. Similarly, there are only two forms for the genitive singular—one masculine *and* feminine, and one neuter. And so on for all the cases in the singular. Only two forms.

(2) Two of the forms are just plain different from those of the relative pronoun. (a) For the masculine and feminine nominative singular, the form is **quis**, not **quî** or **quae** as you might expect. (b) You might expect **quod** for neuter nominative and accusative singular, but the form is **quid**. (c) For the remaining cases of the masculine/feminine forms, the interrogative pronoun uses the masculine forms of the relative pronoun.

Look over this description closely and try to write out the Latin interrogative pronoun (Wheelock 124).

	Singular		Plural		
	Mas./Fem.	**Neuter**	**Masculine**	**Feminine**	**Neuter**
Nom.	quis	quid	quī	quae	quae
Gen.	cuius	cuius	quōrum	quārum	quōrum
Dat.	cui	cui	quibus	quibus	quibus
Acc.	quem	quid	quōs	quās	quae
Abl.	quō	quō	quibus	quibus	quibus

Let's look at some examples of how the interrogative pronoun works in Latin. You'll note that it has some surprising properties, which the English interrogative pronoun *who, what,* etc. doesn't have.

Quis librum tibi dedit, *who gave you the book.*

You can tell this sentence is a question because it is introduced with the interrogative pronoun. But the English translation isn't as precise as the Latin. Why not? Look at **quis**. It's nominative because it is used as the subject of the verb. But what about its number and gender? It's masculine/feminine in gender and singular in number. That means that the question was formed in such a way as to imply that there was only *one* person who gave you the book. Now look at the English *who*. Can you tell whether the person asking the question expects there to be only one person who gave you the book? No, you can't. So, in Latin, the questioner reveals more about the kind of answer expected because the pronoun reveals more about the possible antecedent. How would we translate these into English:

Quî librum tibi dedêrunt?

Quae librum tibi dedêrunt?

We'd have to translate them both as *Who gave you the book.* But look more closely at the Latin. The first question implies that more than one person gave you the book and that they are either all male or mixed male and female. The second question implies that those who gave you the book are plural and all feminine. Look at another example. All of these Latin questions can be translated into English as *Whose book did Cicero give you:*

Cuius librum Cicerô tibi dedit?

Quôrum librum Cicerô tibi dedit?

Quârum librum Cicerô tibi dedit?

The interrogative pronoun in each of these questions is in the genitive case because the point of the question is to learn more about the owner(s) of the book. But each question suggests a different kind of answer. Can you spot the different expectations?

INTERROGATIVE ADJECTIVE

Okay, you know that the interrogative pronoun is a word that takes the place of another noun or idea about which certain information is being sought. Because it asks a question we call it *interrogative*; because it stands in for something else, we call it a *pronoun*: interrogative pronoun.

So what is an *interrogative adjective*? Start from the beginning. *Interrogative* means that it will be asking a question. *Adjective* means that it will be modifying a noun in the sentence and to modify a noun an adjective must agree with it in number, gender, and case. Putting these two parts together, we come up with this: an *interrogative adjective* is a word that modifies a noun in a way that asks more information about it. How does this work? Look at these English questions:

Which fool did this?

What house was burning?

For what reason are we doing this?

In each of these questions, more information is being requested about something that is already expressed in the question. Like this. What's the difference between (a) *Who did this*, and (b) *Which fool did this*? In (a), the answer sought is not restricted to anything specified in the sentence itself. But in the second, the potential responder is directed to limit his reply to something in particular; namely, *the fool*.

Latin also has interrogative adjectives for this purpose, but because Latin is a fully inflected language, the interrogative adjective has many more forms than its English analog. After all, the Latin interrogative adjective is going to have to agree with masculine, feminine, or neuter nouns in any one of the cases and numbers. You'll be pleased to know, however, that you're not going to have to learn anything new, because the Latin interrogative adjective uses the forms of its relative pronoun. Go ahead and write out the forms of the interrogative adjective to refresh your memory. (If you've forgotten, see Wheelock 448.)

Interrogative Adjective

	Singular			Plural		
	Masculine	**Feminine**	**Neuter**	**Masculine**	**Feminine**	**Neuter**
Nom.	quī	quae	quod	quī	quae	quae
Gen.	cuius	cuius	cuius	quōrum	quārum	quōrum
Dat.	cui	cui	cui	quibus	quibus	quibus
Acc.	quem	quam	quod	quōs	quās	quae
Abl.	quō	quā	quō	quibus	quibus	quibus

Because the interrogative adjective is an adjective, its form is determined entirely by the noun with which it is agreeing in the sentence. Like this:

Quem librum legêbâtis, *what (or which) book were you reading?*

The interrogative adjective **quem** is singular, accusative, masculine because the noun about which the question is seeking more information is singular, accusative, and masculine. Study these examples:

Quibus fêminîs librôs illôs dedistis? *to which women did you give those books?*

Â quô virô admonitî sunt? *by which (or what) man were they warned?*

Â quibus virîs admonitî sunt? *by which (or what) men were they warned?*

Â quâ fêminâ admonitî sunt? *by which woman were they warned?*

VOCABULARY PUZZLES

senex, senis This word is much more bizarre than Wheelock lets on. You'll see it mainly as a noun, meaning *old man* or *old woman*. Don't expect to see it modifying a neuter noun. It'll always be masculine or feminine. Because it's really a third declension adjective, it'll decline like:

senex	senês
senis	senium
senî	senibus
senem	senês
senî	senibus

20

Fourth Declension; More about Ablatives

FOURTH DECLENSION NOUNS

Let's review a moment. You know that a noun will belong to one declension and one declension only, and you know that a declension is a pattern of case endings. There are five declensions in Latin, and in each of them some case endings resemble those of the other declensions. You know the **-m** is almost always the ending of the accusative singular; **-s** is almost always the ending of the accusative plural; etc. So what makes these declensions truly different from each other? The truly distinctive characteristic of these declensions is the thematic vowel (that is, the vowel that regularly appears in the case endings):

(1) The thematic vowel of the first declension is **-a-**.

(2) The thematic vowel of the second declension is **-ô-** (the **-u-** in the declension was really an **-ô-** which has been changed).

(3) The thematic vowel of the third declension is short **-e-** (which often changes to a short **-i-**).

And now the fourth and fifth declensions:

(4) The thematic vowel of the fourth declension is **-u-**.

(5) The thematic vowel of the fifth declension is **-e-**. (We'll look at fifth declension nouns later in Chapter 22.)

How can you tell to which declension a noun belongs? The dictionary must give you that information. But instead of listing a number next to the noun, the dictionary does something else. It actually starts to decline the noun for you. The first entry in the dictionary is the nominative singular, followed by the genitive singular, which is then followed by the gender. You deduce the declension by looking at the genitive singular ending, which means you must know the forms of the genitive singulars for all the declensions:

(1) An **-ae** genitive ending means the noun declines in the first declension, because **-ae** is the genitive singular ending of the first declension.

(2) An **-i** genitive ending means the noun is second declension.

(3) An **-is** genitive ending means the noun is third declension.

Now let's look at the fourth declension. Like the third declension, the fourth declension can have nouns of all three genders belonging to it: the masculine and feminine nouns will follow one pattern of endings; the neuter nouns will follow another. (Now it happens that the vast majority of fourth declension nouns are masculine and that there are hardly any feminine nouns, but you should keep your guard up anyway.) Write down the case endings (Wheelock 129-30).

	Singular		Plural	
	Masc./Fem.	**Neuter**	**Masc./Fem.**	**Neuter**
Nom.	-us	-ū	-ūs	-ua
Gen.	-ūs	-ūs	-uum	-uum
Dat.	-uī	-ū	-ibus	-ibus
Acc.	-um	-ū	-ūs	-ua
Abl.	-ū	-ū	-ibus	-ibus

Let's take a closer look. First the masculine and feminine endings:

(1) The nominative singular is short **-us**, so this ending looks exactly like the **-us** type second declension ending for the nominative singular. It also looks like the ending you saw in a couple of neuter nouns of the third declension; remember **corpus**, **tempus**, and so on? To see the difference you must go to the next entry—the genitive singular.

(2) The genitive singular is long **-ûs**, so the dictionary entry for a fourth declension noun will look like this: '**x'us**, **-ûs**, *m./f.*, where '**x**' is the stem of the noun.

(3) The dative singular ending is the **-î** you've seen in the third declension and on the pronouns, which is attached to the thematic vowel **-u-**.

(4) The accusative singular ending is entirely predictable: it's just the thematic vowel with the ending **-m** attached. This is the way all accusative singulars of masculine and feminine nouns are formed in all the declensions.

(5) Equally predictable is the ablative singular: it's just the thematic vowel.

(6) The nominative plural works on the analogy of the third declension: the long thematic vowel plus the ending **-s**.

(7) The genitive plural is odd-looking—**-uum**—but it's made up of the thematic vowel plus the genitive plural ending **-um** you're already familiar with from the third declension.

(8) The dative and ablative plurals **-ibus** look like the third declension endings; notice also that the thematic vowel **-u-** has been replaced. It's **-ibus**, not **-ubus**. Strange.

(9) The accusative plural is the same as the nominative plural. You've seen this phenomenon before in the third declension.

Now let's look at the neuter side of the fourth declension. Wheelock tells you correctly that these are rare. And we're lucky they are, because they're somewhat odd.

(1) The nominative singular ends in just a long **-û**. Odd.

(2) According to the laws of neuters, therefore, the accusative singular will also end in long **-û**.

(3) You would expect the dative singular to have a predictable ending, but look at it: the ending is long **-û**. Take a look at the endings in the singular, now. Four of the cases in the singular have the same ending—long **-û**—which means you may have a devil of a time deciding which case a noun is in when it ends in long **-û**. Context has to help you.

(4) Nothing irregular happens in the plural—if you remember that proposition two of the law of neuters tells you that all neuter nominative and accusative plurals end in short **-a**.

One more thing about the fourth declension which might interest you is that there are no fourth declension adjectives. You recall that the first, second and third declensions are patterns of endings which nouns and adjectives can use. The fourth declension contains only nouns. Isn't that nice? So decline these nouns (Wheelock 129-30).

	metus, -ûs, *m.*	**cornû, -ûs,** *n.*
N/V.	metus	cornū
Gen.	metūs	cornūs
Dat.	metuī	cornū
Acc.	metum	cornū
Abl.	metū	cornū
Plural		
N/V.	metūs	cornua
Gen.	metuum	cornuum
Dat.	metibus	cornibus
Acc.	metūs	cornua
Abl.	metibus	cornibus

ABLATIVE OF PLACE FROM WHICH AND SEPARATION

There's nothing really difficult about this bit of knowledge. You've seen for quite some time now that prepositions take certain cases and that the meaning of such expressions is set by the meaning of the preposition. The case the noun is in really has nothing to contribute to the meaning of the expression. For example, **ad** means *to* or *toward* and it takes its object in the accusative case. Therefore, **ad urbem** means *to/toward the city*. The prepositions **ab, ex, dê** mean something like *from* or *out of* or *away from* and they take the ablative case. So we can say, **Veniunt ex urbe**, *they are coming out of the city*. Got that?

Now here's a new twist. If the verb being used explicitly contains the idea of physical separation, then the prepositions indicating separation (**ab, ex, dê**) are not used. Instead, the thing from which the separation is being made is simply put into the ablative case. We call this prepositionless use of the ablative case the *ablative of separation*. Watch. The verb *to free*, **lîberô** (1), also carries with it the sense *to free from*. Hence, the idea of separation from something is explicit in the verb. So if we wish to say something like this—*The truth will free us from fear*—we write **Vêritâs nôs *metû* lîberâbit** (not **ab metû**). A couple more examples ought to make this clear.

Frûctibus bonîs numquam carêbâmus, *we never used to lack good fruits (or pleasures)*.

Lîberâvistis nôs sceleribus istîus tyrannî, *you have freed us from the crimes of that tyrant.*

VOCABULARY PUZZLES

frûctus, -ûs, *m.* Don't forget the extended senses of the word *fruit: fruits of our labor*, for example.

commûnis, -e It doesn't mean *common* in the negative sense of *ordinary*; it means *common* in the sense that many share it. *General* is a better first translation. **Commûnis opiniô** means *general opinion*; **commûnis salûs**, *general safety.*

careô (2) **caruî**, ——- Pay no attention to the fourth principal part for now, but do look at the construction that follows the verb. **Careô** takes the ablative of separation, not the accusative case, as you might be led to expect by our English verb *to lack.*

21

Finishing Off the Passive Voice of the Present System

PRESENT SYSTEM OF THIRD AND FOURTH CONJUGATIONS VERBS

This chapter completes the picture of the passive voice. In Chapter 18, you studied the passive voice of the present system of tenses (the present, imperfect, and the future), but only for the first two conjugations. The third and the fourth conjugations present nothing strange or frightening in the passive voice. If you can form the active voice of these conjugations, then you can form the passive voice. In fact, let's do that. Form the active voice of the following verbs (Wheelock 452).

agô

	Present	Future	Imperfect
1st	agō	agam	agēbam
2nd	agis	agēs	agēbās
3rd	agit	aget	agēbat
Plural			
1st	agimus	agēmus	agēbāmus
2nd	agitis	agētis	agēbātis
3rd	agunt	agent	agēbant

capiô

	Present	Future	Imperfect
1st	capiō	capiam	capiēbam
2nd	capis	capiēs	capiēbās
3rd	capit	capiet	capiēbat
Plural			
1st	capimus	capiēmus	capiēbāmus
2nd	capitis	capiētis	capiēbātis
3rd	capiunt	capient	capiēbant

audiô

	Present	Future	Imperfect
1st	audiō	audiam	audiēbam
2nd	audīs	audiēs	audiēbās
3rd	audit	audiet	audiēbat
Plural			
1st	audīmus	audiēmus	audiēbāmus
2nd	audītis	audiētis	audiēbātis
3rd	audiunt	audient	audiēbant

REVIEW OF THE PRESENT SYSTEM PASSIVE

You saw in Chapter 18 that there was nothing very difficult about it. The only difference between the active and passive voices is the different set of personal endings each uses. So all you're going to have to do to the forms above (if you have them right) is to take off the active endings and put on the passive endings. The passive personal endings are:

	Singular	Plural
1st	r	mur
2nd	ris	minī
3rd	tur	ntur
Infinitive	ī	

Are you ready? Write out the passive voice of these verbs (Wheelock 135).

agô

	Present	Future	Imperfect
1st	agor	agar	agēbar
2nd	ageris ⁵⁰	agēris ⁵¹	agēbāris
3rd	agitur	agētur	agēbātur

---

⁵⁰Remember, short -e- stays short -e- if the personal ending begins with an -r-. Look at the present infinitive of agô: it's agere, not agire, because the infinitive ending starts with an -r-. Therefore, the form here is ageris, not agiris. Write in the short mark in your list.

⁵¹Tough one, isn't it. The sign of the future is long ê. So the form is agêris. Now look over to your left. How does the present tense differ from the future. Look closely. The only difference between these two tenses is the length of the vowel -e-. In the present tense, it's short, because it represents the original stem vowel, which is a short -e- in the third conjugation. In the future tense, the -ê- is long, because this time the -ê- is the tense sign for the future. The length of the vowel—and hence the location of the stress accent—is the only difference between the present and future second person singular passive: the present ageris is pronounced *AH geh ris*; the future agêris is pronounced *ah GEH ris*.

	Present	Future	Imperfect
Plural			
1st	agimur	agēmur	agēbāmur
2nd	agiminī	agēminī	agēbāminī
3rd	aguntur	agentur	agēbantur

capiô

	Present	Future	Imperfect
1st	capior	capiar	capiēbar
2nd	caperis	capiēris	capiēbāris
3rd	capitur	capiētur	capiēbātur
Plural			
1st	capimur	capiēmur	capiēbāmur
2nd	capiminī	capiēminī	capiēbāminī
3rd	capiuntur	capientur	capiēbantur

audiô

	Present	Future	Imperfect
1st	audior	audiar	audiēbar
2nd	audīris	audiēris	audiēbāris
3rd	audītur	audiētur	audiēbātur
Plural			
1st	audīmur	audiēmur	audiēbāmur
2nd	audīminī	audiēminī	audiēbāminī
3rd	audiuntur	audientur	audiēbantur

THE PASSIVE INFINITIVES

To form the passive infinitive of first and second conjugation verbs, you simply replace the normal **-re** ending with **-rî**. This is how you form the passive infinitive of fourth conjugation verbs as well:

First Conjugation	**amâre**	*to love*	**amârî**	*to be loved*
Second Conjugation	**dêlêre**	*to destroy*	**dêlêrî**	*to be destroyed*
Fourth Conjugation	**audîre**	*to hear*	**audîrî**	*to be heard*

Notice that these three conjugations have something in common. In each the stem vowel is long: **amâ-**, **dêlê-**, and **audî-**. Hence, they form their present passive infinitives the same way. This leaves the third conjugation, both *i-stem* and *non-i-stem* unaccounted for; because third conjugation verbs have a short stem vowel: short **-e-**. To form the passive infinitive of third conjugation verbs, you drop the stem vowel and replace it with long **-î**:

Non-I-Stem	**dûcere**	to lead	**dûcî**	to be led
I-Stem	**capere**	to capture	**capî**	to be captured

DRILLS

Work through Wheelock's Self Tutorials for this chapter to see whether you've thoroughly understood the material.[52] Then try these exercises for a little more practice. Reverse the voice of these sentences. Caution! This means more than just changing the voice of the verb. You've also got ot reverse the subjects and objects! (I'll do the first one for you).

Hômînês saepe malam laudem audiunt.

The translation reads *men often hear wicked praise.* So to change the voice, we have to make it passive; we want it to mean *wicked praise is often heard by men.* Now *wicked praise* is the nominative subject of the verb, and *men* is the agent. Here's the way it goes in Latin: **Mala laus ab hominibus saepe audîtur.**

1.	Quî discipulî hôs versûs legêbant?
	Ā quibus discipulīs hī versūs legēbantur?
2.	Iste tyrannus omnês cîvitâtês capiet.
	Omnēs cīvitātēs ab istō tyrannō capiēntur.
3.	Nostrî amîci nôs adiuvâbant.
	Ā nostrīs amīcis nōs adiuvābāmur.
4.	Tuî amîcî tê nôn neglegent.
	Ā tuīs amīcis tū nōn neglegēris.
5.	Tua domus dehinc â mê vidêrî potest.
	Tuam domum dehinc vidēre possum.

---

[52]You can listen to me teaching the Self Tutorials in RealAudio. The links are at www.uncc.edu/classics/Wheelock.

SYNOPSIS

You've just learned another couple dozen forms of Latin, and it might be getting a little hard to remember everything. The Wheelock text tells you that a good, fast way to get an overview of the verb forms is to drill yourself with a *synopsis*. What you do in a synopsis is produce a verb in a certain person in all the tenses and both voices. Like this. I say *Produce a synopsis of the verb **mittô** in the second person singular*. Then you write out all the second person singular forms in all the tenses and in both voices. In this way, you review the formulae for the different tenses without having to crank out all the forms, which takes a lot of time and paper. Try it:

Synopsis of mittô: 2nd Person Singular

	Active	Passive
Present	mittis	mitteris
Future	mittēs	mittēris
Imperfect	mittēbās	mittēbāris
Perfect	mīsistī	missus es
Pluperfect	mīserās	missus erās
Future Perfect	mīseris	missus eris

VOCABULARY PUZZLES

causa, -ae, *f.* Note well the common use of **causa** to mean *for the sake of.* In this usage, **causa** is used like a preposition: it is put into the ablative case and its object, which actually precedes it, is in the genitive case. E.g. **artis causâ**, *for the sake of art.*

fînis, -is, *m.* Look at what it means in the plural: *boundries, border of a country.*

quod You have to be careful with this word. As you probably remember, **quod** is the form used by the relative pronoun for the neuter nominative and accusative singular.

22

Fifth Declension; Summary of Ablative Uses

THE FIFTH DECLENSION

The fifth declension is simple—probably the simplest declension in Latin. Write down the case endings of the fifth declension (Wheelock 141).

	Singular	Plural
N/V.	ēs	ēs
Gen.	eī	ērum
Dat.	eī	ēbus
Acc.	em	ēs
Abl.	ē	ēbus

Notes

(1) It has no subcategories or deviant set of endings.

(2) The nouns of the fifth declensions never have stems that are not the same as the nominative singular.

(3) Its thematic vowel -ê- is transparent in all the case endings.

(4) There are no adjectives that use the fifth declension endings.

(5) There is only one nominative singular ending.

(6) The vast majority of fifth declension nouns are feminine.

The nominative singular is always -ês, which makes this declension much easier to spot than the second and the third declensions, in which there are a variety of possible endings for the nominative singular. Therefore, a fifth declension noun will always end in -ês—and that is the first entry in the dictionary. But be careful not to make an elementary error in logic. All fifth declension nouns end in -ês in the nominative singular, *but* not all nouns which end in -ês in the nominative singular are fifth declension. **Nûbês**, for example, ends in -ês, but its genitive is **nûbis**, clearly telling you that it's a third, not a fifth declension noun. Be sure to check the nominative *and* the genitive forms for your nouns. A fifth declension noun will look like this: **'x' ês, -eî** (*gender*), where 'x' is the stem of the noun.

The Problem with diês, diêî, m.

Wheelock shows you the noun **diês** separately; and it's possible to get the impression that it is a paradigm for a subdivision of the fifth declension. It is not. Look at the endings carefully. You'll see the case endings on **diês** don't differ from the endings of **rês** in any significant way. The only difference is in the quantity of the thematic vowel **-ê-**.

By nature, the thematic vowel of the fifth declension is long, and it *wants* to stay long. Often, however, it becomes short when certain endings are attached. For **rês**, the thematic vowel **-ê-** becomes short when you add the genitive and dative singular ending long **-î** (and it is also short before the **-m** ending of the accusative singular). But, when the thematic vowel **-ê-** is itself preceded by another vowel—as it is in **diês**—then it stays long before the genitive and dative ending long **-î**. So you get **diêî** for the genitive singular, not **dieî**. Since you're not overly concerned about getting all the long marks right at this point in your study, you might just as well cross out **diês** in Wheelock and forget about it. The stem of **diês** is **diê-** to which you add the fifth declension case endings.

ABLATIVE OF MANNER WITH AND WITHOUT CUM

Now you get a stylistic variation on the ablative of manner construction you've already learned. The ablative of manner, you may recall, is a way to use a noun as an adverb. You use the preposition **cum** with the noun in the ablative case: **Id cum celeritâte fêcêrunt**, *they did it quickly*. You can also modify the noun being used adverbially with an adjective. Latin likes to turn the word order around some, but this is no great problem: **Id magnâ cum celeritâte fêcêrunt**, *they did it with great speed*.

When the noun in this kind of construction is modified by an adjective, Latin has the option of dropping the preposition **cum**. This sentence could also be written: **Id magnâ celeritâte fêcêrunt**. But if the noun governed by **cum** is not qualified by an adjective, the **cum** *must* be used. This is incorrect: **Id celeritâte fêcêrunt**; but this is correct: **Id cum celeritâte fêcit**. And so is this: **Id magnâ cum celeritâte fêcit**; this is fine, too: **Id magnâ celeritâte fêcit**.

SUMMARY OF ABLATIVES

This is just a rehash of old material, but it's good to get all the facts laid out at one time. The uses of the ablative case can be divided into two groups:

(1) Uses of the ablative with a preposition.

(2) Uses of the ablative without a preposition.

When you have a preposition governing an ablative case, you just translate the meaning of the preposition and then translate the meaning of the noun. The fact that the noun is in the ablative case really doesn't contribute anything to the translation. It's in the ablative case because the preposition requires it. That's all.

One preposition that takes the ablative case requires some special caution, however, and that's **cum**. Remember, **cum** means *with* in two different senses: (1) as accompaniment and (2) as manner.

Id cum amîcô fêcit, *he did it with a friend.*

Id cum cûrâ fêcit, *he did it with care.*

It is important, however, that you know all the *prepositionless* uses of the ablative case. Here the ablative case itself, without a preposition in Latin to govern it, takes on special meanings. You simply must know them.

(1) *Ablative of means* shows the instrument with which the action of the verb was effected. Keep it distinct from the *ablative of manner*, which shows in what manner the action was carried out. Common translations of the ablative of means are: *with, by means of, through.*

(2) *Ablative of time* is easy to spot. If you have a unit of time in the ablative case without a preposition, it's expressing time. The problem is that Latin used this construction to indicate two different kinds of time which we keep separate in English. The Latin ablative of time can express either the *time when* or *time within which* of an action. (See Chapter 15.)

(3) *Ablative of separation* is a prepositionless use of the ablative case after verbs that strongly contain the idea of separation; so the normal prepositions **ex** or **ab** are dropped, and the ablative case alone is used.

(4) *Ablative of manner* can be written without a preposition if the noun used as an adverb is modified by an adjective—as you saw above.

VOCABULARY PUZZLES

rês, reî, *f.* Start by scratching off the first translation *thing*. **Rês** doesn't mean *thing* in our common sense of *What's that **thing** on the table?* or *Bring me that **thing**,* or *Wild thing, I think I love you.* It doesn't mean a nondescript object for which we can't quite come up with a name. It means *thing* when we say something like *What's this **thing** about you're not wanting to learn Latin?* or ***Things*** *sometimes get out of control.* It means *matter, affair,* or *business* (non-commercial).

rês pûblica, *f.* First, this is the origin of our *one* word *republic*, but in Latin it is two words—the noun **rês** and the adjective **pûblicus, -a, -um** modifying it. Therefore both **rês** and **pûblica** decline, **reî pûblicae, reî pûblicae, rem pûblicam, rê pûblicâ**, and so forth. Second, it obviously doesn't mean *public thing* as in *public object*, but *public business or affair*, even *power*. Here you can see the real meaning of **rês**.

medius, -a, -um It is an adjective, not a noun, so it can't be used the way our noun *middle* is used. We say *the middle of the city*, putting *city* into the genitive case. Latin can't do this, because **medius** doesn't mean *middle*, but *mid*. Hence, they say **media urbs**; or **mediâ nocte**, *in the middle of the night.*

23

Participles

Despite its disarmingly simple title, this chapter contains a lot of material—some of it simple, some of it potentially perplexing—but all of it overwhelming taken together in one heap. I'm going to break it down into two sections for you. Don't try to do them both in one sitting, unless you find the first section so easy that you need more. The sections are (I) basic concepts, morphology (formation), and rudimentary translations, and (II) Syntax (use) of the participles.

I: BASIC CONCEPTS OF LATIN PARTICIPLES

You already know what a participle is; you've been working with one now for a couple of chapters. A participle is a verbal adjective. That is, an adjective derived from a stem of a verb. The participle you're familiar with is the perfect passive participle—the fourth principal part of the verb—which is used in the formation of the perfect system passive. Let's look at it again, this time with an eye for the finer details.

We call the fourth principal part of a verb a participle because it's a verbal adjective. Now, because it's an adjective it must agree with whatever noun it's modifying. That's what adjectives do: modify and agree with nouns. So to agree with its noun, a participle must be able to decline in some way to get the different numbers, genders, and cases it may need— just as any adjective must. The fourth principle part, therefore, has the adjectival endings **-us, -a, -um** attached to it, and that tells you it declines in the first and second declensions—like **magnus, -a, -um**—to get the endings it needs. So every participle in a sentence will have number, gender and case because it is an adjective and it must be agreeing with something in the sentence of which it is a part.

But a participle is a *verbal* adjective; so it's going to get some of its character from its verbal ancestry. What qualities do verbs have? They have (1) number, (2) person, (3) tense, (4) mood, and (5) voice. So which of these five will participles retain?

(1) *Number:* A participle has number, that's true; but it gets its number—singular or plural—from the noun it's modifying. So a participle will have number, not because it is a verbal derivative, but because it's an adjective.

(2) *Person:* A participle does not have person—first, second, or third. You can't say of a participle, this is in the first person.

(3) *Tense:* A participle will have tense—after a fashion. It will be either present, future, or perfect. The participle you know is the *perfect* participle.

(4) *Mood*: A participle is already a mood of a verb. There are the indicative, imperative, subjective, infinitive, and participial moods of verbs. So to say *participle* is already to designate a certain mood.

(5) *Voice*: A participle has voice—either active or passive. The participle you know is a passive participle; hence, it is the perfect passive participle.

Let's summarize all this. Whenever you see a participle in a sentence, you must be prepared to identify its adjectival and verbal components:

Adjectival	Verbal
number	voice
gender	tense
case	

FORMATION OF LATIN PARTICIPLES

Now for a pleasant surprise: the Latin participial system is not nearly so complicated as the English system. In English, participles are often compounds of verbal stems and auxiliary verbs: *having been seen, having looked*, etc. In Latin, a participle is a one-word show.

You know that the Latin participles have number, gender, and case, all of which it must have because participles are adjectives. They get their number, gender, and case in its adjectival endings. The participle which you already know—the perfect passive participle—is declined in the first and second declensions. This is important to remember: all participles will have number, gender, and case; and they get them by declining. We'll look at this again.

But what about voice and tense? You know only one participle; and it is passive in voice and perfect in tense. But there are other participles with other tenses and voices. In Latin, there are participles of the present, future, and perfect tenses, and of the active and passive voices. Here are the formulae for their formation:

Future Active Participle

The future active participle of any verb is formed by adding **-ûr-** and the adjectival endings **-us, -a, -um** to the stem of the fourth principal part of the verb. For example, the future active participle of **laudô** is: **laudât + ûr + us, -a, -um** → **laudâtûrus, -a, -um**.

Future Passive Participle (The Gerundive)

The future passive participle (also called the gerundive (*jeh RUHN div*) for reasons you'll see in a minute) of any verb is formed by adding **nd** and the adjectival endings **-us, -a, -um** to the *lengthened* stem of the first principal part of the verb. Hence, for the four conjugations:

I.	laudâ	+	nd	+	us, -a, -um	→	laudandus, -a, -um
II.	monê	+	nd	+	us, -a, -um	→	monendus, -a, -um
III.	agê	+	nd	+	us, -a, -um	→	agendus, -a, -um
III-i.	capiê	+	nd	+	us, -a, -um	→	capiendus, -a, -um
IV.	audiê	+	nd	+	us, -a, -um	→	audiendus, -a, um[53]

Present Active Participle

The present active participle is formed by adding the third declension adjectival ending **-ns, -ntis** to the *lengthened* stem of the first principal part. This adjectival ending is the same ending you saw in the adjective **potêns, potentis**. (We'll consider the declension a little later.) So the present active participle of the four conjugations looks like this:

	Stem	Ending	Conjugated Form
I.	laudâ	+ ns, -ntis	laudâns, laudantis
II.	monê	+ ns, -ntis	monêns, monentis
III.	agê	+ ns, -ntis	agêns, agentis
III-i.	capiê	+ ns, -ntis	capiêns, capientis
IV.	audiê	+ ns, -ntis	audiêns, audientis

Perfect Passive Participle

The perfect passive participle is given to you as the fourth principal part of the verb in the dictionary with the adjectival endings **-us, -a, -um**. The only refinement you should make to your knowledge is that the true fourth principal part of a verb is what is left *after* you drop off the adjectival endings. The true fourth principal part of **laudô**, for example, is **laudât-**, not **laudâtus, -a, -um**. **Laudâtus, -a, -um** is the perfect passive participle; **laudât-** is the true stem of the fourth principal part.

DRILLS ON PARTICIPLE MORPHOLOGY

Study the formulae for the Latin participles, then write out the complete participial system of the following verbs.

	Active	Passive
Future	4th prin. part. + ûr + us, -a, -um	1st prin. part + nd + us, -a, -um
Present	1st prin. part. + ns, ntis	
Perfect		4th prin. part. + us, -a, -um

---

[53]As you can see, for the third i-stem and fourth conjugation verbs, the lengthened stem involves inserting an extra vowel. It's the same stem you see used in the imperfect tense of these conjugations: **capiêbam** and **audiêbam**.

dûcô, dûcere, dûxî, ductus -a, -um

	Active	Passive
Future	ductūrus	dūcendus
Present	dūcēns	
Perfect		ductus

mittô, mittere, mîsî, missus -a, -um

	Active	Passive
Future	missūrus	mittendus
Present	mittēns	
Perfect		missus

cupiô, cupere, cupîvî, cupîtus -a, -um

	Active	Passive
Future	cupītūrus	cupiendus
Present	cupiēns	
Perfect		cupītus

DEFECTIVE VERBS

You have already seen many verbs whose fourth principal part is a little odd looking, or which have no fourth principal part listed in the dictionary at all. Verbs that do not have a perfect passive participle as their fourth principal part are called *defective* verbs. But often defective verbs will nevertheless have a future active participle.

Now, this may seem to be an impossibility, because the future active participle is a derivative of the fourth principal part of the verb, right? For example, you get **laudâtûrus** by using the perfect passive participle **laudât-** plus -**ûr** plus *the adjectival ending* -us, -a, -um. So if a verb has no fourth principal part, how can you put together a future active participle?

Look again. The fourth principal part is the perfect *passive participle*, and there are many verbs which have no possible passive voice. Verbs that are intransitive cannot be made passive; so, logically, they'll have no perfect *passive* participle. But the future *active* participle *is* a possible form for intransitive verbs. In this case, the dictionary will list the future active participle as the fourth principal part:

fugiô	fugere	fûgi	fugitûrus
sum	esse	fuî	futûrus
careô	carêre	caruî	caritûrus
valeô	valêre	valuî	valitûrus

TRANSLATING THE PARTICIPLES: THE BASICS

Now let's think about the meaning of these participles. We'll first look at their barest, literal translations. They make really awful sounding English and, I hope, you'll soon discard them. By learning these rudimentary translations first, you'll be certain to understand the grammar the participles involve.

The Future Active Participle

Obviously, the future active participle tells you that the modified noun is about to undertake some action some time in the future (*future active*). But this construction has no convenient parallel in English. To translate this in English we use what is called a *periphrastic (peh ri FRAS tik)* construction. The root of this term is *periphrase* and that's precisely what we have to do to translate the future active participle—we have to find a periphrase for it, some way of approximating the meaning it would have had for the Roman ear. We *talk around it*. The standard periphrases for the future active participle is *about to 'x'* or *going to 'x'*, where *x* is the meaning of the verb. For example, for the participle **laudâtûrus** we would say *about to (or going to) praise*; for **factûrus** we would say *about to (or going to) do*.

The Future Passive Participle

This participle, too, has to be brought into English with a periphrase. Since both future participles make use of periphrastic constructions, the translation for the future *active* participle is often called the *first periphrastic*; the future *passive* participle is called the *second periphrastic*. The periphrase of the future passive participle might be something like this: *about to be 'x'ed*, or *going to be 'x'ed*, where *x* is the meaning of the verb. For example, **dûcendus** might be translated *about to be (or going to be) led*. But the future passive participle in Latin usually has a special sense attached to it you can't foresee simply by examining the grammar of its constituent parts. The future passive participle very often implies a sense of obligation or necessity that the action be performed. We can get a feel for it in our construction *to be 'x'ed* with a conjugated form of the verb *to be*. Like this: *This book is to be put on the shelf; This point is not to be ignored*. The underscored portions would be represented in Latin with the future passive participle. The next chapter will straighten all this out. For now, just remember that the future passive participle involves a special meaning that has to be treated separately.

The Present Active Participle

The key to the translation is *present and active*. This tells you that the noun which the participle is modifying is currently engaged in an action. That is, the noun is the agent of an action, and the action is currently underway. The Latin present active participle can be translated directly into our English present active participle, which is formed from the first principal part of the verb plus the participial suffix -ing; e.g., *walking, running, seeing,* etc.

The Perfect Passive Participle

Once again, with this participle the translation is spelled out in its title. The perfect passive participle tells you that the noun which the participle is modifying underwent (*passive*) an action that is viewed as having been completed (*perfect*). The surest way to get this over into English is with the rather clumsy auxiliary construction *having been* plus the third principal part of the English verb; e.g., *having been seen, having been taken, having been helped.*

Participles and Translations Summarized

	Active	Passive
Future	laudâtûrus, *about to praise*	laudandus, *about to be praised*
Present	laudâns, *praising*	
Perfect		laudâtus, *having been praised*

For some good practice identifying and translating the participles, look at the Self Tutorials in Wheelock, exercises 1-3 (page 377). You really shouldn't go any further in this lesson until you feel comfortable about the morphology and basic translations of the participles. Plus, you should stop here and take a break.

II: THE SYNTAX OF THE PARTICIPLES

Latin is fond of its participles; it uses them much more often and with many more shades of meaning than English. For this reason, it is critically important that you not rush to grab hold of one-to-one equivalent translations from Latin to English. First you must force yourself to understand the *meaning* of the Latin construction, and only then look for an English translation that will faithfully reproduce it. It's in cases like this where basic language instruction truly approaches the realm of the liberal arts. You must understand the meaning of the Latin *before* you reproduce it in English.

Translating Latin Participles as Clauses

In many ways, English is a very precise language, especially when it comes to spelling out the relationship a subordinate clause has to the main clause of a sentence. Consider these complex sentences:[54]

1. When the sailors were seen by Polyphemus, they were frightened.

2. Because the sailors were seen by Polyphemus, they were frightened.

3. Since the sailors were seen by Polyphemus, they were frightened.

4. The sailors, who were seen by Polyphemus, were frightened.

---

[54]By *complex*, we mean a sentence having a main clause and at least one subordinate clause.

Each of these four sentences is doing the same thing syntactically: each is subordinating one thought to another. The main clause—the main thought—is that the sailors were frightened. Subordinate to the main thought is the thought that the sailors were seen by Polyphemus—the one-eyed monster. So syntactically, these sentences are constructed the same way.

But look at the different ways this subordination is realized and look at the different ways the relationship between the two thoughts is being expressed. In sentence (1), the relationship is strictly temporal—they were seen, then they were frightened. And it's very possible that they were seen and frightened at the same time for some length of time. Like this:

they were seen —————————>

    they were frightened ——————>

In sentence (2), by contrast, the relationship is expressly causal—being seen made them fear. Hence the subordinating conjunction *because* is used to tell you explicitly that the action in the subordinate clause *caused* the action in the main clause.

Now look at (3). Does the subordinating conjunction *since* express a chronological or causal relationship? The truth is, it can be indicating both! Let's look at the subordinating conjunction *since* more closely. In these examples, *since* is used temporally: *Since your children were such monsters at the party, Krusty the Klown is charging double his normal fee; Since you called yesterday, I've been busy cleaning the house.*

The first example shows *since* in its causal sense; the second example shows it in the chronological sense. But often you can't tell in which way you ought to understand a *since* in a sentence; and often it has to be taken in both senses at the same time.

In sentence (3) above, clearly, it has to be understood in both senses, because both are accurate descriptions of what happened. The sailors were seen and *then* they were frightened (they weren't frightened until after they were seen); but, just as well, the sailors were frightened *because* they were seen. It's maddening, sometimes. Look at these examples where *since* could be expressing a causal, temporal, or both a causal *and* temporal subordination: *Since the town of Hootersville had grown so much, no one could book a room at the Shadey Rest Hotel; Since you came yesterday, our peaceful home has been reduced to near anarchy.*

Let's have a look at sentence (4) from above. As you can see, the same subordination is present. The main idea is still that the sailors were terrified; and the fact that they were seen by Polyphemus is attached to it. In this sentence, however, this latter idea is put into a relative clause—*who were seen by Polyphemus.* That is, it is presented simply as additional information about something in the main clause, as an adjectival clause.

Now what about translating the Latin participle? As I said at the beginning of this section, English likes to nail down the precise logical and temporal relationships between subordinate and main clauses in its sentences. It accomplishes this with a wide array of subordinating conjugations. Latin, however, isn't so fussy about stating these relationships precisely. All the sentences (1) through (4) could be represented by one Latin sentence: **Nautae, vîsî[55] ab Polyphêmô, territî sunt.** The participial phrase **vîsî ab Polyphêmô** could be translated into English different ways.

Nautae	vîsî ab Polyphêmô	territî sunt
The sailors	having been seen by Polyphemus	were terrified.
	who were seen by Polyphemus	
	because they were seen by Polyphemus	
	since they were seen by Polyphemus	
	after they were seen by Polyphemus	
	when they were seen by Polyphemus	
	although they were seen by Polyphemus[56]	

This is the moral: one way to bring a Latin participle into English is to *promote* it from a single word to a full subordinate clause, one that mixes well with the context. Try your hand at some of the examples in Wheelock's Self-Help Tutorials, and use a variety of subordinating English constructions. Watch the tenses of the main verb and the *relative tense* of the participles.

The Participle as a Noun

There isn't really anything shocking about this. You've seen adjectives used as nouns before. You simply noted the number and the gender, and then plugged in an appropriate pronoun. The participle, since it's an adjective, can do the same thing. The trick is to find a good way to bring the verbal part of the participle out. A simple solution, for starters, is to *promote* it to a relative clause which captures the meaning, tense, and voice of the verbal root of the participle.

Participle	Substantive
opprimêns	*he/she/it who oppresses* or *the oppressor*
opprimentês	*they who oppress* or *the oppressors*
oppressus	*he who was oppressed*
oppressî	*they who were oppressed* or *the oppressed*
oppressûrî	*those who are going to oppress*

The Active Participle Taking Objects

We mustn't ever forget that the participle is a *verbal* adjective, and it always retains its verbal character. The verb **laudô** takes a direct object to complete its

---

[55]Confused by this ending? Don't be. The word **nauta** is masculine despite being a first declension noun. This fact also explains the gender of the participle.

[56]This possibility doesn't make much sense in this example, but, grammatically at least, it's possible.

sense when it's being used in the active voice: **Rômânî ducês bonôs laudâvêrunt**, *the Romans praised the good leaders.* Similarly, when the participle derived from it is in the active voice, it also can take a direct object: **Rômânî *ducês bonôs laudantês* virtûtem amâvêrunt**, *the Romans, who praised good leaders, loved virtue.*

Tense of the Participles

This feature of the Latin participle may be the most difficult for students to comprehend. You know that participles have three different tenses: the present, the future, and the perfect. The present participle indicates an action that is on going; the future, an action that is going to happen, and the perfect, an action that has been completed. But a Latin participle only shows time *relative* to the tense of the main verb of the sentence. Participles only indicate whether an action

(1) Is going on at the same time as the action of the main verb—the present participle.

(2) Will occur after the action of the main verb—the future participle.

(3) Was already completed before the action of the main verb—the perfect participle.

To keep things simple, we refer to these temporal relationships as

(1) Time contemporaneous: the present participle.

(2) Time subsequent: the future participles.

(3) Time prior: the perfect participle.

Therefore, the participle **ductus** does not mean that the action happened in the absolute past, but that it happened before the action of the main verb. If the main verb is in the future tense, then the action of **ductus** might not have happened yet in absolute time. Similarly, the participle **ducêns** does not mean that the action is going on in the real present, but that the action is going on at the same time as the main verb. Therefore, if the main verb is a past tense, the action of **ducêns** may have already been completed by the time the sentence is uttered. And so also for the future participle. The future participle indicates that, relative to the time of the main verb, the action in the participle has yet to take place. **Ductûrus**, therefore, may represent an action that by the time of the real present has already been completed, if the main verb of the sentence was a past tense. Let's study a couple of examples of this problem.

Puellae, vocâtae â patre, ad campum reveniunt

Okay, the participle is perfect, and the main verb is present. So we could translate the sentence, *the girls, since they were called by their father, are returning to the field.* Simple. Now let's change the tense of the verb and see what we have.

Puellae, vocâtae â patre, ad campum revenient

Now the main verb is future, and the participle, being perfect, show time prior to that. So we would translate it, *the girls, when they are called by their father, will return to the field.* Do you see what we did? The participle now shows time prior to a future event, so it has to be handled differently.

Puellae, vocâtae â patre, ad campum revênêrunt

Now we have a main verb in the perfect tense. We might translate the sentence, *the girls, since they had been called by their father, returned to the field.* Now the participle is translated as if it were a pluperfect, and that's because it's showing time prior to another past event—revenêrunt—and that's exactly what the pluperfect tense does.

Okay. Now let's examine a few more such examples that mix the tenses. Remember, the translations offered for each sentence are only one among several approaches. Watch how a change of the tense of the main verb necessitates a change in the way the participle has to be translated.

Puellae ad campum currentês patrem vident, *the girls who are running to the field see their father.*

Puellae ad campum currentês patrem vîdêrunt, *the girls who were running to the field saw their father.*

Puellae ad campum currentês patrem vidêbunt, *the girls who run to the field will see their father.*

Puellae hâs litterâs scriptûrae patrem vocant, *the girls who are going to write this letter are calling their father.*

Puellae hâs litterâs scriptûrae patrem vocâvêrunt, *the girls who were going to write this letter called their father.*

Puellae hâs litterâs scriptûrae patrem vocâbunt, *the girls who will write this letter will call their father.*

SYNOPSIS

Have any place to go? If not, read on for a while. If so, come back to this section sometime soon. Now that you have the complete picture of participles, your notion of a synopsis of a verb needs updating. Now you can be expected to include a survey of the participles. It's customary just to leave the participles in the nominative, masculine or neuter singular. Fill out the synopsis as instructed.

Audiô, -îre, audîvî, audîtus 3rd person , sing. neuter

FINITE FORMS

	Active	Passive
Present	audit	audītur
Future	audiet	audiētur
Imperfect	audiēbat	audiēbātur
Perfect	audīvit	audītum est
Pluperfect	audīverat	audītum erat
Future Perfect	audīverit	audītum erit

PARTICIPLES

	Active	Passive
Future	audītūrum	audiendum
Present	audiēns	
Perfect		audītum

VOCABULARY PUZZLES

Aliquis, aliquid This pronoun means *somebody, something, some people, some things*. It has two parts: the **ali-** and the **quis, quid** part. It is very easy to decline this pronoun because it follows the pattern set by the interrogative pronoun **quis, quid**. The one difference is the nominative and accusative plurals, which are **aliqua** and not the expected **aliquae**.

24

Ablative Absolute; Passive Periphrastic; Dative of Agent

REVIEW OF PARTICIPLES

As you learned in the last chapter, a participle is a verbal adjective. The formation of participles from the different verbal stems obeys a few, very regular rules. Let's run through them again. Write out the formulae for forming the different participles (Wheelock 147, and notice that the table in the text arranges the tenses differently from the way I do!).

	Active	Passive
Future	stem(4ᵗʰ) + ūr + us, a, um	stem (2ᵈ) + nd + us, a, um [57]
Present	stem(2ᵈ) + ns, -ntis	—
Perfect	—	4ᵗʰ p.p. + us, -a, -um

As you can see, all the participles except the present active use the **-us, -a, -um** adjectival endings, and so present no problem in their declensions. The present active participle, however, declines in the third declension, and behaves like a third declension adjective of one termination of the **-ns, -ntis** type, with the exception of the short **-e-** in place of the **-i-** in the ablative singular. If you're a little squishy on this, go back to Chapter 23 now and review!

THE ABLATIVE ABSOLUTE

You remember from Chapter 23 that Latin isn't so fussy as English is about spelling out the exact temporal or logical relationship between a subordinate and main clause. In English, we have a bumper crop of subordinating conjunctions for this purpose: *since, because, although, if, even if, if and only if, being as how, seeing as how, before, after, during, while, inasmuch as, who*, and on and on. Latin has many of these conjunctions, too, but, always aiming at compression and economy, Latin has a tendency to reduce subordinate thoughts to participles. A very popular way of linking two separate ideas without spelling out the exact relationship they have to each other is the *ablative absolute* construction. Let's look at both parts of the description *ablative* and *absolute*.

---

[57] You remember that we didn't work with this participle in the last chapter because the future passive participle, the gerundive, very often is used in a special, idiomatic construction. You'll learn about it in this chapter.

Absolute

We call a subordinate clause *absolute* when it stands entirely outside of the grammar of the main clause and contains no finite verb. We have a common *absolute* construction in English, which we call the *nominative absolute.* Watch:

The door being open, all the flies in the neighborhood could get in.

The key having been lost, I couldn't move the car out of the way of the bulldozer.

That said, we now turn Mr. Vane's portion of this evening's program.

All other things being equal, the procedures are identical.

The first clause in each of these sentences is simply stating a fact that is given as a circumstance under which the action of the main clause takes place. And none of the absolute constructions has a finite verb. Obviously there is a logical or temporal relationship between the absolute clauses and the main clauses in each of these sentences; and you could easily recast the sentences to make them explicit. For example:

Because the door was open ...

Because the key was lost ...

Now that that has been said ...

If all other things are equal ...

But the speaker has chosen to keep the relationship unstated or implicit. For that reason, the verb is left as a participle and—this is important—the participle is not attached to anything in main clause. For example, let's rewrite the original absolute construction in *The key having been lost, I couldn't move the car out of the way of the bulldozer* to *Having lost my key, I couldn't move the car out of the way of the bulldozer.* Now the participle agrees with something in the main clause—*I*—and the act of losing the key is specifically attributed to *I* and not left ambiguous. In the original sentence, the speaker may or may not have been the one who lost the key. It may have been lost by someone else. But in the rewritten version, the guilty party is identified: *I* lost the key. An absolute construction doesn't do that.

So here are two things to remember about clauses that are absolute: (1) the verb is a participle and (2) it agrees with something in the absolute clause, not in the main clause of the sentence.

Ablative

Now for the *ablative* part of the construction called the *ablative absolute.* Just as the word *ablative* tells you, in Latin the participle and the noun it agrees with are both in the ablative case. For example: **Hâc fâmâ nârrâtâ, dûx urbem sine morâ relîquit.** In this sentence, the main clause is **dûx ... relîquit.** The ablative absolute clause is **hâc fâmâ nârrâtâ.** The verb of the clause is the participle **nârrâtâ,** which in turn agrees with the ablative **hâc fâmâ.**

So how do we translate the ablative absolute clause into English? As always, let's start with the roughest, but most accurate, way. The quickest way to translate an ablative absolute clause is to use the preposition *with,* followed by the noun, and then the participle in its correct tense and voice: *with this story having been told.* So this sentence would come out: *With this story having been told, the leader left the city without delay.*

Try your hand at a couple more sentences: **Cane currente, equus magnô cum timôre campum relîquit,** *with the dog running, the horse left the field with great fear;* **Equô cursûrô, canis magnô cum timôre campum relîquit,** *with the horse about to run, the dog left the field with great fear.*

As you can see, the relationship between the clauses of these sentences is clear enough, even though it's unstated. In the first sentence, perhaps we could say, *Because the dog was running, the horse left the field.* That is, the horse has some fear of running dogs. In the second, the dog doesn't like running horses, so when it realized that the horse was going to run, it ran away: *Because the horse was going to run, the dog left the field.*

One last item about the ablative absolute clause is that when the participle is in the active voice, it can be followed by objects of its own which are not in the ablative case. That is to say, not every word in the ablative absolute clause has to be in the ablative case. Only the noun and the participle agreeing with it are necessarily ablative; the rest of the ablative absolute clause will follow the normal rules of Latin grammar. For example: **Rêge haec dîcente, omnês cîvês terrêbantur,** *with the king saying these things, all the citizens were terrified.*

The ablative absolute clause in this sentence is **rêge haec dîcente**, as you can see by looking at the cases of **rêge** and **dîcente** and by recognizing that the verb of the clause is in the participial mood. These are the two parts of an ablative absolute clause: noun and participle in the ablative case. But what about **haec**? Why is it in the accusative case if it's in an ablative absolute clause? The answer is that **haec** is the direct object of the action of the participle **dîcente**; and direct objects are always in the accusative case, regardless of the mood or construction of the verb. Remember, once you have a noun—**rêge**—and a participle—**dîcente**—in the ablative case, you have an ablative absolute construction. Everything else in the clause is simply additional material which follows the predictable rules of Latin grammar. Study a few more examples:

Bonîs virîs imperium tenentibus, rês pûblica valêbit, *with good men holding power, the republic will be strong.*

Cîvibus patriam amantibus, possumus magnam spem habêre, *with the citizens loving the fatherland, we are able to have great hope.*

Hîs rêbus gravibus ab ôrâtôre dictîs, omnis cupiditâs pecûniae expulsa est, *with these serious matters having been said by the orator, all longing for money was driven out.*

THE ABLATIVE ABSOLUTE WITH THE VERB "BEING"

The ablative absolute construction, as you now know, is made up of a noun and a participle agreeing with it in the ablative case. This brings up an interesting problem with the verb **sum**, which has no present participle. How would you say, for example, *The king being good, the people were happy*? The clause you would turn into the ablative absolute contains the present participle *being*, but Latin has no translation for it. In occasions like this, Latin simply leaves the participle out and uses the noun in the ablative case with the adjective agreeing with it: **Rêge bonô, populus beâtus erat**. So if you see a clause set off with commas containing a noun and adjective in the ablative case without a participle, just plug in our participle *being*.

ABLATIVE ABSOLUTE: TRANSLATIONS

Still with me? Just one more thing about the ablative absolute. The literal translation of ablative absolutes—*having.., with . . .*, etc.—makes for some hellish English. A translation is not complete until we've rendered a thought from one language into the target language in a smooth, fluent expression that wouldn't surprise or annoy a native speaker. We have to massage ablative absolutes a little to get them into English.

Because the ablative absolute is essentially a participial construction, the same rules that applied to translating participles will apply to translating the ablative absolute. That is:

(1) The ablative absolute shows time *relative* to the time of the verb of the main clause—future participles show time subsequent, present participles show time contemporaneous, perfect participles show time prior.

(2) The exact logical relationship between the main clause and the ablative absolute has to be reconstructed from the context and expressed by one of our subordinating conjunctions: *because, since, after, although, if, inasmuch as,* and so on.

Recognizing an ablative absolute clause in a Latin sentence and plugging in the *with* to bring it into English is only the first step in translation. Next you might like to *promote* the participial clause into a subordinate clause with a finite verb (a verb with person) and decide on the most likely subordinating conjunction. Obviously, this is going to involve some judgment on your part, since the possible subordinating conjunctions have very different meanings. For example, here are two possible translations of this Latin sentence: **Cîvibus patriam amantibus, possumus magnam spem habêre.**

(1) *Because* the citizens love the fatherland, we are able to have great hope.

(2) *Although* the citizens love the fatherland, we are able to have great hope.

The meaning of (1) and (2) are flatly contradictory; (1) is saying that it's a good thing for citizens to love the fatherland, but (2) says that it's not. Both are possible translations of the Latin sentence. You must first examine the general intention of the author as it appears in the context of his writing before you can translate this sentence into meaningful English. It'll take some practice and patience.

The relationship of tenses should present you little difficulty—your natural instincts will serve you well. But one item should be mentioned. As you know, a perfect participle shows time prior to the time of the verb in the main clause. If therefore, the participle in the ablative absolute is perfect, and if the tense of the main verb is one of the past tenses—imperfect, perfect, or pluperfect—then how should you translate the participle when you promote it to a finite verb?

Think about it a moment. If the perfect participle is showing time prior to another past event, then what finite tense should you use? The tense which shows time prior to another past event is the pluperfect tense, so you should choose the pluperfect tense to represent the perfect participle of the ablative absolute clause.

Like this: **Omnibus bonîs cîvibus ex urbe expulsîs, tyrannus imperium accêpit,** *when all the good citizens had been expelled from the city, the tyrant took power.*

Take a few minutes now do sentences 8-10, 12, 14-17, 22, and 25 from Wheelock's Self-Tutorial (pages 378-9). First analyze the sentence literally, then smooth it over into English you'd expect to hear in civil conversation.

THE PASSIVE PERIPHRASTIC; DATIVE OF AGENT

As I warned you in the last chapter, Latin has an idiomatic use of the future passive participle. If the future passive participle is linked to the subject with a form of the verb **sum**, it takes on a sense of obligation or necessity. When it is used this way, we call the future passive participle a *gerundive* (geh RUHN div). Do you remember the future passive participle? Let's review its formation for a moment. You form the future passive participle this way: 1st principal part[58] + nd + -us, -a, -um. Latin uses this participle as a predicate adjective, linked to the subject of a conjugated form of the verb **sum**, to express obligation or necessity. This construction is called the *passive periphrastic* (peh ri FRAS tik). What do you say we go over it again?

(1) The construction links a participle with the subject through a form of the verb **sum**. Since participles are verbal *adjectives,* the participle—the gerundive—will agree in number, gender, and case with the subject to which it is linked. That is, the gerundive modifies the subject of the verb **sum**.

(2) Because the gerundive is the future *passive* participle, this construction will always be in the passive voice. That is, the construction will always be saying what should *be* done.

(3) When the passive periphrastic construction expresses the person/agent who should be performing the action, the agent is put into the dative case, not, as is normal for the passive voice, into the ablative of personal agent: **ab** + ablative.

---

[58]Remember, that for the third, third i-stem, and fourth conjugations, the stem vowel is lengthened.

Now let's look at a couple of simple examples of the passive periphrastic:

Carthâgô delenda est.

Carthâgô (**Carthâgô, -inis**, f., *Carthage*) is the subject and is feminine; so the gerundive, **dêlenda** (from **dêleô**, *to destroy*) agrees with it. A literal translation, therefore, would be *Carthage is to be destroyed.* Some acceptable variations may be: *Carthage ought to be destroyed, Carthage should be destroyed, Carthage has to be destroyed, Carthage must be destroyed.* Each of these translations has a different flavor in English, but they are all legitimate renderings of the Latin **Carthâgô dêlenda est**.

Carthâgô nôbîs dêlenda est.

What about the **nôbîs**? It is in the dative case, so it is expressing the agent of the passive construction. So we should add to our translation *by us. Carthage is to be (should be, ought to be, has to be, must be) destroyed by us.* Written English tries to be parsimonious of the passive voice; so a final translation of the passive periphrastic might be a conversion to the active voice: *We are to (must, ought to, should, have to) destroy Carthage.*

Haec puella meô fîliô amanda est.

This girl is to be (ought to be, should be, must be, has to be) loved by my son. Or, if you want to invert the voice and put it into the active voice *My son is to (must, ought to, should, has to) love this girl.*

Haec omnibus agenda sunt.

These things are to be (must be, ought to be, should be, have to be) done by everyone. Or *Everyone is to (must, ought to, should, has to) do these things.*

Finally, the conjugated form of **sum** can be in any of the tenses—naturally—so the translation has to reflect the different tenses. Watch:

Haec omnibus agenda erunt, *everyone <u>will have</u> to do these things.*

Haec omnibus agenda erant, *everyone <u>had</u> to do these things.*

VOCABULARY PUZZLES

quisque, quidque The inflected part of the word comes before the suffix **-que**. This is the interrogative **quis, quid** + the suffix; so you already know how it is declined. It means *each one*, so obviously should have no plural forms—and it doesn't until after Classical Latin. And that's not your concern for now.

25

Infinitives; Indirect Statement

TENSES OF THE INFINITIVE: MORPHOLOGY

What are infinitives again? They're the form of the verb you've been translating with our word *to* followed by the meaning of the verb. Until this chapter, you've known infinitives only in the active and passive voice of the present tense. That's about to change. Let's set out the formulae for all the infinitives you're going to study in this chapter, then we'll work with each in more detail. Here we go:

	Active	**Passive**
Future:	fut. act. part. esse	[supine + irî]
Present:	1st prin. part. + re	1st princ. part + rî *or* 1st princ. part + î
Perfect:	3rd princ. part + isse	4th princ. part esse

Future Active Infinitive

Do you remember how to form the future active participle? You use the fourth principle part + **ûr** + the adjectival endings **-us, -a, -um**. (If you're shaky on this, go back to Chapter 23 for a reminder.) The future active infinitive is formed by using the future active participle of the verb with the infinitive of the verb **esse**. So the future active infinitive of the verb **laudô** will be **laudâtûrus (-a, -um) esse**.[59]

Translating the future active infinitive is a little tricky, however, because we have no simple future active infinitive in English. Two common suggestions—clumsy though they are—will at least help you rough out the Latin until you can polish up the translation: try *to be about to x* or *to be going to x*. So **laudâtûrum esse** can be translated *to be about to* (or *to be going to*) *praise*.

Future Passive Infinitive

This infinitive is put in brackets because it's rare in Latin and won't come up in your work this year, nor in the next most likely. The Romans, apparently, didn't particularly care for it either. If they found themselves in a construction that would have required it, they found a way out of it. If it annoyed the Romans themselves, surely we can skip it.

---

[59]When an infinitive form includes a participle, grammars conventionally list the participle in the neuter, accusative singular. So this would be written as **laudâtûr*um* esse**. It is important for you to remember, however, that the participle can actually be in a number of different cases and numbers and genders in a sentence. Because it is an adjective, the participle must agree in number, gender, and case with whatever is on the other side of the verb **esse**. You'll see how this works later in the chapter.

Present Active and Passive Infinitives

These are the infinitives you've been working with all along. No special explanation should be needed. Remember, though, that the passive infinitives of the first, second, and fourth conjugations are formed by adding -**rî** to the stem; but the third conjugation deletes the stem vowel and replaces it with a single long -**î**: **capiô capî**, *to be taken.*

Perfect Active Infinitive

The perfect active infinitive is a new form for you: the third principal part with the ending -**isse** attached. So the perfect infinitive of the verb **laudô** is **laudâvisse**. The literal translation of a perfect infinitive is *to have x,* where *x* is the participle of the English verb. Hence **laudâvisse** can be translated *to have praised.*

Perfect Passive Infinitive

This infinitive, like the future active infinitive, is made up of a participle followed by the infinitive of the verb **sum**. The translation for starters is *to have been xed.* Hence **laudâtum**[60] **esse** may be rendered *to have **been** praised.*

DRILLS

Fill in the infinitives for the following paradigm verbs.

amô (1)

	Active	Passive
Future	amātūrum esse	
Present	amāre	amārī
Perfect	amāvisse	amātum esse

habeô (2), habuî, habitus, -a, -um

	Active	Passive
Future	habitūrum esse	
Present	habēre	habērī
Perfect	habuisse	habitum esse

---

[60] The -**um** ending on the participle is there merely as a placeholder. It will not always be the case that the participle will be neuter accusative singular. Don't confuse this adjectival ending with the infinitive itself.

dûcô (3), dûxî, ductus, -a, -um

	Active	Passive
Future	ductūrum esse	
Present	dūcere	dūcī
Perfect	dūxisse	ductus esse

capiô (3), cêpî, captus, -a, -um

	Active	Passive
Future	captūrum esse	
Present	capere	capī
Perfect	cēpisse	captum esse

audiô (4), audîvî, audîtus, -a, -um

	Active	Passive
Future	audītūrum esse	
Present	audīre	audīrī
Perfect	audīvisse	audītum esse

THE IDEA OF INDIRECT STATEMENT

So now that you know the whole spread of infinitives, what are they good for? One very common use of the infinitive in Latin is in a construction we call indirect statement. I'll explain. So far all the sentences you've been working with in Latin have been in direct speech. In a direct statement, the author casts the thought in a sentence and addresses it directly to the audience. In an indirect statement, a thought is treated as the object of a verb, and the thought is being reported to the audience. The difference between direct and indirect speech is a little difficult to describe completely, but a couple of examples of each may give you a feel for it. In English, we frequently precede the reported thought, the *indirect statement*, with the conjunction *that*, or we may omit it.

Direct	Indirect
She saw her friend.	They told me *(that) she saw her friend.*
The movie was terrible.	He said *(that) the movie was terrible.*
I've had just about enough.	I do believe *(that) I've had just about enough.*

Do you see? On the left, a statement is made directly. On the right, the same statement is reported by another verb. If you analyze these sentences, you see that they are complex sentences (having a main and a subordinate clause). The verb that introduces the indirect statement is the main verb, and the indirect statement, which is treated as an object of the main verb, is the subordinate clause.[61] There are many ways that indirect statements can be initiated, and, naturally enough, most all imply some kind of mental activity or speaking or perceiving: verbs like *to think [that]*, *to say [that]*, *to hear [that]*, *understand [that]*, *to suppose [that]* ... In short, there are dozens of verbs which can introduce an indirect statement; and it would be futile to try to memorize them all outright. Just use your common sense. If a verb is a *head verb*—if it implies mental activity or speaking or sensing—then it can be followed by an indirect statement.

Next point. In English, an indirect statement often doesn't differ at all from the form of the original statement. We just put a *that* in front of the original statement if we feel like it, and away we go. There are some places where we do alter the form of the original statement, and we'll study them later in this chapter. But for now, English mostly leaves the original statement alone and just inserts it as a subordinate clause into another sentence.

THE ACCUSATIVE-INFINITIVE CONSTRUCTION

Latin considerably alters the original statement when it becomes indirect. Two things happen: (1) The subject of the original statement, which is in the nominative case, becomes accusative; (2) The original finite verb (the verb which has person: first, second, or third) becomes an infinitive. We often call this the accusative-infinitive construction, because the infinitive has a subject which is in the accusative case. Study a couple of examples:

	Puella	cum	amîcô	venit	*the girl is coming with her friend.*
		↓		↓	
audiô	puellam	cum	amîcô	venîre	*I hear that the girl is coming with her friend.*

	Amîcî	meî	nôs	adiuvâbunt	*My friends will help us.*
		↓		↓	
putô	amîcôs	meôs	nôs	adiutûrôs esse	*I think that my friends will help us.*

---

[61]In English, we can report a statement by quoting it directly, word for word. In this case, we use quotations marks. For example, *He said, "We're tired of this."* This is not indirect speech, in which the reported speech is subordinated to the main clause of the sentence. This example in an indirect statement would be, *He said that they were tired of this*, with no quotation marks around the reported speech. Notice also the change in person in the indirect statement. He didn't say originally *they* ... he said *We* ... Do you see why that change was necessary?

The literal translation of the first sentence would be *I hear the girl **to be coming***, and we could make sense of that if we heard someone say it in English. In fact, sometimes English can form indirect statements by using this accusative-infinitive construction. For example, you'd have no trouble understanding this: *We think him to be a scoundrel*. The original statement behind this is *He is a scoundrel*, which then becomes *him to be a scoundrel* after the verb that introduces the thought as an indirect statement. The difference is that in English we sometimes have the option of choosing the construction we'll use, but Latin from the period you're studying had only one construction for indirect statement: the accusative-infinitive construction.

In the second example, the original finite verb was in the future tense active, so the infinitive of the indirect statement will also have to be future active. The formula for this infinitive is the future active participle plus the infinitive of the verb **sum**. Please remember that a participle is a verbal *adjective*, so it has to agree with something. Now, look at the ending of the participle **adiutûrôs**. Why does it have this ending? Think.[62]

There is one more item you need to know before we can pause and try some exercises. As you know, because Latin verbs have personal endings, it's not always necessary to have a subject pronoun expressed in the sentence. We simply look at the personal ending on the verb and insert the correct personal pronoun in our English translation. For example:

Meôs amîcôs laudô, *I am praising my friends.*

Meôs amîcôs laudâs, *you are praising my friends.*

Meôs amîcôs laudat, *he is praising my friends.*

Meôs amîcôs laudâmus, *we are praising my friends.*

Meôs amîcôs laudâtis, *you are praising my friends.*

Meôs amîcôs laudant, *they are praising my friends.*

This shouldn't cause you any anxiety. You've been supplying personal pronouns for twenty-four chapters, and by now it's probably second nature for you. You probably don't even notice any longer that you're doing it. But now we have a problem. In an indirect statement, there has to be a subject of the infinitive expressed in the sentence, and that's because infinitives have no personal endings. In other words, an original direct statement could be **Haec dîxit**, *he said these things*. But you can't make it indirect simply by putting the verb into the infinitive: **Audîvî haec dîxisse**. That's because there's no subject or person in the infinitive. What to do?

The solution is really quite simple. You use the accusative case of the personal pronoun which is indicated by the original personal ending on the verb. Like this: **Audîvî eum haec dîxisse**. Do you see what happened? Basically, you rethought the original sentence **Haec dîxit**, and imagined what it would have looked like if there had been a personal pronoun expressed. In this case, it would have been **is**,

---

[62]It's modifying the accusative plural subject of the verb **esse**.

from the third person pronoun **is, ea, id**. And then you made that accusative to complete the accusative-infinitive construction. Study a few variations on this:

Direct Statement		Indirect Statement
Meôs amîcôs laudat	→	Dîcô **eum** meôs amîcôs **laudâre**.
Meôs amîcôs laudâmus	→	Dîcô **nôs** meôs amîcôs **laudâre**.
Meôs amîcôs laudâtis	→	Dîcô **vôs** meôs amîcôs **laudâre**.
Meôs amîcôs laudant	→	Dîcô **eôs** meôs amîcôs **laudâre**.

You can see that all indirect statements *must* have the subject accusative expressed. The infinitive, by its nature, doesn't contain person, so it alone can't tell you its subject. You must have **mê, tê**, etc. or some accusative subject expressed in an indirect statement. Next, are you wondering about the accusative **meôs amîcôs** in the sentences above? You may be wondering how you can tell which accusative is the subject of the infinitive and which is its object, since Latin word order is generally very flexible. That is, what's to keep the first sentence from meaning: *I say that my friends are praising* **me**. Here is one place where word order is very important in Latin. The normal word order in an indirect statement is this:

Subject-Accusative	Direct Object Accusative	Infinitive
mê	amîcôs meôs	laudâre

It usually is the case that the first word in the indirect statement is the subject accusative. The next accusative, if there is one, will be the direct object of the verb in the infinitive.

DRILLS

Change the following direct statements into indirect statements. Remember: (1) the original subject nominative becomes the subject accusative; (2) the original finite verb becomes the infinitive; (3) where there is no subject expressed, you must use the appropriate pronoun in the accusative case.

1.		Veniunt cum amîcîs tuîs.
	Putô	eôs cum amîcîs tuîs venîre.
2.		Hoc signum Caesarî dandum est.
	Putô	hoc signum Caesarî dandum esse.
3.		Spês novârum rêrum mollibus sententiîs alitur.
	Putô	spêm novârum rêrum mollibus sententiîs alî.

4.		Tyrannus multâs copiâs in mediam urbem dûcit.
	Putô	tyrannum multās cupiās in mediam urbem dūcere.
5.		Illa puella dôna multa patrî dat.
	Putô	illam puellam dōna multa patrī dare.

TENSES OF INFINITIVES: RELATIVE TENSE

Now that you've mastered the basics of the Latin indirect statement, it's time for some refinement. Earlier I said that English generally leaves the form of the direct statement alone when it becomes an indirect statement. English often simply subordinates the original statement to a *head verb* with, or without, the conjunction *that*, without changing the original statement at all. But this is not always true. Sometimes we do change the form of the original statement when it becomes an indirect statement.

Let's assume that someone says *I am coming*, and that you wish to report what he said to someone else. You would say, *He says that he is coming*. Except for the natural change in person, you haven't changed the form of the original direct statement at all. But suppose that he said this yesterday. That is, yesterday he said, *I am coming*. To report this statement as an indirect statement, you would say, *He said that he **was** coming*. Here English lets some of the past tense of the main verb of the sentence—*said*—infect the original direct statement: *am coming* is changed to *was coming*. He didn't say *I was coming*, rather he said *I am coming*. But because the leading verb is past tense—*he said*—English makes the original statement a past tense, too, although logically it shouldn't because it distorts what was actually said. What is worse, it introduces the possibility for ambiguity. What did he really say? Did he say *I **am** coming*, or did he really say *I was coming*? You can't tell from the sentence *He said that he was coming*.

Let's change the example slightly. Suppose he is now saying, *I will come*. You would report this as *He says that he will come*. No problem. But suppose he said *I will come* yesterday. You would report his statement as *He said that he **would** come*. Once again, you can see that English changes the form of the original statement when it becomes indirect. Here, when a statement referring to the future is reported as a past event, the original simple future becomes the conditional. It's a great big mess. In Latin there is none of this nonsense.

First you have to recognize something about the tenses of the infinitives in Latin: like the tenses of participles, the tenses of infinitives are not absolute, but are only relative to the tense of the leading verb—the verb that is introducing the indirect statement.

Think of it this way. The future tense of a finite verb depicts an action which has not yet occurred, but a future infinitive depicts an action which occurs after the action of the leading verb. The present tense of a finite verb depicts an action which is currently going on, but the present infinitive depicts an action that is going on at the same time as the leading verb. And, finally, the perfect tense (or any of the past tenses) of a finite verb depicts an action that has already occurred, but the perfect infinitive depicts an action which occurs before the leading verb. To simplify this we say that a present infinitive shows time contemporaneous, a future infinitive shows time subsequent, and a perfect infinitive shows time prior. Let's look at several examples of this:

Putô eum venîre.

Here the tense of the infinitive in the indirect statement is present, so it is showing time contemporaneous with the time of the leading verb **putô**. This means that I think that he is coming now (while I'm thinking). We may translate the sentence, therefore, *I think that he is coming*.

Putô eum ventûrum[63] esse.

Now the tense of the infinitive is future, showing time subsequent to the action of the leading verb. This means that I am thinking now that he will come— not that he is coming but that he will come. So we can translate the sentence *I think that he will come (or that he is going to come)*.

Putô eum vênisse.

The perfect infinitive shows time prior to the leading verb, so at the moment I'm thinking, the action I'm thinking about has already occurred. So the translation is *I think that he has come (or that he came)*.

Putâvî eum venîre.

Since the present infinitive shows time contemporaneous, this means that the sentence must be translated *I thought that he **was** coming*. Do you see why? **Venîre** shows time contemporaneous with the action of the leading verb, which is depicting a past event, so we have to translate the sentence into English to show this relationship. There is a problem, however, with the English translation. It's possible for our English translation, *I thought he was coming*, to mean two things. It could mean either that I was thinking about an event that was prior, or contemporaneous. *I thought he was coming* could mean that yesterday morning I thought he was coming the day before that. Or it could mean that yesterday morning I thought he was coming while I was thinking it. The trouble here is not with the Latin. As you can see, the indirect statement **eum venîre** doesn't change when we use a different tense of the leading verb. The problem is with our English representation of the Latin. **Putâvî eum venîre** can only mean the latter. I thought he was coming at the same time that I was thinking about it.

Putâvî eum ventûrum esse.

How are you going to translate this sentence? The future tense of the infinitive shows time subsequent (after) the time of the leading verb, and how do we do that

---

[63]Notice the number, gender, and case of the participle. Why is it accusative, masculine singular? Well, as a participle it agrees with something. Here it is agreeing with the subject accusative on the other side of the verb **esse**. Since **eum** is accusative, masculine, singular, the participle must be too. If, on the other hand, we were saying *I think that **she** will come*, then the Latin would have been **Putô eam ventûram esse**.

in English? We say *I thought that he* **would** *come.* Here's another instance where the form of the original statement is changed in English. From what I was thinking originally—*he will come*—the indirect statement becomes *he would come.*

Putâvî eum vênisse.

The translation is *I thought that he* **had** *come.* Can you explain why? This actually can get a little sticky in English, because we tend to shy away from the pluperfect tense. We might just as possibly say *I thought that he* **was** *coming* when we mean that he was coming *before* I thought about it. In Latin, though, there is no chance for ambiguity. The perfect infinitive **vênisse** shows time prior to **putâvî**, and **putâvî** is already representing a past event. An event before another event in the past is represented by the pluperfect tense. Hence *I thought that he had come.*

THE THIRD PERSON REFLEXIVE PRONOUN IN INDIRECT STATEMENT

You're going to get plenty of chances to work with the indirect statement and the tenses of the infinitives soon, but there is one more item in the chapter we have to look at—although it's really quite simple. Consider the following sentence: *He said that he was a good leader.* Is there any way you can tell whether the sentence means *he said that he himself was a good leader,* or *he said that he [somebody else] was good leader?* You can't. This is the same problem we saw before with the third person pronoun: English has no convenient way to distinguish the reflexive from the non-reflexive third person pronoun. In Latin, however, the pronoun **is, ea, id** is always non-reflexive, and the pronoun **suî, sibi, sê, sê** is reflexive. Consequently, *He said that he [somebody else] was a good leader* is **Dîxit eum dûcem bonum esse**; and *He said that he [himself] was a good leader* is **Dîxit sê dûcem bonum esse.** Remember also that the reflexive pronoun doesn't show difference in number: **Dîxêrunt sê bonôs dûcês esse** is *They said that they [themselves] were good leaders.*

DRILLS

Now you try some on your own. Translate the verbs of the indirect statement, observing the correct tense sequences.

1.	Putâmus omnês bonôs virôs vîtâs beâtâs agere.		
	We think that all good men	*lead*	happy lives.
2.	Putâmus omnês bonôs virôs vîtâs beâtâs êgisse.		
	We think that all good men	*led*	happy lives.
3.	Putâmus omnês bonôs virôs vîtâs beâtâs actûrôs esse.		
	We think that all good men	*will lead*	happy lives.

4.	Putâvimus omnês bonôs virôs vîtâs beâtâs agere.		
	We thought that all good men	*were leading*	happy lives.
5.	Putâvimus omnês bonôs virôs vîtâs beâtâs êgisse.		
	We thought that all good men	*had lead*	happy lives.
6.	Putâvîmus omnês bonôs virôs beâtâs vîtâs actûrôs esse.		
	We thought that all good men	*would lead*	happy lives.

Now try it the other way. Fill in the correct tense of the infinitive in these sentences.

1.	We hear that you (*pl.*) are coming.	
	Audîmus vôs	venīre
2.	We hear that you (*pl.*) were coming.	
	Audîmus vôs	vēnisse.
3.	We hear that you will come.	
	Audîmus vôs	ventūrōs esse.
4.	We heard that you would come.	
	Audîvimus vôs	ventūrōs esse.
5.	I thought that you had written the letter.	
	Putâvî vôs litterâs	scrīpsisse.
6.	We thought that the letter had been written by you.	
	Putâvimus litterâs â vôbîs	scriptās esse.

VOCABULARY PUZZLES

ait, aiunt, *he, she says/ they say.* Its first and second persons don't appear in this book, and it's used only in its present tense forms.

spêrô (1) **Spêrô** takes its infinitive in indirect statement in the future tense. This makes sense, because you generally hope for something that is not now presently the case. *We hope to see our friends* comes over into Latin as *We hope that we will see our friends:* **Spêrâmus nôs amîcôs nostrôs vîsûrôs esse.**

26

Making Comparisons

DEGREES OF ADJECTIVES

Adjectives are words which attribute qualities to nouns. In Latin, adjectives must agree in number, gender, and case with what they are modifying. You have learned adjectives which decline in the first and second declensions, and those which decline in the third. But up to this chapter the adjectives you've studied attribute qualities to nouns in what is called the positive degree only. That is, they simply attach the quality to the noun. But adjectives can also attribute the quality in a way that compares the noun with other nouns by indicating that the noun has more of the quality than another noun, or that it has the most of the quality than at least two other nouns. We call these two other degrees the comparative (more of the quality) and the superlative (most of the quality).

In English, we form the comparative and superlative degrees of adjectives in two different ways. We use the adverbs *more* and *most*, and we use the suffixes *-er* and *-est* added to the base of the adjectives.[64] For example,

Positive Degree	Comparative Degree	Superlative Degree
blue skies	bluer skies	bluest skies
difficult book	more difficult book	most difficult book

For your concerns now, there is only one way to form the comparative and superlative degrees of adjectives in Latin, and that is by adding suffixes to the base of the adjectives. But Latin's an inflected language: its nouns, adjectives, and pronouns have case endings. This means that whatever you add to the end of an adjective to get the comparative or superlative degrees is also going to have to be able to decline. Here they come.

THE COMPARATIVE DEGREE OF ADJECTIVES

To form the comparative degree of an adjective, you add the ending **-ior**, **-ius** to its stem. The comparative suffix is a third declension ending and declines just like a normal *noun* of the third declension. This is a little odd, since you might expect the comparative suffix to decline like a third declension *adjective*. Let's look at the declension of this suffix. The masculine and feminine nominatives are **-ior**, and the neuter nominative is **-ius**. The stem of the ending is **-iôr-**. Decline the comparative adjectival suffix. Don't forget the rules of the neuter (Wheelock 172).

---

[64]If you trust the standard English grammars, we should use the adverbs *more* and *most* when the adjective has more than one syllable (polysyllabic), and we should use the suffixes **-er** and **-est** when the adjective has one syllable (monosyllabic). So the comparative of the adjective *just* is *juster*, but that doesn't sound right to me. Doesn't *more just* sound better?

	Masculine and Feminine	**Neuter**
N/V.	-ior	-ius
Gen.		
Dat.		
Acc.		
Abl.		
Plural		
N/V.		
Gen.		
Dat.		
Acc.		
Abl.		

How did you do? Do you see the patterns at work? The stem **-iôr-** plus the case endings from the third declension *non-i-stem*. These are the inflected endings you then attach to the stem of the adjectives. So to make any adjective comparative, regardless of its original declension—first and second, or third—you attach these endings to the stem of the adjective and then decline the adjective in the third declension. This is important to remember. As soon as an adjective is put into the comparative degree, it gets its case endings from the third declension, because that's how the comparative suffix declines. Let's look at some examples of this:

Adjective	**Stem**	**Comparative Degree**
beâtus, -a, -um (*happy*)	beât-	beâtior, -ius
fortis, -e (*strong*)	fort-	fortior, -ius
potêns, potentis (*powerful*)	potent-	potentior, -ius
clârus, -a, -um (*famous*)	clâr-	clârior, -ius
turpis, -e (*shameful*)	turp-	turpior, -ius
acerbus, -a, -um (*harsh*)	acerb-	acerbior, -ius
fêlix, -icis (*happy*)	fêlic-	fêlicior, -ius
sapiêns, -ntis (*wise*)	sapient-	sapientior, -iu

THE SUPERLATIVE DEGREE OF ADJECTIVES

The superlative degree of adjectives is even easier to form. It's simply the stem of the adjective plus the suffix **-issim-** plus the first and second declension adjectival endings **-us, -a, -um**. Hence all adjectives in the superlative degree decline like the simplest adjectives you know: the first and second declension types.

Adjective	Stem	Superlative Degree
beâtus, -a, -um	beât-	beâtissimus, -a, -um
fortis, -e	fort-	fortissimus, -a, -um
potêns, potentis	potent-	potentissimus, -a, -um

DRILL

Decline the following expressions. Here are the words you'll need: **sapiêns, -entis**, **cônsilium, -iî**, *n.*; **potêns, -entis, urbs, urbis**, *f.*

	wiser	plan	most powerful	city
N/V.				
Gen.				
Dat.				
Acc.				
Abl.				
Plural				
N/V.				
Gen.				
Dat.				
Acc.				
Abl.				

TRANSLATIONS OF THE COMPARATIVE AND SUPERLATIVE DEGREES

You may well wonder why we need to bother with how the degrees of the adjectives are translated. It's obvious that the comparative will be translated *more X* or *X-er* and that the superlative will be translated *most X* or *X-est*. And, in fact these are common ways of translating them into English. But often, very often, the comparative and superlative degrees are used *absolutely*; that is, without anything being directly compared to the quality depicted in the adjective. Hence the adjective **longior, -ius** can mean *longer*, if there's something being compared, or it can mean just *rather long* or *too long*, if there isn't anything being compared. Similarly, **longissimus, -a, -um**, can mean *longest*, or it can mean *very long* if it's being used absolutely.

THE USE OF THE ADVERB QUAM OR THE ABLATIVE OF COMPARISON

How does Latin directly compare two things? In English, we use the adverb *than*, as in *he's taller **than** I am.* Latin has two ways to do this. One is to put the thing being compared in the ablative case. So you'll see **beâtior mê est** for *he is happier than I.* Another way is to use a word that's like our word *than*, the adverb **quam**: **beâtior quam ego est.** That's easy. But what's hard about comparisons for us is that English, not being an inflected language, isn't very fussy about cases. Although we tend to slop over it in English, you must remember that in Latin the two things being compared must be in the same case. In the example I just gave, we might be tempted to say *he is happier than **me**,* and we probably *should* say *me* if we're in a situation when erudition might be the cause of some scorn or suspicion. But technically, because *he* is the point of comparison, and because *he* is in the nominative case, we should use *I* and not *me.* In Latin, the **quam** is like an equal sign: it requires the same case on each side of the comparison. Study these examples.

Sunt beâtiôrês quam ego, *they are happier than I.*

Ille est beâtior quam hic, *that man is happier than this man.*

Putô illôs esse beâtiôrês quam hôs, *I think that those men are happier than these men.*

Nêmô est stultior quam eî quî librôs numquam legunt, *no one is more foolish than those who never read books.*

Quam can also be used with an adjective in the superlative degree to mean *as X as possible.* In fact, sometimes the whole construction is written out like this: **quam *potest* longissimus**: *as long as is possible.*

THE POSSESSIVE PRONOUN

There is one other issue I'd like to take up, even though it's not in Wheelock. It causes students some confusion. Consider this sentence. *Our city is more illustrious than yours.* The final word in the sentence, *yours*, is standing in for *your city*: *Our city is more illustrious than your city.* But English has a way of simplifying the full construction by using a *possessive pronoun.* Check both words here: *pronoun*, meaning a word that stands in for another, and *possessive*, meaning a word that shows possession. The possessive pronouns in English for the different numbers and persons are: *mine, ours, yours, his, hers, its, theirs.*

Latin has no equivalent of the possessive pronoun, which we find so useful. Instead, it uses the possessive adjective in the number and gender of the noun which has been omitted, and in the case required by the construction of the sentence. Like this:

Vênî cum amîcîs meîs; ille vênit cum **suîs**, *I came with my friends; that man came with his.*

Nostra cîvitâs est clarior quam **vestra**, *our city is more illustrious than yours.*

Mea mâter est sapientior quam **tua**, *my mother is wiser than yours.*

VOCABULARY PUZZLES

quîdam, quaedam, quiddam or **quoddam** This word is an inflected form of the relative pronoun **quî, quae, quod** with an indeclinable suffix **-dam** attached. It has a set of closely related meanings which make its translation a little slippery at first. When used as an adjective, it means *a certain, some,* or just our English indefinite article *a, an*: **quîdam auctor**, *some/an author;* **quaedam terrae**, *some lands,* etc. When it is used as a pronoun, it means *somebody, something, some people, some things.* **Quîdam putant eum stultum esse,** *some people think he is foolish.* **Quoddam** is the neuter form used when the word is being used as an adjective; **quiddam** when it's being used as a pronoun. **Fêcit quoddam cônsilium,** *he made some plan;* **Fêcit quiddam,** *he made something.* You'll have to work some to keep this word distinct from **quidem,** *indeed.* I remembered the difference this way: **quid*em*** has -*e*-, like *ind*eed*;* **quîd*am*** has an -*a*- as when you're saying *ah . . .* because you can't come up with the name for something.

quam You've see this before, meaning *how,* as in **Quam dulce est beâtam vîtam agere,** *how sweet it is to live a happy life.* In this chapter, you learned that it is the adverb of comparison *than,* and that it can also be used with a superlative degree of the adjective to mean *as X as possible,* where **X** is the meaning of the adjective.

vîtô (1) Students always confuse this with **vîvô**, *to live.* Try to remember this: when you see the verb **vîtô**, it's ine*vita*ble (unavoidable) that you'll confuse it with something else.

27

Making Irregular Comparisons

ADJECTIVES WITH IRREGULAR STEMS

The title of this chapter says it all: some adjectives in Latin form their comparative and superlative degrees irregularly. But don't panic. The irregularities are entirely limited either to the stem the adjective uses in the comparative and superlative degrees, or to the way the comparative or superlative endings are attached to the stem. The irregularities do *not* affect the way the adjectives decline in the comparative or superlative degrees. Let's start by drawing from your experience with irregular English adjectives:

Positive	Comparative	Superlative
good	better	best
bad	worse	worst
little	smaller	smallest
much (many)	more	most

If you take a close look at the degrees of these adjectives you can see that for all of them a different stem is used in the comparative and superlative degrees. It's not *good, gooder, goodest*, because English substitutes another stem in place of the one you would expect if you were thoughtlessly following the rules that apply to the regular adjectives. Now look more closely. Even though the stems have changed, you can still often see the regular comparative and superlative endings *-er* and *-est* attached to the irregular stem. That's all you need to know before you turn to Latin irregular adjectives.

We'll start with the Latin adjective that means *good*: **bonus, -a, -um**, a first and second declension adjective. To form the comparative degree, you use another stem, **mel-**, to which you add the comparative adjectival ending **-ior, -ius**. Review the comparative endings **-ior, -ius** from Chapter 26, if you have to, and decline the adjective **melior, -ius**.

	Masculine and Feminine	Neuter
N./V.		
Gen.		
Dat.		
Acc.		
Abl.		

	Masculine and Feminine	Neuter
Plural		
N/V.		
Gen.		
Dat.		
Acc.		
Abl.		

There was really no reason for you to decline this adjective. It follows precisely the same pattern as the regular comparative degree. I just want to convince you that the irregular comparative degree isn't *completely* irregular: its irregularity is limited to the stem it uses and does not affect its declension at all.

Perhaps you have some bad feelings already about all the new forms you're going to have to memorize. There's no escaping the hard fact that you will have to memorize three forms for irregular adjectives, but don't be pessimistic. Being optimistic brings maximum comfort. There's a way to ameliorate (*to make better*) the problem. These irregular stems often are the roots of English words; so, if you learn the English derivatives, it will much easier to fix the irregular stems in your memory. For example, from the stem **mel-** we get the English verb *ameliorate*, which means *to make better, improve*.[65]

Let's move on now to the superlative degree of the adjective **bonus, -a, -um**: it's **optimus, -a, -um**. Obviously we get the English words *optimist, optimal, optimum*, and others from this stem. Notice that the superlative degree simply uses the **-us, -a, -um** endings without the **-issim-** infix which the regular adjectives use. Here are some more irregular adjectives with a few comments.

Magnus, -a, -um

Positive	Comparative	Superlative
magnus, -a, -um (*great*)	maior, maius (*greater*)	maximus, -a, -um (*greatest*)

The comparative degree **maior** will look more familiar if you add a tail to the intervocalic **-i-**: **major**. (A Major is greater than a Captain.) Remember, now, that even though it looks a little odd, **maior** will decline quite normally: **maiôris, maiôrî**, etc., with **ma-** as the stem.

Malus, -a, -um

Positive	Comparative	Superlative
malus, -a, -um (*bad*)	peior, peius (*worse*)	pessimus, -a, -um (*worst*)

---

[65]The Wheelock text gives you a list of English derivatives from the degrees of some of the most common irregular adjectives on page 184. You would do well to look them over.

Use the same trick with the intervocalic **-i-** in **peior**. *Pejorative* means *derogatory, disparaging,* from the Latin sense of *worse.*

Parvus, -a, -um

Positive	Comparative	Superlative
parvus, -a, -um (*small*)	minor, minus (*smaller*)	minimus, -a, -um (*smallest*)

The comparative degree looks odd: the adjectival ending **-ior, -ius** seems to be missing. It's there; only the **-i-** is missing. You decline **minor, minus** as you normally would, but just leave the **-i-** off.

Superus, -a, -um

Positive	Comparative	Superlative
superus, -a, -um (*above*)	superior, -ius (*higher*)	suprêmus, -a, -um (*last*) summus, -a, -um (*highest*)

The only peculiarity of this adjective is the two superlative degrees which are derived from it. **Summus** means *highest,* and so does **suprêmus**, but **suprêmus** can also mean *last.* Think of it this way. In the court system, if you don't like the ruling in a lower court, you can take your suit to a *superior* court; and then next to the *supreme* court, which is the *last* court of appeal. So Latin can say **suprêmô diê**, *on the last day.* The point is, both **summus** and **suprêmus** can mean *highest,* but **suprêmus** often can have the extended meaning *last.*

Pro, prae

Positive	Comparative	Superlative
(prô, prae)(*before*)	prior, -ius (*prior, previous*)	prîmus, -a, -um (*first*)

The adjectives **prior** and **prîmus** are comparative and superlative degrees of an adjective that doesn't exist in the positive degree. **Prô** and **prae** are prepositions, not adjectives; and they can mean *before.*

Multus, -a, -um

Positive	Comparative	Superlative
multus, -a, -um (*much; many*)	plûs, plûris, *n.* plûrês, plura (*more*)	plûrimus, -a, -um (*very many; most*)

The chief difficulty with this adjective, as you can see, comes in the comparative degree. In the singular of the comparative, the adjective **multus** becomes a neuter *noun* **plûs, plûris,** *n.* It isn't an adjective at all. It's a noun which means *more.* Latin uses it with a genitive case of the noun: **plûs pecûniae**, *more of money.* Like this:

N/V.	plûs	pecûniae	more of money
Gen.	plûris	pecûniae	of more of money
Dat.	____[66]	____	____
Acc.	plûs	pecûniae	more of money
Abl.	plûre	pecûniae	by/with more of money

In the plural, however, the word for *more* becomes an adjective, and declines just as you would expect a normal third declension adjective to decline. One set of forms for the masculine and feminine, and one for the neuter:

	Masculine and Feminine	**Neuter**
N/V.	plûrês	plûra
Gen.	plûrium	plûrium
Dat.	plûribus	plûribus
Acc.	plûrês	plûra
Abl.	plûribus	plûribus

There is a distinction to be maintained between **plûs, plûris**, *n.* and **plûrês, plûra**. The adjective **multus, -a, -um** means *much* or *many*. These two words, *much* and *many* are not interchangeable in English. We use the adjective *much* when we're talking about something which can't be counted up individually; we use *many* when it can. For example, we say *much mud*, or *much money*. It would sound odd to say *many muds* or *many monies*.[67] Conversely, we wouldn't say *much towels*, *much rivers*, or *much people*, because these are objects which are countable. Latin uses the singular neuter noun **plûs, plûris** when referring to uncountable objects, and the adjective **plûrês, plûra** when referring to countable objects. **Plûs aeris**, *more [of] bronze*, and **plûrês hominês**, *more people*.

SUPERLATIVE DEGREE OF ADJECTIVES IN -R

To form the degrees of regular adjectives, you simply add **-ior, -ius** or **-issimus, -a, -um** to the *stem* of the adjective. The stem, you remember, is the form you see in all the forms of the adjective except for the masculine nominative singular. The comparative degree of these adjectives is quite regular. You simply use the stem

---

[66]There is nothing mysterious about the lack of a dative case for this noun. It just means that the dative of **plus** was never used in Classical Latin. We can probably guess that the form would have been **plûrî**; but, since no Roman writer ever used it, we leave the place for it on the chart blank.

[67]We could possibly say *many muds* if we're limologists (mud-doctors) and we're talking about many different kinds of muds around the world: Chinese mud, Korean mud, French mud, and so on. In this case the mud types would in fact be countable; and the adjective *many* would be appropriate: *There are many muds in the world today. Some tan, some yellowish, and others that are completely black.*

with the comparative suffix **ior, -ius** attached. But to form the superlative degree of these adjectives you do two things: (1) use the masculine nominative singular as the stem and (2) add the suffix **-rimus, -a, -um**. Thus, according to step (1), even if the true stem of the adjective lacks the **-e-** before the **-r**, you build the superlative degree from a base ending in **-er**. Adding the suffix **-rimus, -a, -um**, you end up with a doubled **r**. So for the adjective **piger, -a, -um**, *slow*, the superlative degree is **pigerrimus, -a, -um**. Now write out the comparative and superlative degrees of these adjectives.

Positive	Comparative	Superlative
pulcher, -chra, -chrum		
lîber, -a, -um		
âcer, âcris, âcre		
celer, celeris, celere		

SOME ADJECTIVES ENDING IN -LIS

There are six adjectives in Latin ending in **-lis, -e** which have an oddity in the formation of the superlative degree. Wheelock concentrates on only three of them. The irregularity of these adjectives is that the suffix **-limus, -a, -um** is used in place of **-issimus, -a, -um**. The comparative degree, however, is entirely regular. Form the degrees of the three adjectives which use this irregular suffix in the superlative, then compare them to three other adjectives in **-lis, -e** which use the regular superlative suffix. (Remember, this irregularity is limited to only six adjectives ending in **-lis, -e**. All other adjectives ending in **-lis, e** form their comparisons regularly.)

Irregular

Positive	Comparative	Superlative
facilis, -e		
similis, -e		
difficilis, -e		

Regular

Positive	Comparative	Superlative
mollis, -e		
mortâlis, -e		
fidêlis, -e		

VOCABULARY PUZZLES

appellô (1) This verb in the passive voice is a copulative verb, linking the subject to a predicate nominative. *He is called Brutus* would be **Appellâtur Brutus**, not **Brutum**.

maiôrês, -ium, *m.* Obviously this noun is derived from the comparative adjective for **magnus, -a, -um**. Used as a noun in the plural, it means *the greaters in age* or the *ancestors*.

similis, -e It takes the dative case as its complement. **Hoc nôn simile illî**, *this is not similar to that.*

28

The Subjunctive I

FORMATION OF THE SUBJUNCTIVE, PRESENT TENSE

In this chapter, you begin your study of the subjunctive mood of verbs. The first real hurdle for students to overcome is the temptation to be told how to translate *the* subjunctive mood. The subjunctive mood has no real translation in itself. The subjunctive mood is one primarily of syntax and is almost always used in subordinate clauses. What you must do is (1) learn the morphology (formation) of the subjunctive mood and then (2) study the different ways the subjunctive is used in Latin to express what. Once you've understood the intent of the Latin sentence or clause in which the subjunctive appears, then you'll be prepared to bring that meaning over into an appropriate English construction.

This all may sound rather metaphysical and frightening, but it isn't really. It just means that the method of assigning one-to-one correspondences from Latin to English and vice versa, which may have served you so well in the past, can't help you anymore. You'll learn to form the subjunctive in the different tenses, while you collect and study the different uses of the subjunctive. Let's start.

FIRST CONJUGATION

To form the subjunctive, present tense, a first conjugation verb simply substitutes the normal stem vowel long **-â-** with a long **-ê-**. The personal endings, active and passive, are not changed (except that the first person singular ending is the variant **-m** instead of **-ô-**). Write out the present subjunctive active and passive of the first conjugation verb **laudô** in the present tense (Wheelock 453-4).

	Active	Passive
1st		
2nd		
3rd		
Plural		
1st		
2nd		
3rd		

This wasn't so difficult; but look at these forms again. If you didn't know that **laudô** was a first conjugation verb, you might think that some of the forms were forms of the indicative from a second or third conjugation verb. The form **laudêtis,** for example, looks as if it could be a present tense from a second conjugation verb, or a future tense of the third conjugation non-i-stem verb. The only way to be sure, if you're not totally familiar with the verb you're examining, is to look the verb up and make a note of its conjugation. When you see **laudô** (1) in the dictionary, then you can be sure that the form **laudêtis** is subjunctive present tense.

SECOND CONJUGATION

As you're about to see, the way a first conjugation verb forms the subjunctive present tense is actually an exception to the general rule. All other conjugations form the present subjunctive by inserting a long **-â-** between the stem and the personal endings. This rule is easily seen in the second conjugation:

Active	monê	+	â	+	m	→	moneam
Passive	monê	+	â	+	r	→	monear

Write out the present subjunctive, active and passive, of **moneô, -êre**.

	Active	Passive
1st		
2nd		
3rd		
Plural		
1st		
2nd		
3rd		

THIRD CONJUGATION

When you insert the long **-â-** between the stem and the personal endings on a third conjugation verb, the stem vowel short **-e-** drops out entirely, leaving only the **-â-** between the stem and the personal endings. Note that many of the resulting forms look exactly like the indicative mood of the first conjugation. Again, you need to take care from now on and look at your dictionary entries thoroughly. Write out the subjunctive present tense, active and passive, of **dûcô, -ere**.

	Active	Passive
1st		
2nd		
3rd		
Plural		
1st		
2nd		
3rd		

THIRD CONJUGATION I-STEMS

In the present tense, the extra **-i-** of an i-stem verb is present throughout the forms:

Active	capi	+	â	+	m	→	capiam
Passive	capi	+	â	+	r	→	capiar

Now produce the present subjunctive of the **capiô**.

	Active	Passive
1st		
2nd		
3rd		
Plural		
1st		
2nd		
3rd		

FOURTH CONJUGATION

The stem vowel of a fourth conjugation verb is a long **-î-**. Like the third conjugation i-stem, the fourth conjugation keeps the **-i-** before the **-â-** of the subjunctive mood.

Active	audî	+	â	+	m	→	audiam
Passive	audî	+	â	+	r	→	audiar

Write out the present subjunctive, active and passive, of **audiô**.

	Active	Passive
1st		
2nd		
3rd		
Plural		
1st		
2nd		
3rd		

You will be pleased to know that there are no subjunctive infinitives, imperatives, or participles. There are also no subjunctives in the future or future perfect tense. You now know all the subjunctive forms of the present tense of all four conjugations. So how is the subjunctive mood used?

THE JUSSIVE SUBJUNCTIVE

The *jussive* or *hortatory* subjunctive is used when a command or exhortation is directed to a first or third person. (When a command is directed toward a second person, as you recall, Latin uses the imperative mood.) To issue a prohibition or negative command in the first or third persons, the negative particle **nê** is used, not **nôn**. In English, we make commands to first and third persons with our construction *let . . .* and make negative commands (also called prohibitions) with *let . . . not . . .* Study these examples and their translations.

Indicative	Jussive Subjunctive
Virôs bonôs laudâmus, *we are praising good men.*	Virôs bonôs laudêmus, *let's praise good men.*
Veniunt, *they are coming.*	Veniant, *let them come.*
Librôs malôs nôn legimus, *we don't read bad books.*	Nê librôs malôs legâmus, *let's not read bad books.*

THE SUBJUNCTIVE IN PURPOSE CLAUSES

A *purpose* clause is, as the name tells us, a subordinate clause that explains the purpose for which the action in the main clause was undertaken. And what's that supposed to mean? English has basically two ways to show purpose: (1) infinitive, sometimes supplemented with *in order* and (2) a subordinate clause introduced by *so that* or *so* or *in order that*, often with the conditional mood of the verb. Let's look at the infinitive showing purpose first:

She is coming *to help* (or in order to help).

They are sending him *to tell* you what to do.

The dog has a long nose *to smell* better.

In order *to serve* you better, our store has installed anti-theft devices.

Let's rewrite these sentences using method (2)—as full subordinate clauses with finite verbs:

She is coming *so that she may help.*

They are sending him *so that he may tell you what to do.*

The dog has a long nose *so that it may smell better.*

In order that we may serve you better, our store has installed anti-theft devices.

Some of these may sound rather over blown; our native English sense leans toward simplicity. But there are many cases where we *must* use the subordinate clause to show purpose. For example, there is no way, short of considerable rewriting, to boil these purpose clauses down to infinitives.

We are coming *so you won't have to work so hard.*

She is writing the paper *so you can leave early.*

The Latin prose you're studying has only one way to show purpose: a full subordinate clause introduced by **ut** for the positive, **nê** for the negative, plus a finite verb in the subjunctive mood. It never uses the infinitive to show purpose the way English does. We can translate the Latin purpose clause in whichever of the two English purpose constructions seems most natural to us. But if you are translating from English to Latin, never translate an English infinitive showing purpose directly into a Latin infinitive. Study these examples carefully:

Id facit ut eôs adiuvet, *he is doing it **to help** them [or in order to help them, or so that he may help them].*

Veniunt nê cîvitâtês dêleantur, *they are coming so that the cities will not be destroyed.*[68]

Haec dicit ut discipulî omnia intellegant, *he is saying these things so that the students will understand everything.*

Multôs librôs legit nê stulta videâtur, *she reads many books so that she won't seem foolish.*

---

[68]Don't be alarmed by the future tense indicative in the English translation. It's logical enough. The purpose you're trying to accomplish in a present action is very often going to be a future event. Give your understanding some room to express itself in these translations.

A FINAL WORD ABOUT SUBJUNCTIVES

Real Latin uses the subjunctive mood nearly as often as the indicative mood so, obviously, you must thoroughly master its forms and uses. But beyond that, you must also begin to read Latin, not word by word, but letter by letter. You must strive to understand every tiny twist and turn of the morphology of the verbs. As you know, the difference between an indicative and subjunctive mood is for the most part just one letter. It seems like a microscopic difference, but if you fail to note it, your entire sentence will come grinding to a halt. You simply must slow down some and watch your steps carefully as you begin the subjunctive. If you get off the path now, you'll get more and more lost in the future.

29

The Subjunctive II

FORMATION OF THE IMPERFECT SUBJUNCTIVE

Wheelock tells you that the imperfect subjunctive is an easy form to recognize and to produce. He tells you that it is, in effect, the present active infinitive plus the personal endings, active or passive. Although this may be a convenient way to look at it, it isn't quite true. The actual morphology is just a little more complicated. To spare yourself some confusion in the future, you should learn the real history of the imperfect subjunctive. The (real) formula for the imperfect subjunctive is:

1st principal part	+	**sê**	+	personal endings

Because the **s** of the infix **se** will be intervocalic, it changes to an **r,** giving the appearance of the regular active infinitive ending **-re**. The personal endings are those you use in the present system. (Use **-m** instead of **-ô** in the first person singular.) So for the first conjugation, the forms look like this:

laudâ	+	sê	+	m	→	laudâsem	→	laudârem
laudâ	+	sê	+	m	→	laudâsês	→	laudârês
etc.								

As you can see, the final form does in fact look an awful lot like the present infinitive plus a personal ending: **laudârem,** and so on. You just might have noticed, however, something slightly different about the second person singular. Notice the length of the vowel right before the personal ending. It's long, **laudârês,** whereas the final -e- of the infinitive is short, **laudâre.** That might tip you off that the imperfect subjunctive is more than just the infinitive plus the personal endings. But still, that hardly seems a sufficient reason to drag you through all this morphology. Stay with me. You'll see soon enough how knowing the true history of the imperfect subjunctive will pay off. For now, let's have a look at the imperfect subjunctive in all its forms in all the conjugations. Produce the imperfect subjunctive active and passive for all four conjugations (Wheelock 194; 453-4).

laudô

	Active	Passive
1st		
2nd		
3rd		
Plural		
1st		
2nd		
3rd		

moneô

	Active	Passive
1st		
2nd		
3rd		
Plural		
1st		
2nd		
3rd		

agô

	Active	Passive
1st		
2nd		
3rd		
Plural		
1st		
2nd		
3rd		

capiô

		Active	Passive
	1st		
	2nd		
	3rd		
Plural			
	1st		
	2nd		
	3rd		

audiô

		Active	Passive
	1st		
	2nd		
	3rd		
Plural			
	1st		
	2nd		
	3rd		

As you can see by looking back over these forms, the imperfect subjunctive does, in fact, look like the present active infinitive with personal endings attached. You can think of it this way if you wish, provided that you're aware that this understanding will have to be revised in the near future.

Wheelock also tells you that the imperfect subjunctive is used in subordinate clauses when the verb of the main clause is a past tense. That's true, but don't worry about it for now. You should merely be alerted to the fact that, just like participles and infinitives, verbs in the subjunctive mood don't have absolute tense, but rather they express time relative to the tense of the main verb. This will all be explained in Chapter 30. Your task in this chapter is to learn to recognize an imperfect subjunctive when you see it.

SUBJUNCTIVE OF SUM AND POSSUM

The present subjunctive of **sum** is the stem **si-** plus the active personal endings. (No passive forms, obviously. What would the verb *to be* mean in the passive voice?) The imperfect subjunctive is the present stem (**es-**) plus **sê** plus the active personal endings (Wheelock 195):

sum, esse

	Present	Imperfect
1st		
2nd		
3rd		
Plural		
1st		
2nd		
3rd		

As you no doubt recall, the verb **possum** in Latin is a compound of the adjective **pot-** and the verb **sum**. If you add the **pot-** to the present subjunctive of **sum,** the **t** of **pot-** will always assimilate to **s,** since all the forms of the present subjunctive of **sum** begin with **s.** The imperfect subjunctive of **possum** is best thought of as the present infinitive plus personal endings—the present infinitive of **possum,** that is, which is **posse.** Write out the present and imperfect subjunctive of **possum** (Wheelock 195).

possum, posse

	Present	Imperfect
1st		
2nd		
3rd		
Plural		
1st		
2nd		
3rd		

THE RESULT CLAUSE

A subordinate clause that shows the consequence or result of something in the main clause is called, naturally enough, a Result (or Consecutive) Clause. We often tip off our listener in English that a Result Clause is coming up by inserting words like *so* or *such* in the main clause. The result clause itself is introduced by the subordinating conjunction *that*.

The eclipse made the sky *so* dark *that* it seemed like night.

His penmanship was *so* awful *that* no one could read the letter.

She was *such* a good athlete *that* she easily jumped over the fence.

Latin result clauses are also frequently anticipated by adverbs or special adjectives in the main clause—**ita, sîc, tam, tantus, -a, -um**. The clause itself is introduced by **ut** when the result clause is positive, and by **ut** with a negative in the clause when the result is negated. The verb is put into the subjunctive mood.

In the positive result clause, when **ut** is used as the subordinating conjunction, you may think that some confusion between a purpose and a result clause is possible: they're both introduced by **ut** and have a subjunctive verb. This is true in theory, but in practice it happens rarely. If you see **ita, sîc, tam,** or **tantus, -a, -um** in the main clause and an **ut** clause, then you know for certain that the **ut** clause is a result clause. In the majority of cases, result clauses are anticipated somehow in the main clause.

There is no possibility of confusing a negative purpose clause with a negative result clause. Negative purpose clauses are introduced with **nê;** negative result clauses start with **ut** and then negate the verb in the clause with **nôn, numquam** etc., or by using a negative pronoun such as **nêmô**.

Id sîc fêcêrunt ut omnês metû lîberârentur, *they did it in such a way that everyone was freed from fear.*

Scrîpsêrunt ita male ut nêmô litterâs legere posset, *they wrote so badly, that no one was able to read the letter.*

Tantum ferrum tenêbat ut territî hostês fugerent, *he was holding such a great sword that the terrified enemy ran away.*

Wheelock gives you several examples in the chapter which show you the difference between purpose and result clauses. You should study them carefully—and by all means work through his Self-Tutorials for this chapter. It takes a while for this all to settle in.

VOCABULARY PUZZLES

ita, sîc, tam The adverbs that anticipate result clauses are not entirely interchangeable. **Sîc** is used primarily to qualify verbs: **Id sîc fêcit ut** . . . The other two, **ita** and **tam**, can qualify verbs, adjectives or other adverbs: **Via erat tam [ita] longa ut** . . . or **Tam [ita] male scrîpsêrunt ut** . . . or **Id tam [ita] fêcit ut** . . .

tantus, -a, -um This adjective for some reason always throws students off at first. It means basically *so great* but some flexibility is required to get this over into smooth English. Study carefully the way this adjective is used.

quidem It's an adverb meaning *indeed, certainly,* and is postpositive (it's never the first word in a sentence or clause.) This poses no problem. But the expression **nê . . . quidem** is sometimes difficult to spot. **Nê X quidem** means *not even X.* Watch out for this. When you see **quidem,** check to see whether there is a **nê** two words back. If you miss this construction, you'll mess up the sentence badly.

30

The Subjunctive III; Sequence of Tenses

PERFECT SYSTEM SUBJUNCTIVE

The perfect system of tenses consists of the perfect, pluperfect, and future perfect, but there will be no future perfect subjunctive. The active voice of these tenses is formed from the third principal part of the verb; the passive voice uses the fourth principal part of the verb as a predicate adjective (it's a participle) with a conjugated form of the verb **sum**. So much by way of review. Now on to the new stuff.

Perfect Tense Active

The formula for the perfect subjunctive active is: 3rd principal part + **erî** + personal endings. The one oddity is that the personal endings used for the subjunctive mood in the perfect system are not the endings you learned for the perfect system in the indicative; the endings are not **-î, -istî, -it, -imus, -istis, -êrunt**. The perfect system subjunctive uses the same endings which are used in the present system: **-m, -s, -t, -mus, -tis, -nt**. Linguists use this fact as evidence that the subjunctive mood is somehow closely related to the present system of tenses.

Pluperfect Subjunctive Active

The formula for the pluperfect subjunctive active is: 3rd principal part + **issê** + personal endings. As Wheelock tells you, this amounts to the perfect infinitive, which is the third principal part + **issê**, with personal endings attached to the end. Again, the personal endings are not **eram, erâs,** etc., as you might expect if you're thinking about the pluperfect indicative. The endings are the personal endings from the present system: **-m, -s,** etc. Let's look at the perfect and pluperfect subjunctive active for a couple of verbs. Write out the forms for the following verbs (Wheelock 453-6).

dûcô, dûcere, dûxî, ductus, -a, -um

	Perfect	Pluperfect
1st		
2nd		
3rd		

	Perfect	Pluperfect
Plural		
1st		
2nd		
3rd		

audiô, -îre, audîvî, audîtus

	Perfect	Pluperfect
1st		
2nd		
3rd		
Plural		
1st		
2nd		
3rd		

FUTURE PERFECT INDICATIVE AND PERFECT SUBJUNCTIVE COMPARED

Wheelock warns you that the perfect subjunctive is very similar to the future perfect indicative. Let's have a close look. The future perfect indicative is built on the third principal part and uses the future of the verb **sum** for its personal endings (except for the third person plural, where it's **erint** and not **erunt**). Compare the future perfect indicative with the perfect subjunctive from the verb **laudô (1)**.

	Future Perfect Indicative	Perfect Subjunctive
1st		
2nd		
3rd		
Plural		
1st		
2nd		
3rd		

As you can see, there is only one person in which these two differ: the first person singular. In all the other forms, they are identical. But you needn't despair. There is an easy way to tell the difference between the future perfect indicative and the perfect subjunctive. You simply look at the context. If you see the form **laudâverint,** for example, in a clause where the subjunctive is required, then the form is perfect subjunctive. If, on the other hand, you're in a clause where the subjunctive is not called for, then the form is future perfect indicative. It's as simple as that.

Perfect Subjunctive Passive

You recall that the perfect indicative passive is formed from the fourth principal part (the perfect passive participle) with a conjugated form of the verb **sum** in the present tense. The perfect subjunctive passive is formed exactly the same way. It's the fourth principal part of the verb with the verb **sum**. To make the verb form subjunctive, Latin simply puts **sum** into in the subjunctive mood: **laudâtus sim.**

Pluperfect Subjunctive Passive

How do you imagine Latin forms the pluperfect subjunctive passive? Remember that the pluperfect indicative passive is the fourth principal part (the perfect passive participle) with a conjugated form of **sum** in the imperfect tense. Take a guess: **laudâtus, -a, -um essem.**

Laudô in the Perfect System Passive Subjunctive

	Perfect	Pluperfect
1st		
2nd		
3rd		
Plural		
1st		
2nd		
3rd		

SYNOPSES OF VERBS

A synopsis of a verb—those handy charts which you fill in with a representative of all possible moods, tenses, and voice—will now include the subjunctive. Take a moment to complete a synopsis of the verb **pellô, -ere, pepulî, pulsus, -a, -um**, *to strike, push* in the third person plural, feminine.

Indicative Mood

	Active	Passive
Present		
Future		
Imperfect		
Perfect		
Pluperfect		
Future Perfect		

Subjunctive Mood

	Active	Passive
Present		
Imperfect		
Perfect		
Pluperfect		

Participles

	Active	Passive
Future		
Present		■
Perfect	■	

Infinitives

	Active	Passive
Future		■
Present		
Perfect		

SEQUENCE OF TENSES

You now know all four tenses of the subjunctive mood—there is no future or future perfect of the subjunctive. So what are you supposed to do with them all? You've seen the subjunctive mood used in the jussive construction, and in the result and purpose clauses. And there you used the subjunctive in the present and imperfect tenses. Everything worked just fine. Now, however, we need to complete the picture, tell the whole story, as it were, of the subjunctive mood.

First you need to recall that verbs show absolute time only when they're in the indicative mood. In every other mood, verbs show only time relative to the verb in the indicative mood. The indicative mood shows real time. When verbs are in the infinitive or participial mood, they indicate only whether their action takes place before, during, or after the action of the main verb. In the infinitive and the participle, the present shows time contemporaneous; the future shows time subsequent; the perfect shows time prior. You have to think of the main verb of the sentence as a point in time, around which the participles and infinitives pivot.

The same thing is true for verbs in the subjunctive mood. They pivot around the time established in the main verb of the sentence. The rules that govern which tense shows which temporal relationship are called the sequence of tenses. Let's be clear on this: the rules governing the sequence of tenses apply *only* to dependent subjunctives (subjunctive verbs in subordinate clauses). These rules have nothing to do with participles or infinitives or any other form of a verb which has relative tense. This is the sequence of tense of *dependent* subjunctives only.

We start by categorizing the tenses of the indicative mood: the primary tenses and the secondary (or historical) tenses.

Primary Tenses:	present	future	future perfect	perfect
Secondary Tenses:	perfect[69]	imperfect	pluperfect	

This means that if the main verb is in one of the primary tenses, then the tenses of the subordinate subjunctive are going to be in the *primary sequence*. If the main verb is in one of the secondary tenses, then the sentence is in *secondary sequence*. Now the rules about the subordinate subjunctive in these two sequences:

Primary Sequence

(1) A present subjunctive shows time contemporaneous *or* it may show time subsequent to the action of the main verb.

---

[69]You'll notice that the perfect tense can be either a primary or a secondary tense. The reason for this is that, although Latin has only one form for the perfect tense, it nevertheless is capable of distinguishing two senses of the perfect tense. We have two different tenses in English which are possible translations of the one Latin perfect tense, as you know. **Vīdī** can be translated *I saw* (the English preterit), or *I have seen* (the present perfect). When the Latin perfect tense can be translated in English with the preterit, then the perfect is a secondary tense. When it can be translated with the present perfect, thus indicating that a past action is having some immediate impact on the present, then the perfect is a primary tense. You'll see how this works very soon.

(2) A construction called the *active future periphrastic* with the present subjunctive of the verb **sum** may be used to show time subsequent to the action of the main verb.[70]

(3) A perfect subjunctive shows time prior to the action of the main verb.

Secondary Sequence

(1) An imperfect subjunctive shows time contemporaneous *or* it may show time subsequent to the action of the main verb.

(2) The active future periphrastic with the imperfect subjunctive of the verb **sum** may show time subsequent to the action of the main verb.

(3) A pluperfect subjunctive shows time prior to the action of the main verb.

Let's look at all this another way:

Main Verb	Subordinate Subjunctive	Temporal Relationship
Primary	Future Periphrastic with **sum**	Time After
	Present	Same Time or After
	Perfect	Time Before
Secondary	Future Periphrastic with **essem**	Time After
	Imperfect	Same Time or After
	Pluperfect	Time Before

Examples of Primary Sequence

Haec dicit ut perîcula comprehendâmus, *he is saying these things, so that we may understand the dangers.*

Via ita longa est ut ad urbem numquam perveniant, *the road is so long that they'll never reach the city.*

Both of these sentences are in primary sequence because the tense of the main verb is one of the primary tenses. Therefore, any subordinate subjunctives in the sentence can be either in the present or perfect tense: the present tense for action contemporaneous or subsequent to the main verb, the perfect for action prior. In the subordinate clause in the first sentence, **ut perîcula comprehendâmus**, the tense of the subjunctive is present. This means that the action being depicted is either contemporaneous or subsequent to that of the main verb.

In the second sentence, the result of an activity or state can never be prior to the event or the state. Consequently, a result clause, just as a purpose clause, can never be prior to the action of the main verb of the sentence. Therefore, **veniant** is a present subjunctive, showing time contemporaneous or subsequent to the main verb **est** in primary sequence.

---

[70]The active future periphrastic is the future active participle of the verb plus a conjugated form of the verb **sum**. For example: **factûrus sum**, *I am going to do*; **venitûrî sunt**, *they are going to come*; **laudâtûrî estis**, *you are going to praise*, etc.

Examples of Secondary Sequence

Now let's change the sequence of these sentences from primary to secondary by changing the tense of the main verb to one of the secondary tenses: the imperfect. What will happen to the tense of the subordinate subjunctives?

Haec *dicêbat* ut perîcula **comprehenderêmus**, *he was saying these things so that we might understand the dangers.*

Via ita longa *erat* ut ad urbem numquam **pervenîrent**, *the road was so long that they never arrived at the city.*

The temporal relationships of the subordinate subjunctive and the main verb are still the same: they're both still showing time contemporaneous or subsequent. But now we're in secondary sequence, so the tense of the subjunctive must change to the imperfect, since the imperfect subjunctive shows time contemporaneous or subsequent in subordinate subjunctives in secondary sequence. The forms will be **comprehenderêmus** and **venîrent**. You'll see many more examples of this soon.

INDIRECT QUESTIONS [71]

The title of this section tells it all: just as statements can be the object of a verb—becoming *indirect* statements—so also direct questions can be objects of verbs—becoming indirect questions. Here are some examples of how this is done in English.

Direct Question		Indirect Question
Are you coming?	I wonder	[if] you're coming.
What's new?	I wonder	what's new.
How many candies do you have?	I wonder	how many candies you have.
When will we be finished?	I wonder	when we'll be finished.

Notice the original direct question is changed very little when we make it indirect. The only change we make in English is to invert the subject and verb: from ***are you*** *coming* to **you are** coming. We also insert an *if* or *whether* when the original direct question was a simple question. Let's look at some more complicated examples of indirect questions in English, because sometimes more of a change is required to go from direct to indirect questions.

Direct Question		Indirect Question
Are you coming?	I wondered	if you were coming.
What's new?	I wondered	what was new.
How many candies do you have?	I wondered	how many candies you had.
When will we be finished?	I wondered	when we'd be finished.

---

[71]Pretty long chapter, eh?

As you can see, when the tenses of the main verb of the sentence is one of the past tenses—*I wondered*—the tense of the verb of the original direct question is often changed when it becomes indirect.

In Latin, as in English, an indirect question is a finite construction—that is, the verb of the indirect question has person. This is unlike the indirect statement in Latin, where the original finite verb becomes an infinitive, and the original nominative subject becomes the accusative subject of the infinitive. The mood of the original verb, however, changes from the indicative to the subjunctive. Here are some simple examples to show you how this works.

Direct	Cûr venis?	*Why are you coming?*
Indirect	Nêsciô **cûr veniâs**.	*I don't know why you're coming.*
Direct	Veniuntne nostrî amîcî?	*Are our friends coming?*
Indirect	Rogat **veniantne nostrî amîcî.**[72]	*He is asking if our friends are coming.*
Direct	Quanta perîcula sunt?	*How great are the dangers?*
Indirect	Videô **quanta pericula sint**.	*I see how great the dangers are.*

OBSERVING SEQUENCE OF TENSE IN INDIRECT QUESTION

As you can see, a sentence with an indirect question embedded in it is essentially a complex sentence, with a subordinate subjunctive in a dependent clause. The part of the sentence which introduces the indirect question is the main clause, and the indirect question itself is a subordinate clause, in which the verb happens to be in the subjunctive. So, because this question involves a dependent subjunctive, the rules of the sequence of tenses come into play.

You remember that the tense of the main verb determines the sequence of the sentences, and hence determines the tenses which subordinate subjunctives in the sentence can have. If the main verb is in one of the primary tenses, then the sentence follows the primary sequence: the subordinate subjunctives can be in the present or perfect tenses. If the main verb is in one of the secondary tenses, then the sentence follows the secondary sequence: the subordinate subjunctives can be in the imperfect or pluperfect tenses. Now let's apply these rules to indirect questions.

Time Contemporaneous

When the indirect question is depicting an event that is conceived of as contemporaneous with the action of the main verb, then the subordinate subjunctive is either in the present tense (primary sequence) or in the imperfect tense (secondary sequence).

---

[72]Notice that the enclitic **-ne,** which is used to ask a simple question, remains attached to the first word in the question even when it becomes an indirect question: *They ask if (or whether) our friends are coming.*

Primary Sequence	Secondary Sequence
Nesciô quid faciâs, *I don't know what you're doing.*	Nescîvî quid facerês, *I didn't know what you were doing.*[73]
Rogat veniantne nostrî amîcî, *he asks whether our friends are coming.*	Rogâvêrunt venîrentne nostrî amîcî, *they asked whether our friends were coming.*

Time Prior

When the indirect question is depicting an event that is conceived of as having been undertaken before the action of the main verb, then the subordinate subjunctive is either in the perfect tense (primary sequence) or in the pluperfect tense (secondary sequence).

Primary Sequence	Secondary Sequence
Nesciô quid fêcerîs, *I don't know what you did.*	Nescîvî quid fêcissês, *I didn't know what you had done (or did).*[74]
Rogant vênerintne nostrî amîcî, *they are asking whether our friends came.*	Rogâvêrunt vênissentne nostrî amîcî, *they asked whether our friends had come (or came).*

Time Subsequent (After)

When the indirect question is depicting an event that is conceived as coming after the action of the main verb, then the subordinate subjunctive is the active future periphrastic with the present subjunctive of **sum** in the present tense (primary sequence) or the active future periphrastic with the imperfect subjunctive of **sum** (secondary sequence).

Primary Sequence	Secondary Sequence
Nesciô quid factûrus sîs, *I don't know what you will do (you're going to do).*	Nescîvî quid factûrus essês, *I didn't know what you were going to do (would do).*
Rogant sintne ventûrî nostrî amîcî, *they ask whether our friends are coming.*	Rogâvêrunt essentne ventûrî nostrî amîcî, *they asked whether our friends were coming (would come).*

---

[73]This means that you were doing something at the same time that I did not know. This construction in English is a little ambiguous, because it can be indicating two different temporal relationships. It can mean contemporaneous time, as in *I was watching you work, but I did not know what you were doing.* Or it can mean prior time, as in *I came into the office this morning, but **I did not know what you were doing** last night.* If it's important to make the time sequence entirely unambiguous, we can use a pluperfect tense to show time prior: *I did not know what you **had** been doing (or **had** done).*

[74]English is sparing in its use of the pluperfect tense, even when it's plainly needed. You'll probably hear *what you did* more often than *what you had done* in indirect questions like this.

DRILLS

Write the correct form of the indirect question, being careful to observe the sequence of tense as established by the tense of the main verb. (Use the future active periphrastic for indirect questions showing time subsequent.)

Direct Question	Main Verb	Indirect Question
Quid faciês?	**Rogô**	
Quid facis?		
Quid fêcisti?		

Direct Question	Main Verb	Indirect Question
Quid faciês?	**Rogâvî**	
Quid facis?		
Quid fêcisti?		

Direct Question	Main Verb	Indirect Question
Venientne nostrî amîcî?	**Rogô**	
Veniuntne nostrî amîcî?		
Vênêruntne nostrî amîcî?		

Direct Question	Main Verb	Indirect Question
Venientne nostrî amîcî?	**Rogâvî**	
Veniuntne nostrî amîcî?		
Vênêruntne nostrî amîcî?		

VOCABULARY PUZZLES

cognoscô The **-sc-** inserted before the ending of the verb is called the *inceptive* (*in SEHP tiv*) or *inchoative* (*in KOH uh tiv*) infix. It denotes the sense that the action of the verb is only in the process of being realized or in the very beginning stages. **Cognoscô**, therefore, means *to get to know* or *to become acquainted with,* not *to know.* In the perfect tense, the verb means *to have gotten to know* or *to have become acquainted with,* and this amounts to our present tense *to know.* Therefore, we translate **cognôvî** not *I knew* but *I know, I got to know.*

comprehendô Look at the range of meanings for this verb. All the meanings are related to the idea of getting hold of something. Also, check the third principal part, **comprehendî**. Some of the forms of the perfect tense will be identical to those of the present tense: **comprehendit**, *she grasps*; **comprehendit**, *she grasped*; **comprehendimus**, *we grasp*; **comprehendimus**, *we grasped.*

31

Cum with Subjunctive; Ferô

CUM AS A SUBORDINATING CONJUNCTION

You're already well acquainted with the preposition **cum** + ablative case. It means *with,* which can signify one of two meanings: ablative of accompaniment: **venit cum amîcîs**, *he is coming <u>with</u> friends*; and the ablative of manner, **venit magnâ cum celeritâte**, *he is coming <u>with</u> great speed.* There is also a word **cum** which is not a preposition at all, but a subordinating conjunction. Even though **cum** the conjunction looks exactly like **cum** the preposition, the two words actually have different histories. They are not the same word at all. The difficulty with translating the conjunction **cum** is that it has a wide variety of meanings and can take either the indicative or the subjunctive mood in its clause.

Even though we can distinguish some broad classes of meanings, it is still difficult sometimes to tell just which one of them **cum** is using in a given sentence, and, therefore, which of our several English conjunctions will best translate it. In this respect, **cum** is similar to our conjunction *as,* which has quite a range of meanings, and at times seems to be using many of them all at once. For example: *As I was coming in the door, I saw my friend.* Does this sentence mean *I saw my friend* **because** *I was coming in the door* or does it mean *I saw my friend* **while** *I was coming in the door.* It's hard to say; and, in fact, both could be true at the same time. If I hadn't been coming in the door at that time, I wouldn't have seen my friend. This same kind of fusion of meanings exists for the conjunction **cum**. It's possible to over analyze the different uses of **cum** as a subordinating conjunction, but there are two broad categories of meanings that will be helpful for you to know. There's what's called the **cum** temporal, and the **cum** circumstantial.

Cum Temporal

This use of **cum** is fairly obvious because the mood of the verb in the clause will be indicative. This construction is used to specify a strictly temporal relationship between the event in the **cum** clause and the event in the main clause.

Scrîpsî hâs litterâs, cum apud mê erâs, *I wrote this letter when you were at my house.*

Cum Circumstantial

A **cum** clause can also be used to indicate the general circumstances under which the action of the main clause occurred. This is a little vague, I know, but it really is a pretty broad category, and it has a number of possible translations, as you'll see. One thing about the **cum** circumstantial clause that makes it stand out is that the mood of the verb is always subjunctive. Let's look at several examples. (Take note how the subordinate subjunctives observe the sequence of tenses.)

Cum respondisset, omnia intellêxistis, *because he had answered, you under-stood everything,* or *when he had answered . . .* or *since he had answered . . .*

Cum respondisset, nôn tamen intellêxistis, *although he answered, you still (nevertheless) did not understand.*

Cum responderit, omnia iam intellegitis, *because he answered, you now understand everything.*

THE IRREGULAR VERB FERÔ, FERRE, TULÎ, LÂTUS

Ferô is a very widely-used verb in Latin, as its stem shows up in more than a dozen compound verbs. It's important to master it thoroughly right now, otherwise it will plague you for as long as you read Latin.

Just by looking at the principal parts of the verb, you can tell that the verb **ferô** is going to be unlike any verb you've seen before. It's a third conjugation verb, so the stem of the present system is **fere-**, with a short **-e-** as its thematic vowel. Indeed, for the most part, the verb conjugates just like a regular third conjugation verb.

If you look at the second principal part, however, the thematic vowel **-e-** is missing: the infinitive ending **-re** is added to **fer-** not to **fere-**. Hence the infinitive form **ferre** instead of **ferere**. This is the main irregularity of the verb **ferô**. In the present tense, the thematic vowel is dropped before some endings. Here's where: the thematic vowel—a short **e**—is dropped before endings that begin with the letters **r, s,** or **t**. Keeping this in mind, try to write out the present system active and passive (Wheelock 459-60).

Present System: Indicative Active

	Present	Future	Imperfect
1st			
2nd			
3rd			
Plural			
1st			
2nd			
3rd			

Did you get them all? As you can see, the irregularity does not apply at all to the future and imperfect tenses, where the intervening vowels and tense signs come between the stem and the personal endings that would have produced the irregularity. Did you follow that? The irregularity of this verb is that the short **-e-** of the stem drops out when certain personal endings attached to it. But in the future and imperfect tenses, the personal endings are *not* attached directly to the stem vowel. They're attached to the tense signs. So the stem vowel has no reason to fall out. Now let's look at the passive voice in the present system indicative. Think now. The stem vowel falls out before a personal ending that begins with **r**, **s**, or **t**.

Present System: Indicative Passive

	Present	Future	Imperfect
1st			
2nd			
3rd			
Plural			
1st			
2nd			
3rd			

How did you do? Try the present subjunctive. Stop and think. You form the subjunctive of a third conjugation verb by, in effect, replacing the stem vowel with **-â-** and then attaching the personal endings.

Present System: Subjunctive Active

	Present	Future	Imperfect
1st			
2nd			
3rd			
Plural			
1st			
2nd			
3rd			

Well, what do you think? Since the personal endings are *not* attached directly after the stem vowel, there aren't any irregularities here. It looks just like a normal third conjugation verb in the present subjunctive.

Finally, let's think about the imperfect subjunctive. The formula for all imperfect subjunctives is: stem + **sê** + personal endings. The **-s-** of the mood sign becomes intervocalic and turns to an **-r-**. The **-r-**, you know, is one of those consonants that the stem vowel doesn't like. So the base form for the imperfect subjunctive becomes **ferre-**. Produce the forms.

Present System: Subjunctive Passive

	Present	Future	Imperfect
1st			
2nd			
3rd			
Plural			
1st			
2nd			
3rd			

Perfect System Active

The perfect system, because it is formed from the third and fourth principal parts, is entirely regular (except that third and fourth principal parts are themselves unusual suppletive forms). For the sake of thoroughness, and to prove to you that the verb is not so irregular as you may think, write out the perfect system for the verb **ferô**.

	Perfect	Pluperfect	Future Perfect
1st			
2nd			
3rd			
Plural			
1st			
2nd			
3rd			

Perfect System Passive

	Perfect	Pluperfect	Future Perfect
1st			
2nd			
3rd			
Plural			
1st			
2nd			
3rd			

Perfect System: Subjunctive Active

	Perfect	**Pluperfect**	**Future Perfect**
1st			
2nd			
3rd			
Plural			
1st			
2nd			
3rd			

Perfect System: Subjunctive Passive

	Perfect	**Pluperfect**	**Future Perfect**
1st			
2nd			
3rd			
Plural			
1st			
2nd			
3rd			

Imperatives

Singular	
Plural	

Participles

	Active	**Passive**
Future		
Present		
Perfect		

Infinitives

	Active	Passive
Future		
Present		███████
Perfect		

VOCABULARY PUZZLES

Conferô, conferre, contulî, collâtus As I warned you, the verb **ferô** is used in a great number of compound verbs—prepositional prefixes added to verb roots. Here the preposition **cum** is prefixed to the root **ferô**, rendering the meaning *to bring **together**,* or *to bring together for comparison.* Notice how the original suffix is changed from **cum** to **con-** before the initial **f-** of the verb stem. This kind of alteration occurs frequently with prepositional prefixes. Now look at the fourth principal part of this verb. It's not **conlâtus** as you may expect, but the **-n-** of the prefix assimilates to the **-l-** of the verbal stem. You've got to be on the lookout for this, because if you saw the form **collâtus** in your reading and tried to look it up under **colferô** you wouldn't find it. You've got to get good at recognizing the stem **lât-** from **ferô** and then allowing yourself some flexibility at coming up with the right prefix. Study what happens to the prefix in each of the verbs as they move from one principal part to the next. Watch carefully!

aufero	auferre	abstulî	ablâtus
adferô	adferre	attulî	allâtus, -a, -um
conferô	conferre	contulî	collâtus
offerô	offerre	obtulî	oblâtus, -a, -um
referô	referre	rettulî[75]	relâtus, -a, -um

Sê conferre A very common idiom with **conferô** is to use the reflexive pronoun to mean *to go* (lit. *to betake oneself*). So **mê conferô** means *I go*, **tê confers** means *you go*, **nôs conferimus** means *we go*, **Vôs contulistis** means *you went*, etc.

---

[75]You might not have suspected the double **t** here. In fact, though, the prefix itself is **red-**. That explains the form **rettulî**.

32

Formation and Comparison of Adverbs; Volô, Mâlô, Nôlô: Proviso Clauses

ADVERBS

Adverbs, of course, are words which modify verbs; that is, they tell you something about the way in which, or the conditions under which, the action of the verb is undertaken: *quickly, stupidly, easily, suddenly*, and so forth. And because they don't agree with anything, adverbs don't decline or take on a variety of endings to match them with their verbs.

The adverbs you've been working with up to now are, shall we say, *obvious* adverbs. Adverbs like **tamen** or **tum** aren't morphologically related at all to any other words in any way. They aren't derived from adjectives or nouns; they are *only* adverbs. But if you look at an English adverb like *quickly*, you can clearly see how this is a form derived from the adjective *quick*. To turn it into an adverb, English simply attaches the ending *-ly*.

This may not seem like a monumental discovery, but it does have an important consequence. Since *quickly* is a form which is derivable from *quick* according to a rather straight-forward rule of English grammar, an English dictionary may not list *quickly* as a separate word. You'll find it mentioned in passing only under the entry for *quick*, which is its ancestor, so to speak.

Latin also has a set of rules for deriving adverbs from adjectives, and it is important that you know them—for the same reason it's important to know the English rules of creating adverbs from adjectives: because an adverb which is a derived form from an adjective will not be given a separate dictionary listing. To look up a derived adverb, you'll first have to deconstruct it, by undoing the rules that made it an adverb in the first place. You have to reduce the adverb to the original adjective; then you can look the adjective up. Once you have the meaning of the adjective, then you can go back to your sentence and *adverbize* the meaning of the adjective. Let's get started.

ADVERBS IN THE POSITIVE DEGREE

Let's have a look at how Latin *adverbizes* an adjective. In English, as you know, we can easily turn most adjectives into adverbs simply by adding *-ly* to the stem: *quickly, speedily, ferociously*, etc. In Latin, to form an adverb in the positive degree, you start with the stem of the positive degree of the adjective. Study these rules for a moment, then form the adverbs in the positive degree from the following adjectives.

(1) Adverbs derived from adjectives of the first and second declension: stem + **-ê**.

(2) Adverbs derived from third declension adjectives: stem + **-iter**.

(3) Adverbs derived from third declension adjectives whose stem ends in **-nt-**: stem + **-er**.

Adjective	Stem	Positive Adverb
âcer, -cris, -re		
sapiêns, -ntis		
fortis, -e		
iucundus, -a, -um		
lîber, -a, -um		
clârus, -a, -um		
celer, -is, -e		

COMPARATIVE DEGREE OF ADVERBS

In English, we compare adverbs by using the word *more* placed in front of the adverb in the positive degree: *more quickly*. Latin forms a comparative adverb simply by using the comparative adjective in the neuter accusative singular form. So, to say *more beautifully*, or *rather beautifully*, or *too beautifully*,[76] Romans said *pulchrius*. Let's try a few.

Adjective	Stem	Comparative Adverb
âcer, -cris, -re		
sapiêns, -ntis		
fortis, -e		
iucundus, -a, -um		
lîber, -a, -um		
clârus, -a, -um		
celer, -is, -e		

SUPERLATIVE DEGREE OF ADVERBS

The English superlative adverb is *most* plus the adverb in the positive degree. To form the superlative degree of an adverb in Latin, you simply use the stem of the superlative degree of the adjective and add a **-ê**. To say *most beautifully*, or *very beautifully*, Romans said **pulcherrimê**.

---

[76]Remember, *more, too,* and *rather* are all possible translations of the Latin comparative degree.

Adjective	Stem	Superlative Adverb
âcer, -cris, -re		
sapiêns, -ntis		
fortis, -e		
iucundus, -a, -um		
lîber, -a, -um		
clârus, -a, -um		
celer, -is, -e		

DRILLS

Write out the positive, comparative and superlative degree adverbs derived from the following adjectives.

Adjective	Positive	Comparative	Superlative
longus, -a, -um			
miser, -a, -um			
pulcher, -chra -chrum			
fêlix, -icis			
potêns, -ntis			
facilis, -e			

DEGREES OF ADVERBS FROM IRREGULAR ADJECTIVES

As you know, there are some common adjectives which form their degrees irregularly. It may seem reasonable to assume that the adverbs derived from these adjectives would just use the irregular stems to form their own degrees. That is, you'd suppose that the positive adverb derived from the adjective **bonus** would be **bonê**, that the comparative adverb derived from the adjective's comparative degree **melior, -ius** would be **melius** (*better*) and that the superlative adverb derived from **optimus** would be **optimê**. Sometimes, that's what happens. But sometimes other irregularities start to creep in. Let's have a full look at this. Just to refresh your memory, write out the comparative and superlative degrees for the common irregular adjectives. Next, we'll study the adverbial forms derived from the three degrees. It'll be easier to note the irregular forms if you keep in mind the regular rules of formation (Wheelock 180).

Adjective	Positive	Comparative	Superlative
bonus, -a, -um			
malus, -a, -um			
magnus, -a, -um			
multus, -a, -um			
parvus, -a, -um			
(prae, prô)[77]			

Bonus

If we were to follow the rules for deriving the positive degree adverb, we'd get a form like this: **bonê**. And that's pretty close to the actual form: **bene**. The comparative degree of the adjective is **melior, -ius**. So, following the standard rules, what would be the comparative adverb? The rule says to use the neuter, accusative singular of the comparative adjective for the comparative adverb, so the form would be **melius**. And that is in fact the real form. For the superlative, the form of the adverb would be **optimê**; and that's what the real form is. Now fill in the spaces in the table above with the degree of the adverb derived from **bonus**.

Malus

The adverbs derived from **malus** are entirely regular—once you remember the irregular degrees of the adjective itself. Fill in the next row of blanks.

Magnus

The adverbs in the positive and comparative degrees from **magnus** are very odd: **magnopere** for the positive degree (not **magnê**) and **magis** for the comparative degree (not **maius**). But the superlative degree follows the rules. Fill them in.

Multus

The adverbs from **multus** are odd, too. Just **multum** for the adverb in the positive degree, **plûs** for the comparative degree, and **plûrimum** (not the expected **plûrimê**) in the superlative degree.

Parvus

The adverbs from **parvus** follow the rule, except for the positive degree, where we have **parum** instead of **parvê**.

Pro

The comparative degree of the adverb is regular; the superlative degree is either **primum** or **primô**, (not **primê**).

---

[77]The reason this is put in parentheses is that there is no positive degree of an adjective meaning *before*. But there are comparative and superlative degree adjectives meaning *prior* and *first*.

Other Adverbs

For a long (longer) (longest) time: Wheelock also shows you degree of an adverb which means *for a long time, for a rather long time,* and *for a very long time.* This adverb is not derived from an adjective; but it does show degrees as if it were. Besides, it's a very common adverb, so you need to recognize it: **diû, diûtius, diûtissimê**.

Magnopere, magis, maximê: Wheelock gives you another set of adverbs which are also derived from the adjective **magnus, -a, -um**. The meanings are straightforward enough—*greatly, more,* and *most*—but there is a fine distinction in usage of these forms from the other adverbs derived from **multus, multum, plus, and plurimum**. In the comparative, **plus** is used to compare amounts of action undertaken: **Videô plûs quam tû,** *I see more than you do.* **Magis,** however, is used to compare certain adjectives: **Hoc idôneum est magis quam illud,** *this is more suitable than that.* This may seem odd, because you learned in Chapter 26 that comparative adjectives are formed by adding the suffixes **-ior, -ius** to the stem.

These rules hold except for adjectives whose stems end in **-e-**, as **idoneus, -a, -um** does. These adjectives use the comparative adverb **magis** to form their comparative degree. Similarly, the superlative degree of these adjectives is **maximê** plus the positive degree. (You won't see **magis** or **maximê** much in this book.)

THE IRREGULAR VERB VOLÔ, VELLE, VOLUÎ, ——

The verb *to wish* has some irregularities in the present system of tenses; and it has no passive voice in either the present or the perfect system (hence, no fourth principal part). The perfect system active, however, is entirely regular. Unfortunately, there isn't any way to predict or explain many of these oddities; so you simply must memorize them. Basically **volô** is a third conjugation verb; so you should be noting how it differs from a regular third conjugation verb. That will give you some standard against which to compare it. In the following tables, I'll fill in the irregular forms; you fill in the rest. (Try to write them all in before you check your work, Wheelock 458-9).

Present system: Indicative Active

	Present	Future	Imperfect
1st			
2nd	vîs[78]		
3rd	vult		
Plural			
1st	volumus		
2nd	vultis		
3rd			

[78]This is a nasty form, since it resembles the word **vîs, vis**, *f.* meaning *power.* You'll have to struggle some to keep these two clear in your mind.

Present System: Subjunctive Active

	Present	Future	Imperfect
1st	velim[79]		vellem[80]
2nd			
3rd			
Plural			
1st			
2nd			
3rd			

Perfect System: Indicative Active

	Perfect	Pluperfect	Future Perfect
1st			
2nd			
3rd			
Plural			
1st			
2nd			
3rd			

Perfect System: Subjunctive Active

	Perfect	Pluperfect	Future Perfect
1st			
2nd			
3rd			
Plural			
1st			
2nd			
3rd			

---

[79]The irregularity of the present subjunctive is that it uses **vel-** as the stem, plus **-i-** plus personal endings. So the second person singular is **velis**, etc.

[80]Just as the regular formation of the imperfect subjunctive looks like the present infinitive plus personal endings, so the imperfect subjunctive of **volō** looks like its present infinitive **velle** plus personal endings.

Infinitives

	Active	Passive[81]
Pres.		
Perf.		
Fut.[82]		

Participles

	Active	Passive
Pres.		
Perf.		
Fut.		

THE RELATED IRREGULAR VERBS NÔLÔ AND MÂLÔ

The two irregular verbs **nôlô**, *not to want,* and **mâlô**, *to prefer,* are derivatives of **volô**. **Nôlô** is a kind of contraction of **nê + volô**, meaning literally *I don't want;* and **mâlô** comes from **magis + volô**, meaning literally *I wish more.* Because these verbs are so closely related, therefore, to the irregular verb **volô**, Wheelock thinks it right to put them together in the same chapter. Write out the conjugations of these two verbs. Again, I'll put in the irregular forms; you should be able to produce the forms that aren't irregular on your own. First, the verb **nôlô, nôlle, nôluî, ——**

Present system: Indicative Active

	Present	Future	Imperfect
1st			
2nd	nôn vîs		
3rd	nôn vult		
Plural			
1st	nolumus		
2nd	nôn vultis		
3rd			

---

[81] The verb **volô** has no passive forms; hence, *a fortiori,* no passive infinitives.

[82] The future active infinitive, you recall, is made up of the future active infinitive plus the infinitive of the verb **sum**. The future active participle is formed from the fourth principal part of the verb plus the endings **-ûrus, -a, -um**. But there is no fourth principal part of **volô**. Therefore, there can be no future active participle and no future active infinitive.

Present System: Subjunctive Active

	Present	Future	Imperfect
1st	nolim[83]		nollem[84]
2nd			
3rd			
Plural			
1st			
2nd			
3rd			

Perfect System: Indicative Active

	Perfect	Pluperfect	Future Perfect
1st			
2nd			
3rd			
Plural			
1st			
2nd			
3rd			

Perfect System: Subjunctive Active

	Perfect	Pluperfect	Future Perfect
1st			
2nd			
3rd			
Plural			
1st			
2nd			
3rd			

---

[83]The irregularity of the present subjunctive is that it uses **nol-** as the stem, plus **-i-** plus personal endings. So the second person singular is **nolis**, etc.

[84]Just as the regular formation of the imperfect subjunctive looks like the present infinitive plus personal endings, so the imperfect subjunctive of **nôlô** looks like its present **nôlle** plus personal endings.

Infinitives

	Active	Passive[85]
Fut.[86]		
Pres.		
Perf.		

Participles

	Active	Passive
Fut.		
Pres.		
Perf.		

Imperatives

Singular	**nôlî**	*Plural*	**nôlite**

MÂLÔ, MÂLLE, MÂLUÎ, ——

Present system: Indicative Active

	Present	Future	Imperfect
1st			
2nd	mavîs		
3rd	mavult		
Plural			
1st			
2nd	mavultis		
3rd			

---

[85]The verb **nolô** has no passive forms; hence, *a fortiori*, no passive infinitives.

[86]The future active infinitive, you recall, is made up of the future active infinitive plus the infinitive of the verb **sum**. The future active infinitive is formed from the fourth principal part of the verb plus the endings **-ûrus, -a, -um**. But there is no fourth principle part of **nolô**. Therefore, there can be no future active participle and no future active infinitive.

Present System: Subjunctive Active

	Present	Future	Imperfect
1st	malim		mallem
2nd			
3rd			
Plural			
1st			
2nd			
3rd			

Perfect System: Indicative Active

	Perfect	Future Perfect	Pluperfect
1st			
2nd			
3rd			
Plural			
1st			
2nd			
3rd			

Perfect System: Subjunctive Active

	Perfect	Pluperfect	Future Perfect
1st			
2nd			
3rd			
Plural			
1st			
2nd			
3rd			

Infinitives

	Active	Passive
Fut.		
Pres.		
Perf.		

Participles

	Active	Passive
Fut.		
Pres.		
Perf.		

PROVISO CLAUSES

As I warned you when you first got the subjunctive mood, there is no one way to translate the *subjunctive*. In fact, when you translate a Latin verb that's in the subjunctive into English, you're not really translating the subjunctive at all. Instead you're translating the construction that the subjunctive is in. The subjunctive mood is simply a form the verb assumes in certain constructions in Latin. What you really have to study and learn is what these constructions are before you can choose an appropriate English translation. So far, you know the following uses of the Latin subjunctive:

Name	Latin Example	English Translation
Hortatory	Vivamus atque amemus.	*Let us live and let us love.*
Purpose Clause	Hoc dicam ut vôs servem.	*I will say this to save you.*
Result Clause	Ita stultus est ut nihil possit.	*He's so stupid he can't do anything right.*
Indirect Question	Rogâvit cûr hoc factum esset.	*He asked why this happened.*
Cum Clause	Cum haec fêcisset, fûgit.	*Since he did this, he ran away.*

Can you see that you're not translating the subjunctive according to any set meaning that it has? Instead, you're examining the construction and then finding the parallel construction in English. The fact that the verbs in Latin are in the subjunctive really isn't important.

The construction you're going to study now is called the *proviso* clause, and the name itself just about tells you what kind of a clause it is. It's a subordinate clause that states the provision under which the action of the main clause can or will be fulfilled. In English, we can introduce such a clause with expressions like: *provided that, if and only if, just so long as,* and so forth. One Latin equivalent to all these is the subordinating adverb **dummodo**, which literally means something like *only while* (**modo** = *only*, **dum** = *while*). To negate a *proviso* clause, the particle **nê** is used, and not **nôn**, which you might expect. And finally, because the subjunctive is subordinate, the rules of the sequence of tenses will apply. That is, if the sentence is in primary sequence, the present subjunctive will be used; if the sentence is in secondary sequence, the imperfect subjunctive will be used. Study a couple of examples in the Wheelock text closely (page 223).

VOCABULARY PUZZLES

dîves, dîvitis (dîtis) This is a third declension adjective of one termination, which also has two possible stems: **dîvit-** or **dît-**. You must work hard to keep the form derived from the stem **dîvit-** and the noun for *riches* (**dîvitiae, -ârum**, *f.*) distinct.

pauper, pauperis Another third declension adjective of one termination. It is very often used to mean *a poor person* or *the poor.*

pâr, paris Once again, a third declension adjective of one termination. Don't confuse this with the noun **pârs, partis**, *f.* **Par** means *equal* and takes the dative case: *equal to.* (Remember the *pari*syllabic (*equal* syllable) rule?)

honor, -ôris, *m.* It very often means *public office*; a position with the government.

lêx, lêgis, *f.* Wheelock reminds you to contrast (*cp.*) **lêx**, which means *a written law*, with **iûs**, which means *right, justice*. Not all rights become written law, and justice is often not entirely recognized in law.

33

Conditions

CONDITIONAL STATEMENTS IN ENGLISH

A conditional sentence is one that goes *if something, then something else*. It has two parts: the subordinate *if* clause, called the *protasis* (*PRAH ta sis*) of the condition, and the main *then* clause, called the *apodosis* (*ah PAH da sis*) of the condition. The protasis states the condition under which the main clause can be thought to occur.

Protasis	Apodosis
If it is raining outside	*then the grass is wet.*
If you saw him yesterday	*then he must have been here.*

Pretty simple so far. But we can shape a condition so as to imply our expectation as to whether the condition will be meet. This is where things get more involved. There are basically two kinds of conditional sentences, categorized by the expectation the speaker has concerning the possibility of the fulfillment of the condition stated in the protasis. Here they are.

Open or Simple Conditions

The speaker may be making no implication as to the fulfillment of the protasis. These conditions are called *open* or *simple* conditions. *If x approaches 2000, then the value of f(x) approaches infinity.* The speaker is not implying that it is doubtful or probable that x is approaching 2000. But if x *is* approaching 2000, then the apodosis holds true. Here's another one: *If you saw him yesterday, then he was here.* The speaker is not doubting or suggesting that you did not see him yesterday, but if you *did*, then he was here. And here's another one: *If you come tomorrow, I will be happy.* Again, the speaker is not saying that it is unlikely that you will come tomorrow, but if you *do*, then ... When a simple or open condition applies to a future event, it is often called the *future-more-vivid,* or the *future real* condition.

Unreal Conditions

In this category of conditional sentences, the speaker imputes some doubt as to the fulfillment of the protasis. These categories of conditions are sometimes called the *unreal* conditions, and are further broken down into the time to which the conditions are being applied. When the protasis applies to a future event, these conditions are called *future-less-vivid, future unreal* or *should-would* condition. *If you should come (or were to come) tomorrow, then I would be happy.* (The speaker doubts that you will come, but if you *should*, then he *would* be happy.) When an unreal condition pertains to a present condition that is not being fulfilled, it is called the *present contrary-to-fact* condition. *If you were eight feet tall, you would be a great basketball player.* (But you are *not* eight feet tall, so you are *not* a great basketball player. But if you *were*...) When an unreal condition pertains to a past condition that was not fulfilled, it is called the *past contrary-to-fact* condition. *If George had been there, we would have won the game.* (But he was *not* there, so we did *not* win the game. But if he *had been* there ...)

Please be advised, however, that these formulae for the conditions aren't hard and fast. We can, and do, mix conditions when we need to. Without much trouble you could probably think of many examples of English conditional sentence that don't fit. My advice: don't do it. You'll only confuse yourself and impede your progress in Latin. For now, these simple, bare descriptions will get you on your way.

Let's summarize the basic formulae for English conditional sentences. Notice that it is the change in tense and mood in the protasis which indicates the kind of condition of the sentences.

Simple or Open Conditions

Protasis	Apodosis	Condition
pres. indic.	fut. indic.	*Future-More-Vivid*
pres. indic.	pres. indic.	*Present Simple*
past. indic.	past indic.	*Past Simple*

Unreal (and Contrary-to-Fact) Conditions

Protasis	Apodosis	Condition
should, were to	would	*Future Less Vivid*
imperf. indic	would	*Present Contrary to Fact*
plperf. indic.	would have	*Past-Contrary to Fact*

CONDITIONAL STATEMENTS IN LATIN

The same classification of conditional sentences, which you just learned for English conditions, applies to Latin conditions as well. Here is a table of the formulae for standard Latin conditions. Don't be frightened. We'll spend lots of time on all these conditions.

Open or Simple Conditions

Protasis	Apodosis	Condition
future indic.[87]	future indic.	*Future More Vivid*
present indic.	present indic.[88]	*Present Open*
past indic.[89]	past indic.	*Past Open*

One feature you should notice about these formulae is that the simple conditions all have the indicative mood in the protasis. If the mood of the verb in the protasis is in the indicative, then the condition is one of the simple or open conditions. Further refinement of the condition is then determined by the tense of the verb in the protasis. For example, if the mood of the verb in the protasis is indicative *and* in the future tense, then the condition is future-more-vivid. Let's move on to the unreal conditions.

Unreal Conditions

Protasis	Apodosis	Condition
present subj.	present subj.	*Future Less Vivid*
imperf. subj.	imperf. subj.	*Present Contrary to Fact*
plpf. subj.	plpf. subj.	*Past Contrary to Fact*

Here you can see that all unreal conditions have a subjunctive in the protasis, and the conditions are further subdivided by the tense of the verb in the protasis. Okay, enough talk. Try to classify and translate the following conditions.

Sî hoc faciet, beâtus erô.

Because the protasis is the indicative mood, it is a simple condition—one that does not imply any doubt about the fulfillment of the condition stated in the protasis. Because the tense of the protasis is future, the condition is a *future open*—a condition which is also called a *future real,* or *future more vivid. If he does this, then I will be happy.* Notice that in the Latin future more vivid, the protasis is future, whereas the English is present.

---

[87]This takes some getting used to, because our English future open condition has a present tense in the protasis. We say *If they say so, we'll do it.* But Latin would say, more logically, *If they **will** say so, we'll do it.* Also watch for the future perfect in the protasis of a future open condition. This is logical too. When we say *If they do it, they will be in trouble,* we mean that they will be in trouble *after* they do it. Since a future action that takes place *before* another action in the future is expressed by the future perfect tense, then it makes sense to say *If they will have done it, they will be in trouble.*

[88]Or its equivalent. We can say, *If they come, call me.* The mood in the apodosis is imperative, but clearly this condition is referring to a future event and is not implying any doubt as to the fulfillment of the condition stated in the protasis.

[89]I.e., any of the past tenses: perfect, imperfect, pluperfect.

Sî hoc facit, beâtus sum.

Present simple or open. *If he is doing this, then I am happy.*

Sî hoc fêcit, beâtus eram.

Past simple or open. *If he did this, I was happy.*

Sî hoc faciat, beâtus sim.

Now the mood of the protasis is subjunctive, so you have one of the unreal conditions. Since the tense is present, the condition is a future less vivid, and is represented in English with *should-would*. *If he should do this (I doubt he will), I would be happy.*

Sî hoc faceret, beâtus essem.

The mood is subjunctive and the tense is imperfect, so this is a present contrary-to-fact condition. *If he were doing this (but he is not), I would be happy (but I'm not).*

Sî hoc fêcisset, beâtus fuissem.

Pluperfect subjunctive in the protasis, so this is a past-contrary to fact condition. *If he had done this (but he did not), I would have been happy (but I wasn't).*

REVIEW

To establish the kind of condition in a Latin conditional sentence, follow these simple steps:

1. Find the protasis.
2. Establish whether the mood is subjunctive or indicative.

    a. If the mood of the verb in the protasis is indicative, then you have one of the simple or open conditions: future, present, or past.

    b. If it is subjunctive, find the tense.

        i.   If the tense is present, the condition is future-less-vivid (also called *should-would* or future unreal).

        ii. If the tense is imperfect, the condition is present-contrary-to-fact.

        iii. If the tense is pluperfect, the condition is past-contrary-to-fact.

I strongly suggest that you go to Wheelock's Optional Self-Tutorial Exercises for this chapter (page 388), and work through the list of conditional sentences. (You can listen to me talk through the exercises at www.languages. uncc.edu/clas-sics/ Wheelock.) The only way to internalize these rules is to practice applying them constantly. Ask yourself what kind of condition the sentence is before you translate a single word. Also, practice writing out the basic formulae for the Latin conditional sentences until you have them thoroughly memorized.

DRILLS

Here's a Latin simple open condition in the present tense: **Hoc dîcis, vêritâtem sciô**, *if you're saying this, then I know the truth.* You're going to change the tense and mood of the verbs to change the condition as instructed.

Past Contrary to Fact

Sî hoc		vêritâtem	

Future Less Vivid

Sî hoc		vêritâtem	

Present Contrary to Fact

Sî hoc		vêritâtem	

Past Open

Sî hoc		vêritâtem	

VOCABULARY PUZZLES

quis, quid When the indefinite pronoun **aliquis, aliquid** is preceded in the sentence by **sî, nisi, num,** or **nê,** then the **ali-** drops off, leaving just the inflected endings **quis, quid.** Consequently, you're going to see lots of things like this: **Sî quis haec faciat, mihi placeat**, *if anyone should do this, I would be pleased.* If you forget that the **quis** is really short for **aliquis**, you'd probably start translating the sentence *if who . . .* , and that will get you nowhere fast. The way I remembered the rule was this little jingle: *After **sî, nisi, num,** and **nê**, all the **ali**'s fall away.*

Deponent Verbs; Ablative
with Special Deponents

DEPONENT VERBS

To master the material in the chapter, you're going to have to undo something you learned earlier in the term. You learned that some forms of a verb indicate the passive voice, and that the passive means the subject of the verb is receiving the action of the verb. So, for example, you learned to translate **amâtur** as *he was loved*, or **visa est**, as *she was seen*. In this chapter, you're going to see that it is not always the case that a passive form is *translated* as a passive voice.

What does that mean? There are many verbs in Latin which have almost no active forms but whose passive forms nevertheless must be translated *as if* they were active. These verbs are called deponent, from **dê + ponô,** because they have *set aside* their active forms. In short, a deponent verb is a verb which can be passive in form but active in meaning.[90]

Relax. Everything will be fine. There is a tendency for beginning students of Latin to assume that a deponent verb is so thoroughly exceptional that nothing they have learned about Latin verbs applies. This is a mistake. Deponent verbs are unusual only in this respect: they drop most of their active forms, and their passive forms must be translated as if they were active. Aside from this, deponent verbs follow the rules of inflection and conjugation to the letter.

DICTIONARY CONVENTION FOR DEPONENT VERBS

Imagine that the verb **laudô** had only passive forms. What would the dictionary entry look like? The first dictionary entry of any verb is always the first person singular, present indicative. If **laudô** had no active forms, then the first entry would be passive instead of active: **laudor** instead of **laudô.**

The second entry of any verb is the present infinitive from which you deduce the conjugation of the verb by dropping the infinitive ending. If **laudô** had no active forms, the present infinitive would be passive: **laudârî** instead of **laudâre.** Although you're working only with passive forms, by dropping the infinitive ending **-rî,** you could still tell that verb belongs to the first conjugation.

---

[90]There are just a couple of exceptions to this, as you will see. Deponent verbs do have two active forms. And they have a passive form—the gerundive—which is translated as a passive.

The third entry of any verb is the third principal part, from which is derived the perfect system *active*. But because we're imagining that **laudô** doesn't have any active forms, there would be no third principal part listed.

The fourth entry of any verb is the fourth principal part, the perfect passive participle, which is used with the verb **sum** to form the perfect system passive. Hence the fourth entry of the **laudô**, if it had no active forms, would still be **laudâtus.** Taken together, then, the dictionary entry of **laudô** with its active forms removed would look like this:

laudor, laudârî, laudâtus.

Similarly for verbs of the other conjugations. Without their active forms, the dictionary would list them like this:

moneor, monêrî, monitus

dûcor, dûcî, ductus

capior, capî, captus

audior, audîrî, audîtus.

In each of these cases, you can still see to which conjugations each of these verbs belong by looking at the infinitive, even if the verbs have no active forms.

So there you have it. If these verbs had no active forms, you'd have three entries, all of them in the passive voice. Since a deponent verb is one which has set aside most all of its active forms, a dictionary entry would look like these. In fact, that's the easiest (and only) way to tell whether a verb you're looking at in the dictionary is deponent. The listings will be passive and not active.

Now tell me what you can about this verb: **hortor, -ârî, hortâtus sum.** From the first entry you can tell the verb is deponent because the dictionary is giving you the passive first person singular instead of the active. The verb has no active voice. Looking at the second entry, you can tell that the verb belongs to the first conjugation, because **-ârî** is what the passive infinitive of a first conjugation looks like. Therefore, the stem from which you'll build the present system of tenses is **hortâ-**.

The third entry is the perfect passive participle with a conjugated form of the verb **sum.** Instead of listing a blank where the perfect active is normally listed in a non-deponent verb, the entry for a deponent verb skips over it and goes directly to the participle and adds **sum** to show that this is the perfect system. But the participle **hortâtus** is entirely predictable, since first conjugation verbs form their perfect passive participle by adding **-tus** to the stem of the first principal part—in this case **hortâ-**.

There are deponent verbs belonging to all four conjugations. Examine this list of deponent verbs and write down their conjugation.

Verb		Conjugation
1.	patior, -î, passus sum	
2.	experior, -îrî, expertus sum	
3.	fateor, -êrî, fassus sum	

Verb	Conjugation
4.	loquor, -î, locûtus sum	
5.	ûtor, -î, ûsus sum	
6.	nâscor, -î, nâtus sum	
7.	morior, -î, mortuus sum	
8.	proficîscor, -î, profectus sum	
9.	cônor, -ârî, cônâtus sum	
10.	arbitror, -ârî, arbitrâtus sum	

It is important not to forget that deponent verbs conjugate in ways that are entirely consistent with other verbs of their conjugation. The only difference is that deponent verbs have *set aside* their active finite forms and the remaining passive forms are translated as it they are active.

PARTICIPLES OF DEPONENT VERBS

Let's review. A participle is a verbal adjective. It has tense (present, future, or perfect) and voice (active and passive). This should be simple for deponent verbs. They'll have participles only in the passive voice. That's a logical inference, but there are a couple of things you're forgetting. Let's look at the participles of a regular, non-deponent verb. Fill in this table for the verb **laudô** (Wheelock 455).

	Active	Passive
Future		
Present		
Perfect		

First, even regular verbs don't have participles in every tense in both the active and passive voice. The present tense has only an active voice. There is no such thing as a present passive participle of any verb in Latin. So if a deponent verb dispensed with the present active participle, it would have no participle at all in the present tense. What does it do? It creates an active participle for the present tense according to the rules governing the conjugation to which it belongs.

Secondly, while it's true that the future tense has participles of both the active and passive voices, the future passive participle is the gerundive. As you may recall, the gerundive has a quirky meaning to it, so it's not really an acceptable, general purpose participle. For that, a deponent verb uses a future active participle, and reserves the gerundive for the future passive periphrastic. And—get this—it translates it *as a passive* voice. So you can see that it's not quite true to say that a deponent verb is one with no active voice and which translates the passive forms as if they're active. It does have two active forms—the present and future participle—and it translates its future passive participle—the gerundive—as a passive. It would be true to say that a deponent verb is one with no active *finite forms* and which translates the passive *finite* forms as if they were active.

INFINITIVES OF DEPONENT VERBS

This is a much simpler matter than participles, and that's because verbs have infinitives of both voices in all the tenses. Here, the deponent verb discards the present and the perfect active forms. In the future, however, we have a problem. The future passive infinitive is so weird that even the Romans avoided it. So if that's true, a deponent verb would have no serviceable future infinitive. What does it do? In the place of the future passive infinitive, it makes a future active infinitive, and uses that.

SYNOPSES OF VERBS

So you can get an overview of a deponent verb, I'm going to write out a synopsis of the verb **arbitror, -ârî, arbitrâtus sum**, *to think* in the third person singular masculine. Study each of these forms carefully.

Indicative Mood

	Active	Passive
Present		arbitrâtur
Future		arbitrâbitur
Imperfect		arbitrâbâtur
Perfect		arbitrâtus est
Pluperfect		arbitrâtus erat
Future Perfect		arbitrâtus erit

Subjunctive Mood

	Active	Passive
Present		arbitrêtur
Imperfect		arbitrârêtur[91]
Perfect		arbitrâtus sit
Pluperfect		arbitrâtus esset

---

[91] This is where you need to remember that the imperfect subjunctive is *not* the present infinitive plus personal endings. If that's what you're thinking, you'd probably be tempted to write some monstrosity like **arbitrâritur.** No, no, no! The imperfect subjunctive is the present stem, in this case **arbitrâ-**, because this is a first conjugation verb, plus **-sê-**, which becomes **-rê-**, plus personal endings.

Participles

	Active	Passive
Future	arbitrâtûrus[92]	arbitrandus[93]
Present	arbitrâns, -ntis[94]	
Perfect		arbitrâtus[95]

Infinitives

	Active	Passive
Future	arbitrâtûrum esse[96]	
Present		arbitrârî
Perfect		arbitrâtum esse

Imperatives

Singular[97]	arbitrâre	Plural	arbitrâminî

---

[92]Deponent verbs also have a future active participle formed, as is required, from the fourth principal part of the verb: **arbitrâtûrus, -a, -um**. It's translated actively: *about to think.*

[93]The future passive participle, as you know, is the gerundive: first principal part + **-nd** + **-us, -a, -um**. The gerundive is passive in meaning even for a deponent verb. Hence the gerundive is the *only* form of a deponent verb which is passive in form *and* passive in meaning.

[94]Deponent verbs have an active present participle. The form is as you would expect: first principal part + the adjectival ending **-ns, -ntis**. So for **arbitror** the form is **arbitrâns, arbitrantis**. It has an active meaning: *thinking.*

[95]How do you translate this? Think about it. It's perfect, and it needs to be translated actively. Hence it's *having thought*, not *having **been** thought.* Another peculiarity about the perfect participle of a deponent verb is that it's also translated very often as a present tense. So **arbitrâtus** might be translated *thinking.*

[96]Deponent verbs have future active infinitives, as they must. The future passive infinitive form is practically non-existent even in non-deponent verbs: it's a form called the supine with **îrî**. The future active infinitive is formed just the way a non-deponent verbs forms it: the perfect passive participle + **ûr** + adjectival endings **-us, -a, -um**. So for **arbitror** the form is **arbitrâtûrum esse.**

[97]The imperatives of deponent verbs are identical in form to the second persons singular and plural of the present tense: here **arbitrâris** (or **arbitrâre**) and **arbitrâminî**. The great god of context will help you decide which it is, an imperative or an indicative.

FATEOR, FATÊRÎ, FASSUS SUM

Now you try one. Fill out these charts with a synopsis of the verb **fateor** in the 3rd person plural, feminine.

Indicative Mood

	Active	Passive
Present		
Future		
Imperfect		
Perfect		
Pluperfect		
Future Perfect		

Subjunctive Mood

	Active	Passive
Present		
Imperfect		
Perfect		
Pluperfect		

Participles

	Active	Passive
Future		
Present		
Perfect		

Infinitives

	Active	Passive
Future		
Present		
Perfect		

Imperatives

Singular		Plural	

VOCABULARY PUZZLES

ûtor, ûtî, ûsus sum The verb takes the ablative case to complete its meaning. It means something like *I enjoy myself with* or, as Wheelock offers on page 238, *I am benefitting myself by means of . . .* Often, however, the translation *I am using* fits the bill. **Ûsus sum multîs librîs**, *I used (lit. enjoyed myself with) many books.*

audeô, -êre, ausus sum A handful of verbs are regular in the present system, but become deponent in perfect system. As you can see by this dictionary entry, the verb **audeô** skips over the perfect system active entirely and goes directly to the participle **ausus.** This is telling you that in the perfect system this verb is deponent, hence **ausus sum** means *I dared.* Verbs of which only one of the tense systems is deponent are called *semi-deponent.*

35

More Uses of the Dative

DATIVE WITH SPECIAL VERBS

You've seen before that Latin sometimes conceives actions differently from the way we with English as our native language might expect. For example, remember the verb **careô, -êre, caruî, caritûrus**? For us it means *to lack*, and when we use the verb *to lack* in English, it is followed by the direct object case. We might be tempted to assume, therefore, that the Latin verb **careô** will also take the accusative case. But it doesn't. **Careô** is construed with the ablative case in Latin. Similarly, our verb *to use* is followed by a direct object, but the Latin equivalent, **ûtôr, ûtî, ûsus sum**, takes the ablative case, obviously because Latin simply doesn't conceive of the action of using something in quite the same way we do in English. So the point of all this is that you've got to be careful not to rely too heavily on your English instincts as you try to feel your way through Latin constructions. But you've known that for some time now.

In this chapter, you're presented with several very common verbs which take the dative case instead of the accusative case, as we might expect simply by examining their English translations. There is no rule we can concoct in advance that will tip you off whether a certain verb in Latin will take the dative case. You simply must note in the dictionary entry that a verb takes the dative and try to memorize it. The only helpful advice is that you memorize the verbs with a definition which will make the dative case object obvious. Here's the list:

1st Prin. Part	3rd Prin. Part	4th Prin. Part	Meaning
crêdô (3)	crêdidî	crêditus	*to believe **in*** (not *to trust*)
ignôscô (3)	ignôvî	ignôtus	*to grant pardon **to*** (not *to forgive*)
imperô (1)	imperâvî	imperâtus	*to give order **to*** (not *to order*)
noceô (2)	nocuî	nocitus	*to do harm **to*** (not *to harm*)
parcô (3)	pepercî	parsûrus	*to be lenient **to*** (not *to spare*)
pâreô (2)	pâruî	———	*to be obedient **to*** (not *to obey*)
persuâdeô (2)	persuâsî	persuâsus	*to be persuasive **to*** (not *to persuade*)
placeô (2)	placuî	placitus	*to be pleasing **to*** (not *to please*)
serviô (4)	servîvî	servîtus	*to be a slave **to*** (not *to serve*)
studeô (2)	studuî	———	*to be eager **for*** (not *to study*)

This is quite a list of verbs, but as you can see, almost all have clear English derivatives, which gives you some insight into their meanings. **Pareô** and **ignôscô** are going to be a little tricky, especially **ignôscô**, since it looks like it ought to be *not to recognize* (from a negative prefix + **nôscô**). Actually, this can be used to your advantage, if you think of it this way: *forgive and forget* means *to put out of mind.*

Another aid to memorizing these verbs might be to cluster them together into groups of actions and their opposites, or into groups of related ideas. Something like this: You trust in and are persuaded by what you find pleasing.

I.   command, obey, serve

II. harm, forgive, spare

III. persuade, trust, please

Wheelock omits an important detail about these verbs: none of these verbs can be used in the passive voice. Only verbs which are truly transitive (*i.e.* take an accusative object) can be used both in the active and in the passive voices. To say *he is trusted* in Latin, consequently, it would be wrong to say **Crêditur.** Instead, Latin uses the verb impersonally: *Trust is shown to him,* which would be **Eî crêditur.** Here are some examples: **Nôbîs nôn pârêbitur,** *we will not be obeyed* (literally *obedience will not given to us*); **Eîs ignotum est,** *they were forgiven*; **Mîlitibus imperâtum est,** *the soldiers were ordered.*

DATIVE WITH COMPOUND VERBS

The point of this section is simple: sometimes verbs alter their configuration of objects when prefixes are added. And that's all really that can be said. You've seen already that verbs can pick up prefixes which slightly change the meaning of the verb. Most of these changes have been trivial: **capiô** to **rêcipiô**, *take back* to **accipiô**, *accept.* Sometimes, however, the addition of a prefix will substantially change the way a verbal root has to be understood. Look at some English examples of this phenomenon: *re*fer, *de*fer, *pre*fer, *dif*fer, *in*fer; *re*voke, *in*voke, *pro*voke.

And we could go on like this for days. Latin is similarly able to change the meaning of a root verb with its differing prefixes; furthermore, sometimes the change of meaning also involves a change in construction. The verb **sum**, as you know, means *to be*, and is intransitive. But add the preposition **prae** to it, and it means *to be in command of* and it takes the dative case. For example, **Dumnorix equitâtuî praeerat** means *Dumnorix was in charge of the cavalry.* Further, add the preposition **ad**, and **sum** means *to support* and takes the dative case (not, as we might expect from the English equivalent, the accusative case): **Caesar amîcîs aderat** means *Caesar supported*—or *was there for*—*his friends.*

Wheelock gives you a list of examples where you can see the change of meaning and change of object that prefixes often create in verbs. You should look them over, but it will not be necessary for you to memorize them. As you gather more experience reading Latin, you'll begin to recognize compound verbs like this which take the dative case. For your purposes now, you should simply think about this. If you're reading a sentence which seems to lack a needed direct object for a verb, check to see whether the verb you're considering is a compound (made up of a root and a prefix). If it is, then look for a dative case, since this may be one of those occasions where the meaning of the verb has been altered by the prefix and now calls for a dative case.

VOCABULARY PUZZLES

antepônô (3), -posuî, -positus Obviously this is a compound of the verb you already know **pônô** and the preposition **ante**: *to place before*, hence to prefer. The meaning is completed with an accusative direct object and the dative: **Antepônô vêritâtem pecûniae**, *I place truth before money* → *I prefer truth to money*.

36

Jussive Noun Clauses; Fiô

JUSSIVE NOUN CLAUSES

Let's first try to define what is meant by the expression *jussive noun clause*. Let's start from the back end. A clause, as you know, is a thought, containing at least a noun or pronoun and a finite verb (i.e., a verb with person). You know, don't you, that a sentence can be made of only one clause—a simple sentence—or it can be made of many clauses strung together or subordinated with conjunctions. A jussive noun clause, therefore, is going to be some thought embedded in a sentence. So what does *noun* mean in this description? A noun, you should remember, is the name for a substance or an idea. A noun clause, therefore, must be a clause which is treated like a noun in a sentence. And what does *jussive* mean? You've seen *jussive* before in the subjunctive construction called the *jussive subjunctive*, which is a kind of wish or command. Put it all together, then, a jussive noun clause is going to be a clause indicating a command, which is treated as a noun in a sentence. And what does that mean?

Another, less accurate, way of visualizing this construction is simply as an *indirect* command. You know how Latin expresses direct commands. It uses the imperative mood or the jussive subjunctive.

| Adiuvâ(te) nôs, *help us!* | Nolî(te) nôs adiuvâre, *don't help us!* |
| Adiuvêmus eôs, *let's help them.* | Nê eôs adiuvêmus, *let's not help them.* |

What happens to these direct commands if they are made indirect? That means, suppose the command is being reported and is the object of a verb? What do we do in English? We rewrite the original command to an accusative-infinitive construction. Like this. Suppose I were to have asked you (plural) to help me, and then a friend of mine reported it to someone else:

Direct Command	Indirect Command
Help me!	He asked *them to help* him.

We change the pronoun of the indirect statement as we need to in order to recapture the intention of the original and to take into account the way the original direct command is being re-presented. But the bottom line is, the original direct command is recast as an accusative-infinitive construction.

How about Latin? How does it form an indirect command—the jussive noun clause? When a direct command is written as an indirect command in Latin, it assumes the form of a purpose clause, using **ut** for an original positive command, and **nê** for an original negative command (which we also can call a prohibition). This shouldn't present you with much of a problem. You'd just rewrite the original command as an **ut** or **nê** clause with the verb in the subjunctive in accordance with the rules of the sequence of tenses. But there is one odd twist. Latin may actually insert the pronoun in the main clause after the main verb, and then repeat the person in the personal ending of verb within the indirect command. Watch:

Direct Command	Indirect Command
Adiuvâte nôs, *help us.*	Rogô vôs ut nôs adiuvêtis, *I ask you that you help us* or *I ask you to help us.*

Do you see? The **vôs** in the main clause of the second sentence is, logically speaking, superfluous, since you've already got the second person plural in the finite form of the dependent subjunctive **adiuvêtis**.) But let's try translating the sentence literally: *I am asking you—that you should help us.* If we break the sentence apart just a little, we can see how the repeated pronoun seems to work. The thing you're asking for, that is, the contents of the indirect command, is treated as if it were an accusative object of the main verb of the sentence. *I am asking you "x"*, where "x" is the indirect command. Let's look at some more examples of indirect commands and try a little variety. Watch for two things: (1) the leading verbs take their objects in cases that are different from what we'd expect; (2) the dependent subjunctive in the indirect command observes the sequence of tenses.

Direct Command	Indirect Command
Adiuvâte nôs.	Orô vôs ut nôs adiuvêtis, *I beg you to help us.*
Adiuvâte nôs.	Hortâti sumus eôs ut nôs adiuvârent, *we encouraged them to help us.*
Adiuvâte vôs.	Imperat eîs ut sê adiuvent, *he orders them to help them(selves).*
Nôlî nôs adiuvâre.[98]	Quaesîvit ab tê nê nôs adiuvâres, *he requested from you that you not help us* → *he asked you not to help us.*
Nôlî nôs adiuvâre.	Persuadêbit eî nê nôs adiuvet, *he will persuade him not to help us.*

Now have a quick look at the pronouns in the main clauses of the sentences with the indirect commands. You have different cases, don't you? In the first sentence, you have an accusative, **vôs**. In the second, you also have an accusative, **eôs**. But in the third, you have a dative, **eîs**. In the fourth, **ab** + an ablative. In the last one, you have a dative, **eî**. What's all this about? The reason has nothing to do with the

---

[98]Latin forms its negative direct command by using the imperative of the verb **nôlô** plus a complementary infinitive. Literally it means something like *Don't wish to . . .*

indirect command that follows it. It's simply that different verbs that can take indirect command have different ways of configuring their object.

The verbs **orô** and **hortôr** put the person to whom you're making the request in the accusative case. But **imperô** and **persuadeô** take the dative case. **Quaerô** takes **ab** + ablative. That's just the way it is.

Now try your hand at a little composition. Put the following direct commands into indirect commands dependent on the indicated leading verb. I'll do the first one. Remember to observe the sequence of tenses and remember that there are a number of ways you can construe the persons. The answers in the back are just one way of writing them. Your main job here is to observe the sequence of tenses.

DRILLS

1.	Facite id. (Imperâvêrunt)
	Imperâvêrunt vôbîs ut id facerêtis. (*They ordered you to do it.*)
2.	Adiuvâ mê. (Persuâsit)
3.	Nê dûx hostibus nôceat. (Persuâsêrunt)
4.	Hoc mihi dent. (Rogâbant)
5.	Nê cîvitâtem tollant. (Imperâbat)

THE IRREGULAR VERB: FIÔ, FIÊRÎ

If you were asked to produce the passive voice of the verb **faciô**, you'd probably start writing: **facior, faceris, facitur**, and so forth. Unfortunately, this wouldn't be right. The verb **faciô** has an unusual passive voice *in the present system*. It uses forms from the verb **fiô, fiêrî**, *to be done, to become, to happen.*

Two things you need to note right away before we start looking at the verb itself: (1) the verb **faciô** has an irregular passive *only* in the present system (*i.e.*, the present, future, and imperfect tenses), but it becomes quite regular in the perfect system, where it uses its 4th principal part **factus, -a, -um** and a conjugated form of the verb **sum**; (2) the forms of **fiô** are active but have passive meanings (just the reverse of deponent verbs!). Despite its irregular meaning, the forms of the verb are quite predictable. Here's everything you need to know about the **fiô** to conjugate it correctly: Except for the infinitive, it conjugates just like a third conjugation verb i-stem, with a root **fe-**.

Now try to conjugate the present system of this verb. Do one tense at a time; stop after each and check your work (Wheelock 255).

Present System: Indicative Active

	Present	Future	Imperfect
1st			
2nd			
3rd			
Plural			
1st			
2nd			
3rd			

Present System: Subjunctive Active

	Present	Future[99]	Imperfect
1st			
2nd			
3rd			
Plural			
1st			
2nd			
3rd			

All the other forms of **fiô** are going to come from its parent verb **faciô, -ere**. (The imperatives **fî, fîte** are rare enough to be ignored. So ignore them.)

VOCABULARY PUZZLES

fiô, fiêri, factus sum Wheelock's way of listing the verb as a separate vocabulary item could cause some confusion. It might lead you to think this a kind of reverse deponent verb. I think it'll cause you less confusion just to remember that the verb **faciô** has an unusual stem it uses to form the present system passive than to think of **fiô** as a verb standing on its own. **Fiô** is an irregularity of **faciô**.

---

[99]No future subjunctives, remember?

The Verb Eô; Place and Time

IRREGULAR VERB EÔ

Like most of the irregular verbs you've had to learn so far, the irregular forms of the verb *to go* in Latin are almost entirely limited to the present system of tenses. As I hope to convince you, even those irregularities aren't so peculiar as they might first seem to be. With just a couple of mild reminders, you can produce all the irregular forms of **eô** without having to be shown them in advance. Let's start by looking at the verb in all its principal parts: **eô, îre, iî, itus, -a, -um**.

What's the stem of the first principal part of this verb? Remembering your rule from Chapter 1, you know that the stem of the first principal part is the present infinitive less the infinitive ending **-re**. Accordingly, the stem of the first principal part of the verb **eô, îre** is **î-**. So to form the present tense of **eô** you should simply add the personal endings. And that's what you do—with the following refinement: when the personal ending starts with a vowel, the stem changes from **î-** to **e-**. Now conjugate the present tense of **eô** (Wheelock 260).

	Singular	**Plural**
1st		
2nd		
3rd		

What about the other tenses of the present system, the imperfect and the future? Well, the formula for the imperfect tense for all verbs is first principal part + **bâ** + personal endings. The verb **eô** follows the rule without exception. Next, the future. The future tense of **eô** is slightly odd. As a fourth conjugation verb, it should form the future tense using the tense sign vowels **-â/ê-**. Instead, **eô** uses the **-be-** tense sign before its personal endings—the tense sign used by the first and second conjugation verbs. Okay, knowing all this, you should be able to conjugate the imperfect and future tenses. Give it a try, and then check your work (Wheelock 260).

	Imperfect	Future
1st		
2nd		
3rd		
Plural		
1st		
2nd		
3rd		

And what about the subjunctive mood of the present and imperfect tenses? There are no irregularities here at all. The present subjunctive is, as you should expect, the present stem + **â** + the personal endings; the imperfect subjunctive is, in effect, the present infinitive plus personal endings. So conjugate the present and imperfect subjunctive of **eô**.

	Present	Imperfect
1st	[100]	
2nd		
3rd		
Plural		
1st		
2nd		
3rd		

The perfect system, as I promised you, contains hardly any irregular forms. The third principal part is **iî**, which means the stem for the perfect system of tenses is **i-**, to which you then add the appropriate tense/personal endings. The only oddity is that in the perfect tense, when the ending begins with **-is-**, such as the second person singular and plural, the two **i**'s contract to one. That's an understandable simplification. The same thing happens in the perfect infinitive, where **i-** + **isse** gives you **îsse**, not **iisse**. So conjugate the perfect system of tenses (Wheelock 260-1).

---

[100]Don't forget now, the first principal part is **î-**, which changes to **e-** when followed by a vowel.

	Perfect	Pluperfect	Future Perfect
1st		[101]	
2nd			
3rd			
Plural			
1st			
2nd			
3rd			

Finally the perfect system in the subjunctive mood—the perfect and pluperfect tenses—are likewise entirely regular: perfect → **i-** + **-erî-** + personal endings; pluperfect → perfect infinitive + personal endings.

	Perfect	Pluperfect
1st		[102]
2nd		
3rd		
Plural		
1st		
2nd		
3rd		

And that's the whole picture. Wheelock omits the passive voice of **eô** for the obvious reason that it can only be used in a few rather special constructions. (What would the passive voice of *to go* be, anyway?)

PLACE CONSTRUCTIONS

This section will present you very little trouble. For the most part, as you know, Latin uses prepositions to show place where, to which, and from which. Like this:

In urbe sunt, *they are in the city.*

Ex urbe vênêrunt, *they came from the city.*

In urbem îbunt, *they will go into the city.*

---

[101]Don't be confused by this one. You might be thinking that the **i-** stem should become **e-** before the vowel of the ending. Not so. This **i-** is from the third principal part of the verb, not from the first, and only the first principal part **i-** changes before vowels.

[102]See the previous note.

There are all kinds of prepositions which will indicate spacial relationships: **ad**, **sub**, **dê** . . . Most *place constructions*, therefore, will be covered by any one of a number of prepositions. However, when the location to or from which is a named city or a small island, Latin discards the prepositions or uses the locative (*LAH kuh tiv*) case.

The Locative Case

It seems clear that Latin originally had more cases than the five or six which survived into the historical period. One of them was a case used to show location, which we reasonably call the *locative* case, but we might just as easily call it the *place-where case*. These locative case endings are nearly entirely limited to the names of cities and small islands in Classical Latin. Here's the rule for its formation:

(1) For singular nouns of the 1st and 2nd declension, the form is identical to the genitive singular of the noun's normal declension.

(2) The locative of 3rd declension nouns in the singular is identical to the ablative singular.

(3) For plural nouns of all declensions the form is the same as the ablative plural.

You might have a question right now: *How can the name of a city be plural?* Good question. It just happens that the names of some cities are plural in Latin, but it doesn't mean that there are more than one of the city. For example, *Athens* in Latin is **Athênae, -ârum (f)**; for the city Syracuse, **Syrâcûsae, -ârum (f)**. It's probably because the word refers not to the city itself, but to the inhabitants: the Athenians—i.e., where the Athenians live, and so on.

Motion Toward/From Cities, Small Islands, and Home

In place of the regular prepositions **ad**, **dê** and so on, which show motion toward or away from, Latin simply uses the names of the cities and small islands in the accusative case or the ablative case without the prepositions. This holds true also for the Latin noun for *home*: **domus, -ûs** *m*. You won't see **ad domum eô**, but **domum eô**, *I am going home*.[103] Latin didn't need the preposition because, just as in English, the word for *home* often contains a sense of motion toward. When I was in France a while back, I saw this advertizement outside a hotel: *English spoken here, feel yourself home*. There's something odd about this, isn't there, and that's because you get the picture of someone down on his hands and knees groping his way home along the road. There's just enough of a feeling of movement in our word *home* to make this translation laughable.

There is one peculiarity with the Latin word **domus**. As you can tell from the dictionary entry, **domus** is a fourth declension noun. But when it's used in a construction involving motion to or from a location, then **domus** takes on second declension endings. Consequently, the locative for **domus** isn't **domûs**—the genitive case—but **domî**, which would be the genitive case if **domus** were second declension. Similarly, to show motion from home, Latin uses **domô**, not **domû**. Let's

---

[103]For more help on this, see the "Latin lesson" in Monty Python's *Life of Brian*.

look at some examples of these place constructions side-by-side with a typical construction with prepositions:

	urbs, -is	Rôma, -ae	Athênae, -ârum	domus, -ûs/î
Place From	dê/ab/ex urbe	Rômâ	Athênîs	domô
Place Where	in urbe	Rômae	Athênîs	domî
Place To	ad urbem	Rômam	Athênâs	domum

And now some more examples with a little more context:

Ibit Syrâcûsâs, *he will go to Syracuse.*

Ibit ad urbem, *he will go to the city.*

Hoc Athenîs factum est, *this happened at Athens.*

Hoc in urbe factum est, *this happened in the city.*

Meî amîcî Rômae sunt, *my friends are at Rome.*

Eôs Delphôs mîsit, *he sent them to Delphi.*

Vênit domô, *he came from home.*

Domî librôs scrîpsit, *he wrote the books at home.*

Litterâs domum mîsêrunt, *they sent the letter home.*

TIME CONSTRUCTIONS

Let's review for a moment the time construction you already know. You've been working with the ablative of time for several chapters now.

Paucibus diêbus domum ibunt, *they will come home in a few days.*

Illô diê profectî sunt, *they set out on that day.*

As you can see, the Latin ablative of time has two possible translations into English. In the first example, the ablative of time means the time *within* which something is going to be accomplished; in the second, it is simply time *when* something happened. For that reason you often see the Ablative of Time divided into two descriptions. It's sometimes called the *Ablative of Time When* or the *Ablative of Time Within Which,* because there are two different English meanings possible for this one Latin construction. Okay, enough review.

The new time construction you get in this chapter does not use the ablative case, rather it puts the unit of time in the accusative case. Its name completely describes its meaning: accusative of duration of time. Like this:

Multôs complûrês diês fugiêbant, *they fled for several days.*

Unum annum rêgnâbimus, *we will rule for one year.*

VOCABULARY PUZZLES

ut + indic. You know that the subordinating conjunction **ut** can introduce purpose, result and jussive noun clauses. When it does, the mood of the verb in the **ut** clause is subjunctive. But **ut** can also be used to begin a comparison or simile or even a clause of attendant circumstance, like a **cum** clause. When it does, the verb of the clause is in the indicative mood. This is how you can tell the difference between **ut** meaning *so that* etc., where the verb is subjunctive, and when it means *as* or *like* or just *when*.

licet (2) licuit The principal parts of this verb should tip you off that something's odd about it. It is used only in third person or the infinitive. Verbs that work like this are called *impersonal* verbs. It requires an infinitive and a dative case. Some examples: **Nôn licet vôbîs abîre**, *it is not permitted for you to leave* or *you can't leave*; **Pûtô licêre nôbîs venîre**, *I think we are allowed to leave*—lit. *I think it is permitted for us to leave*.

soleô (2), solitus sum First, notice that the verb is semi-deponent, as you can tell by the third entry. Therefore, **solitus sum** means *I was accustomed*. Next, **soleô** is a little tricky to translate. **Soleô transîre viam** doesn't really mean *I am accustomed to crossing the road,* but it means that I cross the road regularly or usually: *it is my custom* or *habit to cross the road*. Try this when you see a form of **soleô**: translate the verb as the adverb *customarily* or *usually* or *normally*, then promote the complementary infinitive to the main verb. Like this: **Solêtis nôbîs vêritâtem dîcere**, *you customarily—normally, usually—tell us the truth*.

38

Relative Clauses of Characteristic

RELATIVE CLAUSE (REVISITED)

By now you should have a fairly good mastery of the basics of the relative clauses. A relative clause picks out something in the main clause—the antecedent—and gives you more information about it. Like this:

> Amîcus vester, quî Romae consul erat, tôtam pecûnciam consûmpsit, *your friend, who was consul at Rome, used up all the money.*

> Haec opera omnibus placuêrunt quî vênerant, *these works pleased everyone who had come.*

RELATIVE CLAUSE OF CHARACTERISTIC

Now turn your attention to the relative clause in this sentence: *Brutus is the kind of guy **who would give you the toga off his back**.* The relative clause is still adjectival in nature, in the sense that it's telling you more about a noun in the main clause, but the sort of information it's providing is slightly different. What's the difference between saying *Brutus is the guy who <u>is giving</u> you the toga off his back* and *Brutus is a guy who <u>would give</u> you the toga off his back?* Obviously, in the first case, you learn that Brutus, for whatever reason, is physically, literally giving you his toga. The relative clause is qualifying the antecedent, *Brutus,* with concrete reality. In the second case, by contrast, you learn something a little more hypothetical about Brutus; not that he is really giving you his toga, but that his character is such that he just might give you his toga, if the occasion should ever arise. In other words, you're learning something a little less concrete about the antecedent.

In English, we even tip off the reader that this manner of less specific relative clause is coming up by using the indefinite article—*Brutus is **a** guy who . . .*—not the definite article—*Brutus is **the** guy who . . .* And there are other linguistic formulae we might use to indicate that Brutus is going to be qualified in this hypothetical way. We might say, *Brutus is **the sort of** guy who . . .* or *Brutus is **the kind of guy** who . . .*

In Latin, this sort of relative clause isn't anticipated in the main clause as it is in English. Instead, Latin simply puts the verb of the relative clause in the subjunctive mood. Like this:

> Brutus est quî togam tibi dê tergô *det, Brutus is the kind of fellow* (or *sort of fellow,* or *a fellow*) *who'd give you the toga off his back.*

This kind of relative clause is called the *relative clause of characteristic,* which describes the construction fairly well, since the relative clause isn't stating a concrete fact attributable literally to Brutus. Instead, it's identifying a character trait—something true about him, but less tangible.

You will see, however, that this description *relative clause of characteristic* is too narrow to cover all the different ways Latin uses a subjunctive in a relative clause. Perhaps a wider description of this phenomenon in Latin might be the *conditioned relative clause* or the *hypothetical relative clause*. Let's look at a few other situations in which Latin uses the subjunctive in a relative clause.

Sunt quî tam acêrba numquam dicant.

You obviously have a generalized sort of modification going on here because the sentence isn't talking about any people in particular. It's simply saying that somewhere there exist people who are of such genteel disposition that no unkind words ever leave their mouths. If, however, the verb **dicant** had been **dicunt**, then everything is different. Then the sentence is identifying a very specific group of people who really don't say harsh things. Our translation would have to be something like *There are the people who never say such harsh things.* Perhaps the speaker might be pointing into a church or something.

Quis est quî haec scelera faciat?

The modification here obviously can't be specific because the sentence is casting about for someone who'd fit this qualification. It's a question. Change the verb **faciat** to **facit** and then the meaning is substantially altered. The translation would be *Who is the one who commits these crimes?* In this case, the question is an interrogation, looking for the specific person who is really committing these crimes.

Nemô est quem vidêre mâlim.

When the antecedent is *nobody*, then the modifying relative clause is always hypothetical, non-concrete. How could you attribute specific attributes to *nobody*?

The only way to get comfortable with this use of the subjunctive in Latin, alas, is through lots of deliberate reading. I'd recommend that you pause now and have a look at Wheelock's sentences for this chapter in the Self-Tutorials (page 393). Work through them slowly, and watch carefully for subjunctives in the relative clauses. If you are dealing with a relative clause of characteristic, try out a couple of translation strategies and see which you prefer.

DATIVE OF REFERENCE

Let's think about the different uses of the dative case you know so far. There's the indirect object, which we can translate with the prepositions *to/for*, or by position: **Caesar eî multam pecûniam dedit**, *Caesar gave much money <u>to him</u>* or *Caesar gave **him** much money.* You've also seen the dative case used after certain adjectives: ***Tôtî populô** cârus erat*, *he was <u>dear to the whole nation</u>*. Some verbs and compound verbs, for which our English equivalents are transitive, require the dative case to complete their sense: **Studeô *Graecîs litterîs***, *I am studying (eager for) <u>Greek literature</u>*; **Eum secûtus est**, *he chased him* but **Eî obsecûtus est**, *he obeyed <u>him</u>*. Finally, the dative case shows agent in the passive periphrastic construction with the gerundive: **Hoc *tibi* faciendum est**, <u>*you*</u> *should do this.*

The dative of reference is another use of the dative case, but it's a little difficult to define precisely. It sometimes goes by the name of the dative of interest and the ethical dative, but I prefer to call it the "dative of the interested bystander." What that means is there is someone mentioned in the sentence, or pointed to rather, who is not directly involved in what's going on, but who still has some opinion about it, or has stake or involvement in it. This person may be one to whom the sentence is being directed, or the spectator might be passing a judgment on the sentence. Something like this: *For Krusty the Klown, life's one big joke.* Here the meaning is *According to Krusty* or *As far as Krusty is concerned* or *In Krusty's way of looking at things . . .* There are all sorts of different ways you can paraphrase *for Krusty the Klown* and still preserve its intent.

But there are instances of the dative of reference in Latin that are a little more slippery. We just don't have a clean, one-to-one equivalent for the dative of reference. Wheelock suggests a few techniques, but you need to remember that these are only suggestions. A frequent misunderstanding beginning Latin students make is to assume that the dative of reference means *are you sure?* or *in my heart* or *as I see it.* The dative of reference indicates that someone who has some involvement in the meaning of the sentence is being pointed to and drawn into the sentence. How you interpret and then translate that involvement is really up to you. Do you see what I'm trying get you to understand? Don't get imprisoned by just a few stock translations for the dative of reference. It won't get you very far, and it won't help you understand the meaning behind the Latin. Explore and enjoy the different possibilities.

SUPINES

The supine is a kind of verbal noun, and to some degree it resembles a gerund. The difference is that the supine is a fourth declension verbal noun, and it appears only in the ablative and accusatives cases. We call the first the *supine in -û*, and we call the second, logically, the supine in **-um**. Both of them are formed from the fourth principal part of the verb, and both, as you'll see, are limited to very specific constructions.

The supine in -û isn't very difficult to spot and to understand. If you see something that looks like the fourth principal part of a verb with a fourth declension ablative case ending, then you have a supine in -û: **laudâtû** from **laudô**; **nâtû** from **nâscôr**, **vîsû** from **videô**, and so on and so one. What makes this supine even easier to deal with is that it's pretty much limited to one construction. It's used to specify an adjective and appears regularly in stock expressions. For example:

mirâbile vîsû, *wondrous to behold*

dictû nefâs, sinful to say

maior nâtû, *older.*

The supine in **-um**, by contrast, is a real monster. It looks as if it can be a regular form of the perfect passive participle—a neuter nominative or accusative singular, or a masculine accusative singular. As a result, only the most experienced readers of Latin can instantly spot a supine in **-um** in a text and distinguish it from the participle. Fortunately, however, this supine is limited to one construction only: it's used as the direct object of a verb of motion to show purpose. Have a look:

> puella iêrat extra moenia petitum aquam, *the girl had gone outside the walls to get water* .

Do you see **petitum**? There's the supine in **-um,** from **petô, -ere**, indicating the purpose of **iêrat**. You can tell that it's not the participle because it's not agreeing with anything in this sentence. It's also taking **aquam** as its direct object, and that shows you the verbal idea is active. If this had been a perfect passive participle, it could not have taken an object. Here's are some more examples:

> Aequî et Volscî aliâs urbês praedâtum abeunt, *the Aequi and the Volsci march away to plunder other cities.*

> Vênit illôs captîvôs postulâtum, *he came to demand the hostages.*

VOCABULARY PUZZLES

ergâ + acc., *toward* The word looks so much like the adverb **ergô,** *therefore* that you're bound to mess it up the first several times you see it: **magnam fidem ergâ rêgem praebuêrunt,** *they showed great loyalty to the king.*

39

Gerund and Gerundive

THE GERUND

Consider the following sentences:

Running is a good exercise.

Not many people actually enjoy *running*.

People become healthier *by running*.

Strained knees and sore muscles are an unavoidable consequence *of running*.

Dedicate yourself, therefore, *to running*.

In the construction of each of these sentences, the act of running is treated as if it were a noun. In the first sentence, *running* is the subject of the sentence; in the second it's the direct object of the verb *to enjoy*; in the third it's used as an adverb showing means; in the fourth it's the object of the preposition *of*; and in the fifth it's the indirect object of the verb *dedicate*. So here you have a form, derived from a verb, that is being used as a noun. We can think of it as a *verbal noun*. And in grammar we call a verbal noun a *gerund* (*JEHR uhnd*).

As you can see, a verbal noun is a convenient way to talk about an action, without the action becoming, as it were, activated in the sentence. In none of these sentences is anyone actually running, but each of them has the action of running written into its grammar. The action is conceived of as an idea in these sentences. It's turned into a noun: a gerund. In English, we turn a verb into a gerund simply by adding *-ing* to the first principal part of the verb: *think-ing, laugh-ing, see-ing*, and so on. Latin, just like English, can make a noun out of a verb and weave it into a sentence, by putting the verb into a certain form. But that's not the end of it.

Because English, for the most part, is not an inflected language, we don't need to make special provisions for case endings to show the grammatical relationship the gerund has to other words in the sentence. We show grammatical function by position or by using prepositions. In Latin, however, the gerund must be able to decline to show case. So how does it do that?

The nominative of the gerund is simply the present infinitive, and it's considered to be a neuter noun: **Currere est bonum**,[104] *running is good*; **Videre est credere**, *seeing is believing*. And what about the rest of the cases? The Latin gerund for the oblique cases (all the cases except the nominative) is the first principal part + **nd** + neuter endings from the second declension. Here are a couple of gerunds declined:[105]

---

[104]Note the gender of the adjective **bonum**. It's nominative because **currere** is nominative, and it's neuter because a gerund is always neuter in gender.

[105]Obviously, there will be no plural forms for the gerund. Think about it: *runnings*?

Nom.	laudâre	monêre	dûcere	capere	audîre
Gen.	laudandî	monendî	dûcendî	capiendî	audiendî
Dat.	laudandô	monendô	dûcendô	capiendô	audiendô
Acc.	laudandum	monendum	dûcendum	capiendum	audiendum
Abl.	laudandô	monendô	dûcendô	capiendô	audiendô

A quick inspection shows you that the gerund looks very much like the gerundive in the oblique cases. The gerundive, as you should remember, is the first principal part of the verb plus **-nd-** plus the adjectival endings **-us, -a, -um**. You can keep these two distinguished in the following way: the gerund is a neuter singular noun, declined in the second declension; but the gerund*ive* is an adject*ive*, and therefore will have all possible genders, cases, and numbers. So if you see a form like **laudandôs** or **capiendîs** in a sentence you'll know immediately that it can't be a gerund. A gerund (a neuter singular noun) can't possibly have those endings. It has to be the gerundive. Remember, the gerund*ive* is an adject*ive*. Here are some examples of the gerund used in different cases.

Discêmus legendô, *we will learn by reading*.

Nôn mihi currere placet, *running does not please me*.

Omnês arbitrantur currendum esse bonum, *everyone thinks that running is good*.

Hûc vênî ad currendum, *I came here to run*.[106]

Currendô igitur te da, *dedicate yourself therefore to running*.

Hîc nûlla facultâs currendî dabâtur, *there is no possibility of running here*.

Another twist: because it's a verbal noun, the gerund can also take objects. For example, look at the grammar of this sentence: *Kicking the dog is no solution to your problem.* What's the case of *dog* here? Well, *kicking* is the gerund in the nominative since it's the subject of the verb *is*, and *dog*, as the direct recipient of the action in the gerund, is the direct object of *kicking*. Therefore *dog* is in the accusative case.

Do you see? Even though it has become a noun, the verb doesn't entirely shed its verbal nature. It can still take an object if it's transitive. Let's have a look at a few more examples of this in English.

Only intelligent, perceptive students enjoy learning Latin.

Learning is the object of *enjoy*;

Latin is the direct object of the gerund *learning*.

---

[106]Here's a very common use of the gerund: **ad** + the gerund in the accusative equals a purpose clause.

We learn many things by reading books.

Reading is adverbial (ablative in Latin);

books is the direct object of *reading.*

Humiliating one's students is widely recognized as an effective pedagogical method.

Humiliating is the gerund, subject of *is;*

students is the direct object of *humiliating.*

So how does this work in Latin? Let's start with the gerund in the nominative case. When the gerund is the subject of the sentence, the object of the gerund assumes the expected form.

Legere librôs multôs adiuvat discipulôs, *reading many books helps students.*

Vidêre amîcôs suôs omnibus placet, *seeing one's own friends pleases everybody.*

That's pretty easy. But ... when the gerund is itself in one of the oblique cases and has an object dependent on it, Latin prefers another construction. Are you ready? It's going to be a little complicated. When the gerund is itself in an oblique case, the object of the gerund assumes the case the gerund would logically have, and the gerund becomes a gerundive (without the sense of obligation or necessity) which agrees with the noun in number, gender, and case. Read on.

Let's run through this again. How would you translate this into Latin: *We will learn by reading books.* You'd probably try to write something like this:

We will learn	→	discêmus
by reading	→	legendô (gerund in the ablative of means)
books	→	librôs (object of legendô)

And so you'd write **Discêmus legendô librôs.** But that's not idiomatic Latin. Latin thinks this way: *We will learn by books being read.* Do you see the difference? Latin puts the noun that was the object of the gerund—*books*—into the case that the gerund would have been in—ablative—and then turns the gerund—*reading*—into the gerund*ive* and makes it agree with the noun. So it goes from *by reading books* to *books being read.*

So in idiomatic Latin, our thought *We will learn by reading books,* comes out **Discêmus librîs legendîs.** Do you get it? **Legendîs** is now the gerund*ive* modifying the noun **librîs,** which is in the ablative case—the case we put our English gerund in. Let's look at another example of this: *I came to see my friends.*

<u>Expected:</u>   Vênî ad videndum amîcôs, *I came for seeing my friends.*

In practice: Vênî ad amîcôs videndôs,[107] *I came for my friends being seen.*[108]

Now try it another way. Rewrite these sentences into idiomatic Latin, and translate. (I'll do the first one).

1.	Hinc vênit videndî amîcôs causâ.
Idiomatic:	Hinc vênit amîcôrum videndôrum causâ.
Translation:	He came from there to see [his] friends.
2.	Faciendô haec omnês petunt multam pecûniam.
Idiomatic:	
Translation:	
3.	Magister diem omnem cônsûmpsit in docendô discipulôs.
Idiomatic:	
Translation:	
4.	Omnês sunt cupidî exponendî hâs însidiâs.
Idiomatic:	
Translation:	
5.	Cîvês sequuntur virtûtem vitandô hôs malôs.
Idiomatic:	
Translation:	

VOCABULARY PUZZLES

cupidus, -a, -um Here's an example of an adjective which governs the genitive case: *desirous* **of** *something or someone.* **Nêmô tam pecûniae cupidus quam hic,** *no one is so covetous of money as this man.*

necesse is very common, as you might expect, and it is often construed with the dative case: **necesse Hannibalî est Alpês transîre,** *it is necessary for Hannibal to cross the Alpes,* or *Hannibal has to cross the Alpes.* **Necesse** can also be accusative when in indirect statement: **certior factus est necesse esse Alpês transîre,** *he was informed that it was necessary to cross the Alps.*

---

[107]**Videndum** of the expected sentence is the object of the preposition **ad**, and **amîcôs** is the object of **videndum.** Therefore, **amîcôs** is converted to the case of **videndum** while retaining its plural number, and **videndum** becomes the gerundive and agrees with it in number, gender and case.

[108]Obviously we don't go around talking like that—*for my friends being seen.* Instead we'd just say *to see my friends.* I put the translation as literally as I could so that you could see the grammar of the Latin.

40

More about Questions; Clauses after Verbs of Fearing

QUESTIONS IN LATIN

Latin poses questions in a number of different ways. It can use the enclitic **-ne** at the end of the first word of the sentence, or it can use interrogatives: adjectives, pronouns, or adverbs. Like so:

-ne

Bellumne in Galliâ gessit, *did he wage war in Gaul?*

Vidêsne hunc puerum, *do you see this boy?*

Estisne vôs legâtî â populô Collatinô missî, *are you the ambassadors sent by the people of Collatia?*

Interrogative Pronouns and Adjectives

Quanta vîs hôrum oppidôrum fuit, *how great was the power of those forts?*

Quae verba ab eô audîta sunt, *what words were heard by him?*

Quis eâ tempestâte Romae regnum obtinêbat, who held the kingship at Rome at this time?

Interrogative Adverbs

Quô dûcere hunc iuvenem potestis, *to what place can you lead this young man?*

Ubi illam reperiam, *where will I find her again?*

Cûr Cicerô male dê Caesare opînâtus est, *why did Cicero think badly of Caesar?*

NUM, NÔNNE IN QUESTIONS

Life would be pretty boring, though, if all we could do with questions were simply to solicit information from each other. In everyday life, we frequently ask questions that aren't questions at all. Take for example, the notorious but popular interrogative imperative: *Were you going to clean your room today? Will you help me with the lawn tomorrow?* These aren't really questions at all. They're commands. Or how about the psychological torment of the coercive interrogation, *Is that really how you're going to fix the oven?* Or *Wouldn't you rather go to the opera with the Joneses instead of sitting on the couch and watching the Simpsons?* Most of these rhetorical tricks can only be understood contextually, and hardly ever have direct syntactical expressions. But two very common ones do.

Suppose you want to ask a question, and at the same time you want to encourage an answer of *No*. Try it. Take this question *Do you want the Grande Fries with that?* Now recast it so that it expects the answer "No." You'd start it off with a negative—*You don't want the Grande Fries with that, do you?* Can you almost feel the reply, *Well, gosh, I suppose I don't. What was I thinking?* The first part of the question is almost a negative command, a statement of what the speaker doesn't want to be true—*you don't want*—and the final tag is merely asking you to agree with it.

Latin can sometimes achieve this effect by using the interrogative participle **num** at the beginning of the sentence.[109] Thus:

Num Rômânî equôs suôs fatigâvêrunt, *the Romans didn't exhaust their horses, did they?*

Num mê in matrimonium dûcere vîs, *you don't want to marry me, do you?*

Now try it the other way. Try to ask a question so that you expect the answer *Yes*. There are a couple of different ways. First state what you want to be true, and then answer whether or not it's true. *You're taking the next semester of Latin—aren't you* or perhaps, *right?* The Latin equivalent to this has a direct descendant in the French, Spanish and Italian *no?* that often comes at the end of questions. *You like wine from Italy, no? They want to come back, no?* In Latin, the interrogative that expects the answer *Yes* is simply the negative **nôn** with the interrogative enclitic **-ne** stuck on at the end: **nônne**. Thus:

Nônne satis pecûniae habês, *you have enough money, no?* or *don't you?*

Nônne amîcum repperit, *he found his friend, didn't he?*

FEAR CLAUSES

What we're talking about here are clauses that follow verbs that express fear; sort of noun clause that completes a verb of fearing. *I'm afraid*—of what?—*that it'll rain on my parade*. The clause *that it'll rain on my parade* is the fear clause. The Latin fear clause is a standard noun clause—**ut** or **nê** plus a subjunctive. That's easy. What follows will be a little tricky because Latin completely inverts our normal expectation for how a fear clause should be constructed.

The way to start is to think of the fear clauses as independent commands, where **ut** begins a statement of what you want to happen, and **nê** begins a statement of what you don't want to happen. Let's try two:

Ut hostês ex agris nostrîs dêcêdant, *let the enemy leave our fields*.

Nê urbs nostra dêleâtur, *let our city not be destroyed*.

---

[109]You should be aware, however, that the participle **num** doesn't always convey this sense. Sometimes it simply begins an open question: **Num (ali)quid vîs**, *would you care for anything else?* Not *you don't want anything else, do you?* And used in indirect question, it functions just like **-ne**: *whether*. **Velim scire num amîcî veterês meliôres quam novî semper essent**, *I wonder whether old friends are always better than new ones*.

Okay, so here we have two statements of wish—voluntative subjunctives we could call them. Now let's slowly introduce the idea of fear. In the first—**ut hostês ex agrîs nostrîs dêcêdant**—what would be the thing that would cause you fear? You'd be afraid if you're not going to get your wish and the enemy is *not* going to leave the field. That is, you're thinking *oh! let the enemy leave the field, but . . .I'm afraid.* What are you afraid of? You're afraid that they will *not* leave. So you put these two together and what do you have: **timeô ut hostês ex agrîs nostrîs dêcêdant** which have to translate as *I'm afraid that the enemy won't leave.* How are you feeling? A little dizzy? Let's have another go at it.

In this example, what you want to happen is **ut meam pecûniam reperiam**, *let me find my money!* But if there's something about this proposition that frightens you it's not that you'll get want you want but that you won't. So **timeô ut meam pecûniam reperiam**, *I'm afraid—let me find my money.* What are you afraid of—that you won't get your wish—what is your wish—to find my money—so you're afraid you won't find your money—right, *I'm afraid I won't find my money*, **timeô ut meam pecûniam reperiam**.

In the case of the fear clause introduced by **nê** everything is simply reversed. **Nê urbs nostra dêleâtur**, *let our city not be destroyed*, but I'm afraid—of what—that it *will be* destroyed, so **timeô nê urbs nostra dêleâtur**, *I'm afraid that our city will be destroyed.*[110] Still gasping for air? Try a few drills on this:

DRILLS
Translate into English

1.	Veritus est nê rêgnum suum âmitteret.
2.	Metuis nê puer haec saxa iaciât.
3.	Omnês veritî sunt ut rêx lacrimâs tenêret.
4.	Tôta urbs timuit ut Herculês interfectus esset.
5.	Timêbat ut Caesar castra servâre posset.

---

[110]There is another, somewhat archaic way of translating a fear clause beginning with **nê**, but if you understand it, it works every time. Just translate the **nê** as *lest*: **timeô nê urbs nostra dêleâtur**, *I fear lest our city be destroyed.*

KEY

Answers to Selected Exercises

CHAPTER 1

Latin	English	Latin	English
dêbêmus	we owe, ought	monet	he/she/it advises
dêbêtis	you (*pl.*) owe, ought	monês	you advise
dêbent	they owe, ought	moneô	I advise

Stem	Infinitive Ending	Infinitive Form	Translation
laudâ-	re	laudâre	to praise
monê-	re	monêre	to warn
amâ-	re	amâre	to love
vidê-	re	vidêre	to see

CHAPTER 2

	Stem	Case Ending	Inflected Form
N/V.	pecûni-	a	pecûnia
Gen.	pecûni	ae	pecûniae
Dat.	pecûni	ae	pecûniae
Acc.	pecûni	am	pecûniam
Abl.	pecûni	â	pecûniâ
Plural			
N/V.	pecûni	ae	pecûniae
Gen.	pecûni	ârum	pecûniârum
Dat.	pecûni	îs	pecûniîs
Acc.	pecûni	âs	pecûniâs
Abl.	pecûni	îs	pecûniîs

	Singular		Plural	
	magna	**rosa**	**magna**	**rosa**
N/V.	magna	rosa	magnae	rosae
Gen.	magnae	rosae	magnârum	rosârum
Dat.	magnae	rosae	magnîs	rosîs
Acc.	magnam	rosam	magnâs	rosâs
Abl.	magnâ	rosâ	magnîs	rosîs

CHAPTER 3

	Singular		Plural
Nom.	amîcus	Nom.	amîcî
Gen.	amîcî	Gen.	amîcôrum
Dat.	amîcô	Dat.	amîcîs
Acc.	amîcum	Acc.	amîcôs
Abl.	amîcô	Abl.	amîcîs
Voc.	amîce	Voc.	amîcî

	Singular		Plural
Nom.	puer	Nom.	puerî
Gen.	puerî	Gen.	puerôrum
Dat.	puerô	Dat.	puerîs
Acc.	puerum	Acc.	puerôs
Abl.	puerô	Abl.	puerîs
Voc.	puer	Voc.	puerî

	Singular		Plural
Nom.	vir	Nom.	virî
Gen.	virî	Gen.	virôrum
Dat.	virô	Dat.	virîs
Acc.	virum	Acc.	virôs
Abl.	virô	Abl.	virîs
Voc.	vir	Voc.	virî

	Singular		Plural
Nom.	fîlius	*Nom.*	fîliî
Gen.	fîliî	*Gen.*	fîliôrum
Dat.	fîliô	*Dat.*	fîliîs
Acc.	fîlium	*Acc.*	fîliôs
Abl.	fîliô	*Abl.*	fîliîs
Voc.	fîlî	*Voc.*	fîliî

	Singular		Plural	
	magn-	**sapienti-**	**magn-**	**sapienti-**
N/V.	magna	sapientia	magnae	sapientiae
Gen.	magnae	sapientiae	magnârum	sapientiârum
Dat.	magnae	sapientiae	magnîs	sapientiîs
Acc.	magnam	sapientiam	magnâs	sapientiâs
Abl.	magnâ	sapientiâ	magnîs	sapientiîs

	Singular		Plural	
	great	**poet**	**great**	**poet**
N/V.	magnus	poêta	magnî	poêtae
Gen.	magnî	poêtae	magnôrum	poêtârum
Dat.	magnô	poêtae	magnîs	poêtîs
Acc.	magnum	poêtam	magnôs	poêtâs
Abl.	magnô	poêtâ	magnîs	poêtîs

CHAPTER 5

	our	free	fatherland
Nom.	nostra	lîbera	patria
Gen.	nostrae	lîberae	patriae
Dat.	nostrae	lîberae	patriae
Acc.	nostram	lîberam	patriam
Abl.	nostrâ	lîberâ	patriâ

	our	free	fatherland
Plural			
Nom.	nostrae	lîberae	patriae
Gen.	nostrârum	lîberârum	patriârum
Dat.	nostrîs	lîberîs	patriîs
Acc.	nostrâs	lîberâs	patriâs
Abl.	nostrîs	lîberîs	patriîs

CHAPTER 7

Entry	Stem	Entry	Stem
corpus, -oris, *n.*	corpor-	honor, -ôris, *m.*	honôr-
hûmânitâs, -tâtis, *f.*	hûmânitât-	frâter, -tris, *m.*	frâtr-
mûtâtiô, -ônis, *f.*	mûtâtiôn-	pater, -tris, *m.*	patr-
pestis, -is, *f.*	pest-	scrîptor, -ôris, *m*	scrîptôr-
valêtûdô, -inis, *f.*	valêtûdin-	cupiditâs, -tâtis, *f.*	cupiditât-
uxor, -ôris, *f.*	uxôr-	môs, môris, *m.*	môr-
nômen, -inis, *n.*	nômin-	carmen, -inis, *n.*	carmin-

	Singular		Plural	
N/V.	vêra	virtûs	vêrae	virtûtês
Gen.	vêrae	virtûtis	vêrârum	virtûtum
Dat.	vêrae	virtûtî	vêrîs	virtûtibus
Acc.	vêram	virtûtem	vêrâs	virtûtês
Abl.	vêrâ	virtûte	vêrîs	virtûtibus

CHAPTER 9

	Number	Gender	Case
illae cîvitâtês	plural	feminine	nominative
illâs cîvitâtês	plural	feminine	accusative
istî puerô	singular	masculine	dative
istô puerô	singular	masculine	ablative
illî amôrês	plural	masculine	nominative

	Number	Gender	Case
illôs amôrês	plural	masculine	accusative
hae puellae	plural	feminine	nominative
huic puellae	singular	feminine	dative

CHAPTER 12

1.	They will have had.	Habuerint.
2.	I had seen.	Vîderam.
3.	You (pl.) remained.	Remânsistis.
4.	We will have called.	Vocâverimus.
5.	She will be strong.	Valêbit.
6.	You (s.) have tolerated.	Tolerâvistî.
7.	They had taught.	Docuerant.
8.	You (pl.) had had.	Habuerâtis.
9.	We have loved.	Amâvimus.
10.	They thought.	Putâvêrunt.

	Perfect	Pluperfect	Future Perfect
1st	dûxî	dûxeram	dûxerô
2nd	dûxistî	dûxerâs	dûxeris
3rd	dûxit	dûxerat	dûxerit
Plural			
1st	dûximus	dûxerâmus	dûxerimus
2nd	dûxistis	dûxerâtis	dûxeritis
3rd	dûxêrunt	dûxerant	dûxerint

1.	I came.	Vênî.
2.	I saw.	Vîdî.
3.	I conquered.	Vîcî.
4.	I will have begun.	Coeperô.
5.	She had taught.	Docuerat.
6.	They lived.	Vîxêrunt.
7.	We had.	Habuimus.

8.	You (*pl.*) have written.	Scrîpsistis.
9.	They sent.	Mîsêrunt.
10.	They have been.	Fuêrunt.
11.	We have found.	Invênimus.
12.	He had fled.	Fûgerat.
13.	You (*s.*) couldn't see us.	Nôs vidêre nôn potuistî.
14.	You (*s.*) had seen.	Vîderâs.
15.	They came.	Vênêrunt.

CHAPTER 14

	Singular	Plural
N/V.	urbs	urbês
Gen.	urbis	urbium
Dat.	urbî	urbibus
Acc.	urbem	urbês
Abl.	urbe	urbibus

	i-stem (yes/no)	Relevant Rule
ignis, ignis, *m.*	Yes	Parisyllabic Rule
dêns, dentis, *m.*	Yes	Double Consonant Rule
cîvitâs, -tâtis, *f.*	No	
rêx, rêgis, *m.*	No	
opus, operis, *n.*	No	
tempus, -oris, *n.*	No	
nox, noctis, *f.*	Yes	Double Consonant Rule
môlês, môlis, *f.*	Yes	Parisyllabic Rule
urbs, urbis, *f.*	Yes	Double Consonant Rule
sôl, sôlis, *m.*	No	
hostis, hostis, *m.*	Yes	Parisyllabic Rule
dux, ducis, *m.*	No	
ôrâtor, -tôris, *m.*	No	
fînis, fînis, *m.*	Yes	Parisyllabic Rule
gêns, gentis, *f.*	Yes	Double Consonant Rule
laus, laudis, *f.*	No	

	i-stem (yes/no)	Relevant Rule
genus, generis, *n.*	No	
vêritâs, -tâtis, *f.*	No	
aetâs, -tâtis, *f.*	No	

CHAPTER 15

	Roman	English	Roman	English
1.	XL	40	6. XXXIV	34
2.	XXIV	24	7. LXXVIII	78
3.	LXXIV	74	8. CDXXLIII	443
4.	DCCXLVIII	748	9. MMMDCCLXXXIV	3,784
5.	MMCMLX	1960	10. CMXCI	991

CHAPTER 16

Latin	Case(s)
omnium puerôrum	genitive
celerem puellam	accusative
potentî rêgî	dative
potentibus virîs	dative/ablative
fortês fêminae	nominative
fortis fêminae	genitive
fortî fêminae	dative
acrês mortês	nominative/accusative
acrî memoriâ	ablative
acrî bellô	dative/ablative

CHAPTER 17

1.	Vidî canem quî ex Asiâ vênit. (**canis, -is**, *m.*, *dog*)	
	Relative Pronoun:	qui
	Translation:	I saw the dog which (that) came from Asia.

2.	Vidî canês quôs amâs.	
	Relative Pronoun:	quôs
	Translation:	I saw the dogs which (that) you love.
3.	Puellae, quârum pater est parvus, sunt magnae.	
	Relative Pronoun:	quârum
	Translation:	The girls, whose father is short, are tall.
4.	Vidî puerôs quibus librôs dedistis.	
	Relative Pronoun:	quibus
	Translation:	I saw the boys to whom you gave the books.
5.	Vidî puerôs quibuscum (= cum quibus) vênistis.	
	Relative Pronoun:	quibus
	Translation:	I saw the boys with whom you came.
6.	Cîvem quem mîserâtis laudâvêrunt.	
	Relative Pronoun:	quem
	Translation:	They praised the citizen, whom you had sent.

1.	Tyrannus urbês dêlêvit *from which* cîvês fûgerant.	ex quibus
2.	Vênistî cum cîvibus *to whom* vîtâs commîserant.	quibus
3.	Cîvês vidî *with whom* fûgistî.	quibuscum
4.	Pecûniam habent *with which* urbem tyrannus cêpit.	quâcum
5.	Pater *whose* fîliî stultî erant ex Asiâ vênit.	cuius

CHAPTER 18

1.	Haec perîcula vôs terrêbant.
	Hîs perîculîs terrêbâminî.
2.	Discipulî meî hôs librôs cum celeritâte legent.
	Hî librî â discipulîs meîs cum celeritâte legentur.
3.	Tê in viâ vidêbô.
	Ab mê in viâ vidêberis.
4.	Magna îra cîvês movêbat.
	Cîvês magnâ îrâ movêbantur.

CHAPTER 21

1.	Â quibus discipulîs hî versûs legêbantur?
	By which students were these verses being read?
2.	Omnês civitâtês ab istô tyrannô capientur.
	All the cities will be captured by that tyrant.
3.	Â nostrîs amîcîs adiuvâbâmur.
	We were being helped by our friends.
4.	Â tuîs amîcîs nôn neglegêris.
	You will not be neglected by your friends.
5.	Tuum domum dehinc vidêre possum.
	I can see your house from here.

	Active	Passive
Present	mittis	mitteris
Future	mittês	mittêris
Imperfect	mittêbâs	mittêbâris
Perfect	mîsistî	missus es
Pluperfect	mîserâs	missus erâs
Future Perfect	mîseris	missus eris

CHAPTER 23

	Active	Passive
Future	ductûrus	dûcendus
Present	dûcêns	
Perfect		ductus

	Active	Passive
Future	missûrus	mittendus
Present	mittêns	
Perfect		missus

	Active	Passive
Future	cupîtûrus	cupiendus
Present	cupiêns	
Perfect		cupîtus

	Active	Passive
Present	audit	audîtur
Future	audiet	audiêtur
Imperfect	audiêbât	audiêbâtur
Perfect	audîvit	audîtum est
Pluperfect	audîverat	audîtum erat
Future Perfect	audîverit	audîtum erit

	Active	Passive
Future	audîtûrus	audiendus
Present	audiêns	
Perfect		audîtus

CHAPTER 25

	Active	Passive
Future	amâtûrum esse	
Present	amâre	amârî
Perfect	amâvisse	amâtum esse

	Active	Passive
Future	habitûrum esse	
Present	habêre	habêrî
Perfect	habuisse	habitum esse

	Active	Passive
Future	ductûrum esse	
Present	dûcere	dûcî
Perfect	dûxisse	ductum esse

	Active	Passive
Future	captûrum esse	
Present	capere	capî
Perfect	cêpisse	captum esse

	Active	Passive
Future	audîtûrum esse	
Present	audîre	audîrî
Perfect	audîvisse	audîtum esse

1.		Veniunt cum amîcîs tuîs.
	Putô	eôs cum amîcîs tuîs venîre.
2.		Hoc signum Caesarî dandum est.
	Putô	hoc signum Caesarî dandum esse.
3.		Spês novârum rêrum mollibus sententiîs alitur.
	Putô	spêm novârum rêrum mollibus sententiîs alî.
4.		Tyrannus multâs copiâs in mediam urbem dûcit.
	Putô	tyrannum multâs copiâs in mediam urbem dûcere.
5.		Illa puella dôna multa patrî dat.
	Putô	illam puellam dôna multa patrî dare.

1.	Putâmus omnês bonôs virôs vîtâs beâtâs agere.		
	We think that all good men	**lead**	happy lives.
2.	Putâmus omnês bonôs virôs vîtâs beâtâs êgisse.		
	We think that all good men	**led**	happy lives.
3.	Putâmus omnês bonôs virôs vîtâs beâtâs actûrôs esse.		
	We think that all good men	**will lead**	happy lives.
4.	Putâvimus omnês bonôs virôs vîtâs beâtâs agere.		
	We thought that all good men	**led (were leading)**	happy lives.
5.	Putâvimus omnês bonôs virôs vîtâs beâtâs êgisse.		
	We thought that all good men	**had led**	happy lives.
6.	Putâvimus omnês bonôs virôs beâtâs vîtâs actûrôs esse.		
	We thought that all good men	**would lead**	happy lives.

	ar that you (pl.) are coming.		
	vôs	venîre.	
	hear that you (pl.) were coming.		
	Audîmus vôs	vênisse.	
3.	We hear that you will come.		
	Audîmus vôs	ventûrôs esse.	
4.	We heard that you would come.		
	Audîvimus vôs	ventûrôs esse.	
5.	I thought that you had written the letter.		
	Putâvî vôs litterâs	scrîpsisse.	
6.	We thought that the letter had been written by you.		
	Putâvimus litterâs â vôbîs	scrîptâs esse.	

CHAPTER 26

	wiser	plan	most powerful	city
N/V.	sapientius	cônsilium	potentissima	urbs
Gen.	sapientiôris	cônsiliî	potentissimae	urbis
Dat.	sapientiôrî	cônsiliô	potentissimae	urbî
Acc.	sapientius	cônsilium	potentissimam	urbem
Abl.	sapientiôre	cônsilio	potentissimâ	urbe
Plural				
N/V.	sapientiôra	cônsilia	potentissimae	urbês
Gen.	sapientiôrum	cônsiliôrum	potentissimârum	urbium
Dat.	sapientiôribus	cônsiliîs	potentissimîs	urbibus
Acc.	sapientiôra	cônsilia	potentissimâs	urbês
Abl.	sapientiôribus	cônsiliîs	potentissimîs	urbibus

CHAPTER 27

Positive	Comparative	Superlative
pulcher, -chra, -chrum	pulchrior, -ius	pulcherrimus, -a, -um
lîber, -a, -um	lîberior, -ius	lîberrimus, -a, -um
âcer, âcris, âcre	âcrior, -ius	âcerrimus, -a, -um
celer, celeris, celere	celerior, -ius	celerrimus, -a, -um

CHAPTER 30

Direct Question	Main Verb	Indirect Question
Quid faciês?		quid factûrus sîs.
Quid facis?	**Rogô**	quid faciâs.
Quid fêcisti?		quid fêcerîs.

Direct Question	Main Verb	Indirect Question
Quid faciês?		quid factûrus essês.
Quid facis?	**Rogâvî**	quid facerês.
Quid fêcisti?		quid fêcissês.

Direct Question	Main Verb	Indirect Question
Venientne nostrî amîcî?		sintne ventûrî nostrî amîcî.
Veniuntne nostrî amîcî?	**Rogô**	veniantne nostrî amîcî.
Vênêruntne nostrî amîcî?		vênerintne nostrî amîcî.

Direct Question	Main Verb	Indirect Question
Venientne nostrî amîcî?		essentne ventûri nostrî amîcî.
Veniuntne nostrî amîcî?	**Rogâvî**	venîrentne nostrî amîcî.
Vênêruntne nostrî amîcî?		vênissentne nostrî amîcî.

CHAPTER 32

Adjective	Stem	Positive Adverb
âcer, -cris, -re	âcr-	âcriter
sapiêns, -ntis	sapient-	sapienter
fortis, -e	fort-	fortiter
iûcundus, -a, -um	iûcund-	iûcundê
lîber, -a, -um	lîber-	lîberê
clârus, -a, -um	clâr-	clârê
celer, -is, -e	celer-	celeriter

Adjective	Stem	Comparative Adverb
âcer, -cris, -re	âcr-	âcrius
sapiêns, -ntis	sapient-	sapientius
fortis, -e	fort-	fortius
iûcundus, -a, -um	iûcund-	iûcundius
lîber, -a, -um	lîber-	lîberius
clârus, -a, -um	clâr-	clârius
celer, -is, -e	celer-	celerius

Adjective	Stem	Superlative Adverb
âcer, -cris, -re	âcr-	âcerrimê
sapiêns, -ntis	sapient-	sapientissimê
fortis, -e	fort-	fortissimê
iûcundus, -a, -um	iûcund-	iûcundissimê
lîber, -a, -um	lîber-	lîberrimê
clârus, -a, -um	clâr-	clârissimê
celer, -is, -e	celer-	celerrimê

Adjective	Positive	Comparative	Superlative
longus, -a, -um	longê	longius	longissimê
miser, -a, -um	miserê	miserius	miserrimê
pulcher, -chra, -chrum	pulchrê	pulchrius	pulcherrimê
fêlix, -icis	fêliciter	fêlîcius	fêlîcissimê
potêns, -ntis	potenter	potentius	potentissimê
facilis, -e	facilê	facilius	facillimê

CHAPTER 33
Past Contrary to Fact

Sî hoc	dîxissês	vêritâtem	scîvissem.

Future Less Vivid

Sî hoc	dîcâs	vêritâtem	sciam.

Present Contrary to Fact

Sî hoc	**dîcerês**	vêritâtem	**scîrem.**

Past Open

Sî hoc	**dîxistî**	vêritâtem	**scîvî.**

CHAPTER 34

	Verb	Conjugation
1.	patior, -î, passus sum	3rd i-stem
2.	experior, -îrî, expertus sum	4th
3.	fateor, -êrî, fassus sum	2nd
4.	loquor, -î, locûtus sum	3rd
5.	ûtor, -î, ûsus sum	3rd
6.	nâscor, -î, nâtus sum	3rd
7.	morior, -î, mortuus sum	3rd i-stem
8.	proficiscor, -î, profectus sum	3rd
9.	cônor, -ârî, cônâtus sum	1st
10.	arbitror, -ârî, arbitrâtus sum	1st

	Active	Passive
Present		fatêminî
Future		fatêbiminî
Imperfect		fatêbâminî
Perfect		fassî estis
Pluperfect		fassî erâtis
Future Perfect		fassî eritis

	Active	Passive
Present		fateâminî
Imperfect		fatêrêminî
Perfect		fassî sîtis
Pluperfect		fassî essêtis

	Active	**Passive**
Future	fassûrus	fatendus
Present	fatêns	
Perfect		fassus

	Active	**Passive**
Future	fassûrum esse	
Present		fatêrî
Perfect		fassum esse

Singular	fatêris (fatêre)	Plural	fatêminî

CHAPTER 36

1.	Facite id. (Imperâvêrunt)
	Imperâvêrunt vôbîs ut id facerêtis. (*They ordered you to do it.*)
2.	Adiuvâ mê. (Persuâsit)
	Persuâsit tibi ut mê adiuvârês.
3.	Nê dûx hostibus nôceat. (Persuâsêrunt)
	Persuâsêrunt ducî nê hostibus nôcêret.
4.	Hoc mihi dent. (Rogâbant)
	Rogâbant eôs ut hoc mihi dârent.
5.	Nê cîvitâtem tollant. (Imperâbat)
	Imperâbat eîs nê cîvitâtem tollerent.

CHAPTER 39

1.	Hinc vênit videndî amîcôs causâ.
Idiomatic:	Hinc vênit amîcôrum videndôrum causâ.
Translation:	He came from there to see [his] friends.
2.	Faciendô haec omnês petiunt multam pecûniam.
Idiomatic:	Hîs faciendîs omnês petiunt multam pecûniam.
Translation:	They all seek much money by doing these things.

3.	Magister diem omnem cônsûmpsit in docendô discipulôs.
Idiomatic:	Magister diem omnem cônsûmpsit in discipulîs docendîs.
Translation:	The teacher spends each day teaching students.
4.	Omnês sunt cupidî expônandî hâs însidiâs.
Idiomatic:	Omnês sunt cupidî expônandârum hârum însidiârum.
Translation:	They are all desirous of exposing this plot.
5.	Cîvês sequuntur virtûtem vîtandô hôs malôs.
Idiomatic:	Civês sequuntur virtûtem hîs malîs vîtandîs.
Translation:	The citizens are pursuing virtue by avoiding these evils.

CHAPTER 40

1.	Veritus est nê rêgnum suum âmitteret.
	He feared that he would lose his kingdom.
2.	Metuis nê puer haec saxa iaciat.
	You're afraid that the boy will throw these rocks.
3.	Omnês veritî sunt ut rêx lacrimâs tenêret.
	Everyone feared that the king wouldn't hold back his tears.
4.	Tôta urbs timuit nê Herculês interfectus esset.
	The whole city feared that Hercules had been killed.
5.	Timêbat ut Caesar castra servâre posset.
	He was afraid that Caesar wouldn't be able to save the camp.

MORE WHEELOCK RESOURCES

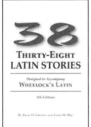

38 LATIN STORIES

Anne H. Groton and James M. May

Originally designed as a supplement to the Latin course by F. M. Wheelock, this book is well suited for use in any introductory course.

> *I would enthusiastically recommend THIRTY-EIGHT LATIN STORIES to all those who teach elementary Latin via Wheelock and wish to provide their students from the start with continuous passages of interesting and idiomatically sound Latin prose.*
> — Richard A. LaFleur, *Classical Outlook*

vi + 104 pp. (5th edition, 1995) Paperback, ISBN 978-0-86516-289-1

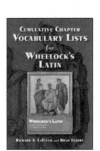

VOCABULARY CARDS AND GRAMMAR SUMMARY FOR WHEELOCK'S LATIN

Richard A. LaFleur and Brad Tillery

This indispensable study aid contains nearly 900 cards on perforated card stock, arranged chapter-by-chapter to accompany all 40 chapters of *Wheelock's Latin*, each with full, unabbreviated Latin vocabulary entry, chapter number, and card number on one side, and English meanings and derivatives or cognates on the reverse side. Also included are: an alphabetical list of all words with their card numbers, suggestions on vocabulary study and use of the cards, a handy Summary of Forms for grammar review, and easily assembled storage boxes.

(2003) ISBN 978-0-86516-557-1

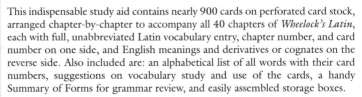

CUMULATIVE CHAPTER VOCABULARY LISTS FOR WHEELOCK'S LATIN

Richard A. LaFleur and Brad Tillery

Cumulative vocabulary lists for the 40 chapters of *Wheelock's Latin*. The list for each chapter contains all the words for that chapter as well as for all chapters preceding; e.g., the chapter 10 list includes all the words introduced in chapters 1–10, usefully sorted by part of speech; nouns and adjectives are further sorted by declension, and verbs by conjugation; all English meanings are included, as are macrons and accents. An invaluable study and review aid for students; helpful for teachers in designing tests and in-class drills.

shrink-wrapped, hole-punched 8 ½ x 11" pages, ISBN 978-0-86516-620-2

READINGS FROM *WHEELOCK'S LATIN*

Mark Robert Miner (readings and performances)
and Richard A. LaFleur (producer)

A 4-CD audio package, with recitation (in Restored Classical Pronunciation) of all vocabulary and paradigms for the 40 chapters of *Wheelock's Latin*, as well as dramatic readings of *Sententiae Antiquae* and narrative passages in the 40 chapters, and lively performance of brief representative selections from the *Loci Antiqui* and *Loci Immutati*. Comes with an 8-page introductory booklet.

4 CD-Roms with Introductory booklet, ISBN 978-0-86516-638-7

BOLCHAZY-CARDUCCI PUBLISHERS, INC.
WWW.BOLCHAZY.COM

1000 Brown Street, Unit 101, Wauconda, IL 60084; *Phone:* 847/526-4344; *Fax:* 847/526-2867